Situated Ethics in Educational Research

Ethics have traditionally been seen as a set of general principles which can be applied in a range of situations. This book challenges the notion of universal ethics, arguing that all ethical acts are situated in socio-political contexts that require the researcher to make complex and sensitive decisions in particular cases and settings.

Situated Ethics in Educational Research develops this notion of situated ethics and explores how ethical issues are practically handled by educational researchers in different fields. The issues discussed include:

- ethics in healthcare research;
- ethics and research in education markets;
- ethics in quantitative research;
- feminist, postcolonial and image-based research;
- emancipatory and race research;
- ethical and political dilemmas in evaluation.

This book fills a gap in the current literature on both educational research and ethics, offering detailed examples of situated ethical research practice. It will be of particular interest to postgraduate students studying education and research, educational researchers and practitioners in all sectors of education.

Helen Simons is Professor of Education and Evaluation in the Research and Graduate School of Education, Faculty of Social Sciences, University of Southampton. She was a key author of the British Educational Research Association *Ethical Guidelines*.

Robin Usher is Professor of Education and Director of Research and Consultancy in the Faculty of Education, Language and Community Services, RMIT University, Australia. He has published widely in the field of educational research.

Situated Ethics in
Educational Research

Edited by Helen Simons and
Robin Usher

London and New York

First published 2000 by RoutledgeFalmer
11 New Fetter Lane, London EC4P 4EE

Simultaneously published in the USA and Canada
by RoutledgeFalmer
29 West 35th Street, New York, NY 10001

RoutledgeFalmer is an imprint of the Taylor & Francis Group

© 2000 Selection and editorial matter Helen Simons and Robin Usher;
individual chapters, their contributors

Typeset in Goudy by Florence Production Ltd, Stoodleigh, Devon
Printed and bound in Great Britain by MPG Books Ltd, Bodmin, Cornwall

British Library Cataloguing in Publication Data
A catalogue record for this book is available from the British Library

Library of Congress Cataloging in Publication Data
Situated ethics in educational research / edited by Helen Simons and
   Robin Usher.
     p. cm.
   Includes bibliographical references and index.
   1. Education–Research–Moral and ethical aspects.
   2. Situation ethics. I. Simons, Helen. II. Usher, Robin, 1944–

   LB1028 .S514 2000
   370'.7'2–dc21 99–088323

ISBN 0–415–20667–7 (Pbk)
ISBN 0–415–20666–9 (Hbk)

Contents

Contributors

Helen Simons is Professor of Education and Evaluation in the Research and Graduate School of Education, University of Southampton where she specialises in evaluation and the teaching of qualitative research methodology. Her conduct of external evaluation and training in the theory and practice of evaluation extends across the professions (including health, medicine and nursing), to different agencies, and to many countries in Europe, Central and Eastern Europe and Australasia. Research interests cover Case Study Research, Policy, Programme and Institutional Self-Evaluation, Arts in Education and the Ethics and Politics of Research. Recent publications include: *Evaluacion democratica de intituciones escolares*, Madrid, Ediciones Morata, S.L. (1999), and 'The Paradox of Case Study', in *Cambridge Journal of Education*, Vol.26, No.2, 1996. She is currently working on a text in case study research to be published in 2001. Convenor of the Ethics portfolio of the British Educational Research Association for many years, she was a key author of the published BERA *Ethical Guidelines*.

Robin Usher is Professor of Education and Director of Research and Consultancy in the Faculty of Education, Language and Community Services, RMIT University, Australia. He is also Adjunct Professor in the Faculty of Education, University of Technology, Sydney. His research interests include epistemological issues in the research process and the impact of postmodernism in education. His books include *Postmodernism and Education: Different Voices, Different Worlds* (1996) (with R. Edwards), *Understanding Educational Research* (1996) (co-editor with D. Scott), *Adult Education and the Postmodern Challenge* (1997) (with I. Bryant and R. Johnston), *Understanding Social Research* (1997) (co-editor with G. McKenzie and J. Powell) and *Researching Education* (1999) (with D. Scott).

Peter Figueroa is Professor of Education in the Research and Graduate School of Education, University of Southampton. He has been a Lecturer in Sociology at the Australian National University (1985), and a Visiting Professor at the Universities of Frankfurt (1979) and Dar es Salaam (1981).

His interests lie mainly in intercultural, antiracist and equal opportunities education; Caribbean-heritage pupils; racialized and ethnic relations; and auto/biography and the phenomenology of Merleau-Ponty. He has published extensively in the fields of racialized and ethnic relations and of intercultural/antiracist education, and he is known internationally for this work. His books include *Sociology of Education: A Caribbean Reader* (edited with G. Persaud), *Education and the Social Construction of 'Race'* and *Education for Cultural Diversity* (edited with A. Fyfe).

Nick Foskett is a Senior Lecturer in Education in the Research and Graduate School of Education, University of Southampton. His main research interests are in the nature and operation of education markets, and he is Director of the university's Centre for Research in Education Marketing (CREM). Recent research projects have focused on the organization of marketing in secondary schools and further education, and the decision-making of students in post-16 markets. Key publications include *Managing External Relations in Schools* (1992), *Student Decision-Making in Post-16 Markets* (1996) (with A. Hesketh) and 'Constructing Choice in Contiguous and Parallel Markets: Institutional and School Leavers' Responses to the New Post-16 Marketplace' in *Oxford Review of Education* (1997) (also with A. Hesketh).

Sally Glen is Professor of Nurse Education and Dean of the School of Nursing and Midwifery at City University, London. She undertook post-graduate studies in Education and Philosophy at the University of London and held staff posts and a charge nurse's post in various children's units before becoming a Nurse Lecturer in the 1980s. Since then she has held academic posts at the Institute of Education, University of London; the University of Glasgow; South Bank University, London and Dundee University, Scotland. Her particular research interests include ethics, values, multi-professional education and skills development, and she has published widely in these areas in the nursing literature.

Rennie Johnston is a Lecturer in Adult and Community Education at New College, University of Southampton. He is responsible for undergraduate and postgraduate programmes in Community Studies, Community Education and Adult Learning and Teaching, and is currently Director of the Widened Provision Project, which engages with non-traditional students looking to enter higher education. He has considerable experience of participatory action-research work with unwaged adults, and his current research interests include the theory and practice of experiential learning and life-long learning, particularly with adults from under-represented groups. Recent publications include *Adult Education and the Postmodern Challenge: Learning*

Beyond the Limits (with R. Usher and I. Bryant) (Routledge, 1997) and 'Lifelong Learning and Unemployment: A UK Perspective', in *Lifelong Learning and Disadvantage: Hungarian and British Perspectives* (K. Percy (ed.)) (University of Lancaster, 1997).

Keith Jones is a Lecturer in Education in the Research and Graduate School of Education, University of Southampton. His specialisms are mathematics education and quantitative methodology in education research. With more than twenty publications to his name, he has participated, by invitation, in two international studies, one on the teaching of geometry and the other on the teaching of mathematics at university level. His jointly authored text *Quantitative Analysis in Education Research* (published by the University of Southampton) is now in its second edition.

Saville Kushner is Associate Dean and Professor of Applied Research at the University of the West of England, Bristol. He is a theorist and practitioner of educational evaluation whose interest and experience have focused on case study. Prior to this post he worked with a group of evaluators at the Centre for Applied Research in Education (CARE) at the University of East Anglia, perhaps best known for its advocacy of Democratic Evaluation.

Mary McKeever is a PhD student in the Research and Graduate School of Education, University of Southampton. She also works as a part-time tutor in Study Skills and English Literature. She has spent eleven years doing literacy work in South Africa and teaching English for Academic Purposes at the University of the Witwatersrand.

Jon Prosser is Senior Lecturer in International Management Education at the University of Leeds. His research interests are in qualitative research methods, particularly the application of images in the research process; school culture, improvement and effectiveness; and child abuse investigation. He has published in the *British Education Research Journal* and *Visual Sociology* and is the editor (and a contributing author) of both *Image Based Research: A Source Book for Qualitative Researchers* (Falmer Press, 1998) and *School Culture* (Paul Chapman Publishing, 1999).

Pat Usher is Head of the Quality Assurance Unit, University of Southampton. She is also a part-time tutor with the Open University and the Research and Graduate School of Education, University of Southampton. Her research interests are in gender issues in post-compulsory education, feminist theory and feminist approaches to research, and the relationship between feminism and postmodernism, She has contributed chapters to *Understanding Educational Research* (ed. D Scott and R. Usher) (Routledge, 1996), *Understanding Social Research* (ed. G. McKenzie, J. Powell and R. Usher) (Falmer, 1997) and *Transitions, Loss and Change* (ed. R. Weston and T. Martin) (Blackwell, 1998).

Chapter 1

Introduction

Ethics in the practice of research

Helen Simons and Robin Usher

This book is intended to fill a gap in the current literature on both educational research and applied ethics. Although there is now no shortage of literature on educational research, little of this has focused explicitly on applied ethical issues. Moreover, when it has, a somewhat traditional view of ethics has been taken. At the same time, the literature on ethics, particularly applied ethics, has burgeoned and questions about the possible situated nature of ethics have come to the fore. One reason for this is that traditional conceptions of ethics have had to be reconfigured in the face of the challenges posed on the one hand by contemporary feminist and postmodern thinking, and on the other, by an increasing awareness on the part of educational researchers of the changing and increasingly complex nature of the environment in which they have to work.

The aim of the book, then, is to bring together situated ethics and educational research by showing the place and role of the former in the latter – in other words, to show how ethical judgements come about within particular fields and practices of educational research; how, in effect, an ethics is constructed and practised. While ethics has traditionally been seen as a set of general principles invariantly and validly applied to all situations, it will be argued that, on the contrary, ethical principles are mediated within different research practices and thus take on different significances in relation to those practices. The book therefore is located at the interface of ethical practice and educational research, and attempts to show what an applied ethics means and how it works in the practices of educational research.

What we have tried to do is exemplify this interface by developing the notion of situated ethics through examining how ethical issues are handled in practice by educational researchers in the field. While some of the chapters have a more theoretical emphasis, all the contributions are located in the diversity of practices that characterize educational research and many have drawn on their author's experience to demonstrate what a situated ethics means in the context of that practice.

We believe that what emerges is a book that will be of interest to academic educationalists, educational researchers and practitioners in all sectors of education. In particular, those involved in conducting research into their own policy contexts, where ethical issues are assuming an increasingly politicized status, will find much of relevance here. As we have noted, there is little in existence that addresses the consequent dilemmas and the ethical problems that need to be resolved in these contexts. Furthermore, given that most of the contributions deal with qualitative research, all those working in this way should find something of interest. There is also much here that would interest researchers and practitioners in other professions, particularly where research and continuing professional development are intimately linked and where issues of applied ethics have become increasingly critical. While the main focus here is on education, the ethical issues are treated in a sufficiently general way to speak to all those engaged in social research.

When we first started work on this book, we envisaged that at some point, probably in this Introduction, we would need to set out a theorization of situated ethics. We felt that it would be necessary to try to nail this notion down by providing a reasonably full explanation. However, as the book progressed and as the time arrived to start thinking about an introduction, we realized that such an explanation was unnecessary because in a very real sense the contributing chapters themselves exemplify the nature of situated ethics. At the same time, through reflecting on what had happened in the compiling of this volume, we came to understand that any attempt to theorize situated ethics would be an impossible and self-contradictory enterprise.

For us, the whole point about a situated ethics is precisely that it is *situated*, and this implies that it is immune to universalization. A situated ethics is local and specific to particular practices. It cannot be universalized, and therefore any attempt to formulate a theory of situated ethics, given that any theorization strives for universality, must be doomed to failure. This is not to say that in any particular practice universal statements or principles of a general nature are inappropriate and unhelpful. However, it is to say that any such statements or principles will be mediated by the local and specific – by, in other words, the situatedness which constitutes that practice. This realization of ours was reinforced by our belief that education research is a social practice, or more accurately a variety of social practices, each with its own set of ethical issues. Researchers cannot avoid weighing up often conflicting considerations and dilemmas which are located in the specificities of the research situation and where there is a need to make ethical decisions but where those decisions cannot be reached by appeal to unambiguous and univalent principles or codes.

Of course, it is very clear by now that we as editors do have a particular philosophical and political stance, one shared in varying degrees by all the contributors. This position is one influenced in a very eclectic way by postmodern, feminist and postcolonial ideas and democratic intent. For want of a better term, we can characterize this position as post-positivist. It has in common a questioning of notions of scientific objectivity and value neutrality, and a recognition of the significance of the socio-political context of all research. While we would not wish to be understood as espousing an 'anything goes' relativism, we do question universalism and foundationalism. But in so doing we do not thereby abandon ethics, as some critics of this position would claim. On the contrary, we emphasize the inescapable necessity for making ethical decisions and the difficulty and complexity of such decision-making in situations where recourse cannot be had to indubitable foundations and incontrovertible principles. Whatever relativistic tendencies may be discerned are more apparent than real, although perhaps the kind of ethics we are talking about is not located within the mainstream canon of Western philosophy.

We have elected therefore to allow each chapter to speak its own story about ethics and ethical decisions. We believe that each chapter tells a story of how practical moral reasoning is developed within particular research practices. By doing so we believe that what follows is an implicit problematizing of dominant notions of objective and universalistic morality – notions which we would argue have usually served to disguise class, race and gendered explanations about 'sameness' that privilege dominant groups and exclude equally valid difference and diversity – a difference and diversity which is mirrored in the book.

Our hope, then, is that even though we have eschewed an overarching explanation, this Introduction will at least allow readers to locate themselves within the book and to obtain some idea of what follows. We proceed now with a brief description of each of the chapters to further this process and to highlight the common linking themes as well as the significant differences.

We begin with a chapter by Sally Glen on integrity, with the intriguing title 'The dark side of purity or the virtues of double-mindedness?'. Although the chapter is written in the context of healthcare practitioner action research, the issues it raises have theoretical and practical implications for all researchers. Glen's essential thesis is that an adequate formulation of integrity as an ethical concept cannot be derived from ethical theory alone, but needs to engage pragmatically with the researcher's own reflective practice discourse. She demonstrates this through both an exploration of pertinent ethical theory and a case example.

While adherence to a core set of principles or commitments grants us authenticity and honesty as researchers in one sense, many of the conflicts and challenges we encounter in research also require a fundamental re-examination of our own value stance. Glen uses the concepts of external and internal integrity to mark this distinction. Integrity is about wholeness as much as it is about consistency of action. 'Being true to one's self' and one's most cherished values (internal integrity) is integral to a 'moral career'.

She also makes a clear distinction between simple integrity – that undeniable belief and commitment to principles that tells us we are right – and complex integrity which recognizes and needs to take into account the multifaceted and conflictual nature of much experience. The attraction of restricting oneself to a small, coherent and absolute set of values and principles is clear: the absence of conflict where there is no need to question courses of action and the self-confidence that comes from knowing one is right. One can act decisively. However, taken too far, adhering too rigidly to the singleness of purpose and unity of self associated with simple integrity may be ultimately self-limiting. The failure to reflect becomes habit, formulae and algorithms replace thinking and problematizing, but most importantly, opportunities for growth of oneself and of others may be lost. Complex situations require a researcher to act reflexively with complicated sets of issues and values, constantly re-examining one's values in interactive contexts – hence the conclusion and virtues referred to in the title of the chapter, not of purity, but of double-mindedness.

Chapter 3, 'Feminist approaches to a situated ethics' by Pat Usher, also addresses the complexity of practice but distinctly from a feminist perspective. Usher begins by asking what is distinctive about feminist ethics and, through an analysis of feminist philosophy, shows how concepts and issues – such as reason, truth, objectivity, virtue, for example – that might seem neutral are in reality coded by masculine assumptions. Feminist ethics, she claims, challenges ethical norms that are derived from abstract ideas of a universally shared interest, as such traditions do not respect either individual or social differences. Space for women to represent their own self-images, choices and patterns of moral evaluation is essential to a feminist ethics.

Usher makes a strong case for researchers positioning themselves clearly in the text, and exemplifies this in her own case in declaring her discussion of ethical practice to be located within feminist approaches which 'believe that moral and social life are completely intertwined and that all knowledge, including moral knowledge, is situated'. Drawing on both feminist theory and postmodern philosophy, she then explores the essential characteristics of feminist ethics, first by examining feminist epistemology and its critique, and second by relating this to issues of gender difference and morality. One critical question she explores is how the contrasting debates about an ethics based on justice and rights and one based on care and responsibility open up the possibility of an ethics that can incorporate insights from both. The chapter explores the implications of these debates for the relationships we create in research, the role of the self and the consequences for how we regard 'experience', 'voice' and 'authenticity'. In conclusion Usher reaffirms the commitment in a feminist ethics to document and understand that subjectivities and moral voices are constituted from their distinctive social, cultural and historical settings.

The next two chapters stem from the field of evaluation, which raises a distinctive further dimension: that of the explicit political intent and repercussions of the production and sharing of knowledge gained in highly politicized and sensitive contexts. Chapter 4, 'Damned if you do, damned if you don't: ethical and political dilemmas in evaluation' by Helen Simons, both reinforces the importance of a situated ethics in practice and directly explores this political dimension. Simons argues that in evaluation all ethics are situated, since the very task of evaluation is particular, practical and inherently political. Making decisions as to how to act involves complex ethical and political judgements. While this may be true in all forms of educational research – the argument of this book, in a sense, for the situatedness of ethical judgement – the inherent political nature of evaluation brings it centre stage. Politics and ethics are inextricably entwined. This refers not only to the need to be responsive and fair in the process and dissemination of evaluation to the many different interest groups who have a stake in the evaluation, but to how the evaluation strategically manages the politics of the site being evaluated.

Simons illustrates this essential connection between ethics and politics through an analysis of two specific dilemmas she faced in conducting programme evaluations, one funded by a major government department, the other by the European Union. The two case studies, or 'scenarios', are long, but deliberately so, as she outlines the dilemmas she faced in each and reflects on the many and varied factors she had to take into account in the complex ethical/political judgements she had to make in each case.

Chapter 5 by Saville Kushner, '"Come into my parlour": ethical space and the conduct of evaluation', explores the multiplicity of factors that an evaluator confronts in conducting evaluations in highly sensitive contexts. Drawing on his experience of evaluation in different cases, in some very intimate contexts such as a hospice, Kushner demonstrates not only the diversity and uniqueness of ethical decisions that need to be made but the effect that coming to such decisions had on himself. The social world, he says, 'lays multiple traps' for the evaluator. There is no point in searching for an elusive principle to arbitrate in the midst of conflicting ethical impulses. Ethical decisions have to be taken against a background of institutional complexities, personal responses and multiple, often conflicting, expectations. The evaluator needs to respond in multifarious, unique ways with the 'complex integrity', in effect, that Glen raises in her chapter.

The practice of evaluation creates an ethical space in which some people are invited to make novel judgements about the work of others, guided by rules governing the conduct of evaluation. But that ethical space is not neutral, nor can it be impartial with regard to particular stakeholders. What is exposed are moral decisions that previously may not have been explicit, and these may conflict with the ethical decisions reached in the evaluation. Through the presentation of a number of vignettes, Kushner illustrates the ethical dilemmas he faced in operating in this ethical space, dilemmas such as when an institutional and a personal ethic conflict, when the case contaminates the context, and when evaluators confuse private morality for public ethics. The ethical space is central both to the role of evaluation and to its goals. Like Simons, Kushner claims that the evaluator needs to be independent of the ethics of the prevailing political culture in order to put this itself under scrutiny. Similarly, the evaluation needs to consider how the process – the journey in the ethical space – needs to incorporate a dialogue about ends rather than take them as givens. The chapter concludes with a commentary on how difficult it is to maintain a sensitive ethics in a contemporary political context that seems hostile to the very concept of ethics itself.

These four chapters in different fields of educational research together present an argument for the complex integrity that Glen outlines, illustrating the need for researchers to act self-reflexively and in the process constantly to re-examine their own values and position in relation to themselves and to what or whom is being researched.

The next three chapters, 6, 7 and 8, address the ethical issues that arise when one is researching disadvantaged groups in society. In the first, the focus is on the unemployed and the explicit intent of trying to make a difference to their experience through the adoption of an emancipatory methodology. In the second, the emphasis is on researching race in a predominantly white urban society. In the third, the focus is on schooling for black manual workers in South Africa. While the emancipatory methodology adopted in Chapter 6 is not explicitly adopted in Chapters 7 and 8, the clear intent is to understand and validly represent the experience and voice of other groups. The contexts of these chapters are markedly different, yet many of the issues raised in all three chapters have a common aim: to enhance awareness and improve the external life prospects for the respective groups involved in the research.

Chapter 6 by Rennie Johnston, 'Whose side, whose research, whose learning, whose outcomes? Ethics, emancipatory research and unemployment', explores key ethical issues in emancipatory research primarily through the example of a participatory action research project, led by the author, of unemployment in a city in the United Kingdom. The project in question was one of a series of local development projects funded through the Department of Education and Science in the Thatcher regime's first concerted response to the dramatic increase in unemployment following its rise to power. The chapter first locates the discourse of emancipatory research within the broad spectrum of research practices that are designed to bring about social change, and outlines its essential advocacy position, which is to try, through one's research practices, to play a part in the emancipation of oppressed groups – those who suffer from social and economic inequality and a lack of social justice. Unlike some research practices that aspire to political neutrality, emancipatory research is clearly about acting politically, and ethically, in the world.

The central part of the chapter then explores, through the case example, the ethical issues that arise in conducting research with this aim. Key issues that are addressed are partisanship and objectivity, research for empowerment, the interrelationship between methodology and outcomes, ownership of the research process, researcher reflexivity and appropriate evaluation and dissemination. The author is aware of the dangers of claiming too much for this style of research, and imposing, for example, yet another 'regime of truth' upon research subjects. 'Giving power to the people' may have a hollow ring to it in a political system dominated by an ideology of power and control. Yet in specific local contexts over time, much can be achieved. This chapter therefore explores the extent to which a degree of emancipation was possible in the particular case in question, and the ethical issues that were confronted and to some extent resolved along the way.

In Chapter 7, 'Researching education and racialization: virtue or validity?', Peter Figueroa begins by making the point that 'racism, "race" and anti-racism are among the most sensitive issues in public discourse' and that therefore the ethical issues raised in researching this field are 'complex, controversial and pressing'. The chapter explores these issues in depth, presenting many examples from actual field practice that exemplify significant ethical questions whose relevance is not confined exclusively to racism research.

Among many critical questions raised, the key one probably is to do with whether an emphasis on ethical issues militates against sound research and valid impartial knowledge. Figueroa asks, 'Is the educational researcher focusing on issues of cultural diversity, inequality, racism and antiracism confronted with a choice between virtue and validity, between social justice and truth?' The answer is that there are no easy answers. The only thing that is clear is that while ethics can provide guidance, the ethical process is mainly about articulating perplexity. Thus while there is always a need to make decisions and take action, particularly when in the field, there is no abstract set of principles that can indubitably point to what decisions need to be made and what actions have to be taken. Furthermore, there is a uniqueness to every situation which means that ethical issues are never resolvable in a once-and-for-all way. All we can do, therefore, he concludes, is to be constantly vigilant and reflexive, adopt a critical approach, and seek to build a sustainable case for what we do as researchers.

In Chapter 8, 'Snakes and ladders: ethical issues in conducting educational research in a postcolonial context', Mary McKeever draws our attention to the ethical dilemmas a white researcher confronts when conducting research in South Africa, in this particular case in a school set up by university black manual workers who themselves had not had the opportunity to attend places of learning. McKeever locates the ethical dilemmas she faced working in and researching this school within a history of the rise of the colonial university and Bantu education and within some of the issues raised by postcolonial theorizations. What right has she, she asks, to research black experience? Is there a danger in privileging imported educational practices, thereby contributing to the demise of traditional understandings? How fair is it to produce knowledge that, given the power base from which research is conducted – the university – possibly perpetuates a colonialist ethics? In exploring these questions and having to make difficult decisions about how to act, McKeever not only listens to her own voice but seeks out the voice of the workers as to whether and how she can fairly represent their experience and context.

Some of the ethical issues discussed – such as whom to report to and how – have resonance in other cultures, but in the particular context McKeever describes, the differential power of the knowledge producers is more sharply contrasted with the power of the researched, and the danger of exploitation that reinforces the dominant culture is ever present. The chapter concludes by re-examining the central issue of whose knowledge is at stake in researching in postcolonial contexts.

The next two chapters, 9 and 10, take us into relatively new fields in which to examine ethical issues in educational research. Both explore how some familiar ethical issues in educational research need to be reassessed in these new contexts; in the first case where images speak louder than words and in the second where a dominant ideology threatens to label and complicate the researcher's access and exit from the field.

Chapter 9, 'The moral maze of image ethics' by Jon Prosser, explores the use of visual images in educational research. Visually oriented research is a relative 'newcomer' to the field of qualitative educational research and its ethical principles and precepts are yet to be fully established. Early practice in the fields of visual sociology and visual anthropology, says Prosser, has done more to discredit than enhance image-based research, and currently there is little ethical consensus about how to use images in educational research.

While some of the ethical issues that confront image-based researchers are the same as those which 'wordsmiths' experience, there are others that are unique to the visual image. There is no possibility of anonymizing the person photographed by changing the face in the way that one can change the name in a written text; there is also little scope for disguising the context. Participants see themselves and are seen by others. The notions of informed consent, deception, construction of reality and whose construction it is, take on a different complexion when there is a lasting image that the world can see. Then there are other questions. Does the aesthetics of the image communicate or distort? How does the image change when used with words? To what extent is the use of photographic techniques to highlight images valid and ethical? How do you overcome the belief in the veracity of the photograph, 'the camera never lies' – or does it only lie more effectively than do words?

The chapter is divided into two parts, each exploring some twists and turns in the moral maze. The first examines still photography, providing examples from the author's own work to illustrate the ethical dilemmas he faced in conducting research using photographs. The second explores moving images, with the emphasis on documentary-type film and video. The chapter concludes by suggesting that image-based researchers need to step back, in a sense, to develop a code of practice to establish consensus of conduct and confidence in the field – although as with all chapters in this book, such a code will provide only a guiding framework for action. In situ, in practice, in the ethical moment that Usher speaks of in the final chapter and the politics of the site that Simons raises, many factors interact in the ethical decisions that have to be taken.

The title of Chapter 10, 'Dancing with the devil: ethics and research in educational markets' by Nick Foskett, is invoked to highlight some of the dilemmas a researcher encounters researching educational markets in a climate dominated by a market culture. '"Markets" and "marketing" are not neutral terms from a values perspective for most working in educational environments,' says Foskett. The researching of educational markets therefore poses new ethical challenges for educational researchers. These centre around questions of access, the researchers' intervention in the market, inequitable benefit from research into markets, and ethical issues involved in researching life decisions. The chapter takes these four sets of issues and illustrates, with examples from published research into educational markets, how the researchers handled the issue in the particular context.

The question of gaining access, for instance, takes on a different perspective in researching education markets as the researcher has to contend with the ethical objection many make to the ideology of markets, and with the possible perception that one may be 'dancing with the devil' – or alternatively that one might have an anti-market stance and an a priori prejudice to critique market processes. What to do in this situation? Is deception ever justified? The critical issue of 'winners and losers' from research findings also takes on a different status in a competitive environment, where organizations can gain market (and financial) advantage from early data release, from disadvantaging data or even by merely participating in the research. Furthermore, certain groups of people and institutions know how to use such 'institutional cultural capital' to their advantage. The chapter concludes by suggesting that if researchers do not address the ethical issues it raises, they may find themselves the losers in the education marketing research marketplace!

The penultimate chapter, Chapter 11 by Keith Jones, 'A regrettable oversight or a significant omission? Ethical considerations in quantitative research in education', at first sight may seem an anomaly in a book devoted primarily to situated ethics in qualitative educational research. However, it would have been a regrettable oversight had the book not acknowledged and included a chapter which explores the relevance of ethical issues in quantitative research. The chapter starts with a vignette from an international study that illustrates the potential harm that can arise when nations fight over results and when the technical reports show no explicit consideration of ethical issues. The chapter has three sections. The first, through data from a small-scale survey, demonstrates the omission of discussion of ethical issues in standard texts on quantitative research. The second indicates where, in the quantitative research process, ethical issues need to be considered. The third examines the extent and impact of variations in use of these issues in four kinds of research studies which use quantitative measures: intelligence testing, gender differences in achievement, teaching methods and school effectiveness. The chapter concludes by returning to the question in the title, indicating (with reference to the lack of attention to ethics in quantitative research texts) that what once might have seemed a regrettable oversight is indeed a significant omission

Like several authors in this volume who are arguing for ethical decisions to be made *in situ* in relation to specific contexts, Robin Usher in the final chapter, 'Deconstructive happening, ethical moment', argues that there is an ethical moment in the research process that is not purely a function of the application of ethical codes and principles of practice. These have their place, but his concern is with the conditions of possibility that exist in the very process of research itself and that precede the application of codes and applications. He argues further that the deconstructive happening, in the title of the chapter, reveals this ethical moment because deconstruction *is* an ethics, though not perhaps one that is commonly understood as such.

The chapter begins by locating some relevant concepts of deconstruction, including those of boundaries and certainties, binaries and hierarchies, drawn from the work of Jacques Derrida. There follow two examples of research texts that embody deconstructive readings, where the author shows how deconstruction works to reveal the ethical moment in the research process. In the final part of the chapter, further explication is offered of this concept of the ethical moment in any act of knowledge production. In exploring the implications of the position that 'there is no safe ground upon which to base decisions, no pure criteria to be used for judgements, instead there is only radical undecidability', Usher reminds us that research, whichever paradigm is adopted, is a rhetorical practice, as much about values as it is about method and outcomes. Furthermore, in accepting the inseparability of knowledge and power, the emphasis on reflexivity, and the positioning of the researcher, the notion of research is itself transformed, with both researcher and researched as active creators of knowledge and where the aim becomes that of *exploring* what reality could become, rather than simply *explaining* what it is. With this analysis, Usher comes to a conclusion similar to that of earlier chapters. The methodologies and field of practice may be different but the aspiration for a research practice and empirical enquiry that is more open, less certain and potentially more liberating for the researcher as well as the researched is the same.

While it is difficult to summarize fully the content of the various chapters, they nevertheless have a number of themes in common related to situated ethics. These include:

- the challenge to universal principles and codes;
- the importance of being sensitive to socio-political contexts;
- the scope for being fair to disadvantaged groups; and
- taking account of the diversity and uniqueness of different research practices.

In presenting detailed examples of how researchers actually came to make ethical decisions in these different practices, this collection offers a kind of guidance different from that generally presented in literature on ethical codes. What the examples also demonstrate is that making ethical decisions, in whatever situated context, is a process of creating, maintaining and justifying an ethical integrity that is more dependent on sensitivity to politics and people than it is on ethical principles and codes.

Chapter 2

The dark side of purity or the virtues of double-mindedness?

Sally Glen

INTRODUCTION

This chapter takes a critical look at the concept of integrity and argues that this concept is a golden thread which runs through healthcare practitioner action research. Action research is becoming increasingly popular among nurse researchers. It is seen to offer a means of narrowing the gap between theory and practice, of promoting the development of the nurse as a 'practitioner/researcher', and of empowering nurses and users to bring about change in their lives and work (Greenwood 1984; Webb 1989, 1990; Titchen and Binnie 1993; Hart 1995). Moreover, the combination of enquiry, intervention and evaluation which powers the action research cycle mirrors the iterative processes employed by healthcare staff in assessing the needs of vulnerable people, responding to them and reviewing progress. Thus, many healthcare practitioners are familiar with an action research approach, even though they might not explicitly label what they do as action research (Hart and Bond 1995).

An adequate formulation and defence of integrity as a complex ethical concept rests not simply in appeal to ethical theory but on a complex pragmatic process and the healthcare action researcher using his or her own reflective practical discourse. In the broadest sense, integrity entails being true to the person so identified, acting in accordance with that core set of principles or commitments that make us who we are. Although integrity entails this, the notion of authenticity, there is more to it than that. For integrity involves wholeness as well as consistency. It locates itself not just in isolated, discrete instances of authentic adherence to principles, but rather in consistent exemplification of the latter over a professional lifetime. The principal subject of integrity is an entire life, conceived temporally as having a beginning, a middle and an end (Benjamin 1990). An analysis of integrity in healthcare practitioner action research brings to the surface moral tensions which healthcare professional action researchers experience both in themselves (i.e. 'internal integrity' – resolving conflicts among competing values, principles and desires within a single person) and in relationships with other healthcare professionals ('external integrity' – compromise between parties, social groups or organizations). Goffman's (1961) work focuses on the notion that each person's life can be viewed as a 'moral career'. He suggests that each moral career has two sides. Internally, it involves how persons see themselves, how they experience their identities and the motivations that influence them. Externally, it involves the influence of social groups, and the influence of hierarchical systems and organizations. Maintaining moral careers involves regular changes in how persons view themselves and their criteria for judging themselves and others.

The person of integrity is someone whose life is 'of a piece'; whose self is 'whole and integrated' (Taylor 1981). Since a human life, throughout the course of its existence, characteristically encounters and interacts with a multifarious array of values and principles, not all of which can be pursued, this second sense of integrity – wholeness – necessitates ordering these into some coherent, integrated pattern (Kekes 1983). There may be something inappropriate, hard-nosed and uncompromising about popular renditions of the concept of integrity when analysed within the context of an ethical practice such as nursing. Or as Rand (1964) unrelentingly advocates, 'There can be no compromise on basic principles nor on fundamental issues . . . [w]hen people speak of "compromise" what they mean is . . . the betrayal of their principles' (quoted in Benjamin 1990: 4).

Such a conceptualization of integrity may be incongruent with the complex pragmatic process which constitutes action research within health-care practice.

CHARACTERIZATION OF INTEGRITY

The most famous conception of integrity is Polonius's notion of being true to oneself. Integrity here is associated with personal ideals or conviction, the notion of being true to those values and principles of whose import one is utterly and completely convinced. Integrity insists that a merely conventional relationship to one's values and principles is not enough. Instead, one must genuinely or authentically espouse them, one must speak 'in the first person' and make one's principles one's own (McFall 1987). We might thus characterize integrity as involving 'a coherent and stable set of highly cherished values and principles'; 'verbal behaviour expressing those values and principles'; and 'conduct concretising those values and principles consistent with what one says' (Benjamin 1990). Implicit in the notion of owning one's principles is the existential dictum that such things as principles, goals and so forth are not pre-ordained givens to which one must conform. Human beings, and most certainly healthcare action researchers, can always stand back from their ongoing world and evaluate the beliefs and values thrust on them. They can always envision further possibilities, always conceive of and opt for alternative beliefs, alternative values. Porter (1993) argues that the values of the research are, in fact, central to the research process, particularly as nurse researchers are part of the social situation they study. Similarly, Reason and Rowan (1981, preface) advocate the need to make it clear 'where one is coming from'. This stance, they suggest, contributes to making research 'objectively subjective', which is the basis of their 'new-paradigm research'.

A growing number of philosophers are raising doubts about the possibility of a complete and wholly integrated set of moral values and principles – even for one person (Nagel 1979; Hampshire 1983; Williams 1985). These philosophers argue that a complete and fully integrated set of moral values and principles is unattainable. Personal and professional identity in healthcare practice and healthcare action research are constituted by a complex constellation of values and principles. And, 'to pursue the course of action that seems on balance to follow from the preponderance of one's central and most highly cherished values and principles cannot be regarded as betraying one's integrity' (Benjamin 1990: 37).

The moral nature of healthcare practice and action research is inherent in the healthcare professional–client/patient relationship (Yarling and McElmurray 1986; Kelly 1990) and therefore inherent in the practice of the healthcare practitioner action researcher. Moral conflicts are of course deliberately avoided if one restricts one's values and principles to a small set which are coherent and closely related – a belief in the absolute sanctity of life, for example. While such a move might serve to maintain overall consistency, it does so at a cost, the cost of our humanity. 'Wholeness' has another meaning besides undividedness. It also indicates totality or entirety – the extent of the diverse range of goods in the world. Opening ourselves to the comprehensiveness of such goods in healthcare, and in society more generally, almost inevitably engenders conflict. Yet if we do otherwise – if we sharply limit, in the name of undividedness, our values and principles – then we also sacrifice wholeness. One sense of the word is achieved at the expense of the other. Furthermore, moral disagreement attributable to moral complexity will often be with us – or rather will always be with us (Strawson 1985). Aggravating disagreement in situations of moral complexity is thus our need for integrity. As Strawson (ibid.: viii) observes,

> Truth in philosophy though not to be despaired of, is so complex and many-sided, so multi-faceted that any individual philosopher's work, if it is to have any unity and coherence [this is integrity] must at best emphasise some aspects of the truth, to the neglect of others which may strike another philosopher with greater force.

What is true of philosophy in general is true of ethics or moral philosophy in particular. Paraphrasing Strawson, one might argue that the ethical issues in healthcare presented by moral complexity are often compounded by practical constraints. As Kuflick (1977: 50) notes, limitations of time, energy and circumstances are often such that individuals become sensitive or are increasingly preoccupied with different aspects of the same reasonably complex moral problem. In the following example, the nurse/practitioner/action researcher has to balance her obligations among three parties: the young girl, her mother and her potential child – whose needs or claims are to be given priority when a nurse cannot respond to all of those to whom she has a prima facie obligation.

Case example

Sandy Wilson, 14 years old, had just completed a six-month check-up for a fractured ankle. The fracture had healed completely without complications, but her haemoglobin was in the low normal range. As a precautionary measure she was sent to Kate Stewart, a nurse practitioner, for diet counselling. Before long, Sandy confided that she thought she was pregnant and that she did not want anyone else to know, especially her mother. Upon brief questioning it became evident to Kate that Sandy had no clear idea of what she was going to do about the suspected pregnancy. However, before Kate could begin to help her think the situation through, Mrs Wilson came in. Mrs Wilson said that Sandy had been nauseous and very tired lately and she asked Kate if she had any idea what could be causing it. As Kate prepared to respond, Sandy remained silent and glared at her.

In considering this example, Schon's (1983) phrase about professional knowledge being constituted by a 'reflective conversation with a unique and changing situation' is an important starting point, with its assumption that a living, developing dialogue is embodied in the very nature of the way reflective practitioners act and think. Collingwood (1924), referring to Plato, puts forward a similar view that 'true knowledge' is dialectical, based on 'the interplay of question and answer'.

What is the nature of Kate's dilemma here? Although there is a presumption that nurses should *maintain confidence*, there is also a *presumption* about the need to reply almost immediately to Mrs Wilson. The moral complexity in this case is due to a conflict between these presumptions. The practical constraints relate to the limited information available to Kate. Hesitancy itself could signify to Mrs Wilson that Kate is being less than honest and direct. Choosing between maintaining confidence and avoiding deception is very difficult. Kate may choose to become preoccupied with the fact that teenage pregnancies pose a high risk to both mother and baby. If Sandy decides (or has already decided) not to have an abortion, obtaining good parental care is important, and Sandy's mother may be instrumental in helping her to get it. Another reason for being truthful with Mrs Wilson is to refrain from reinforcing Sandy's avoidance of her problems. If Kate were to support Sandy's deception, she would undercut her own professional efforts to help Sandy develop effective ways of coping with difficult problems. Alternatively, Kate may become preoccupied with the importance of maintaining trust in the nurse–client relationship. Kate is well aware that a young pregnant girl's trust in her, as a nurse, must be preserved. The questions and answers of the dialectical form described here are not separate from Kate's practice, conceptualized as a form of action research; they are part of it, emerging from it, and feeding back into it. Reflection is not concerned just with being thoughtful, but is about turning experience in practice into learning (Jarvis 1992; Rogers 1992).

COMPROMISE: AN ETHICAL POSSIBILITY?

Can healthcare professionals ever compromise on matters of ethical principles without compromising their integrity? If so, when and how? (Benjamin 1990: ix). In ethics, compromise is usually regarded as a sign of weakness or lack of integrity. One of the most basic questions is whether two (or more) parties to a disagreement rooted in highly cherished but conflicting ethical convictions can compromise without sacrificing their integrity. Many believe that on matters of ethical significance, there can be no compromise – no compromise, one might say, without somehow being compromised. However, contrary inclinations, while often painful and frustrating, have the benefit of inducing careful consideration on one's attachment. Or as Sophocles (1965) writes in Antigone, 'There is something to be said, my lord, for his point of view, and for yours as well; there is much [to be] said on both sides.'

Kate's dilemma illustrates, as suggested above, that when one is drawn in different directions, one is forced to reflect deeply on one's professional commitments, to re-evaluate their importance and to decide thereafter which of them to satisfy, which to thwart. We usually choose to make partial, though not necessarily equal, sacrifices of the competing goals and obligations. Sometimes we do this unconsciously; at other times we engage in what might be called deep or reflective self-evaluation (Dennett 1976; Taylor 1976), debating, arguing, negotiating and bargaining with ourselves just as we do with others. Although we may continue to experience tension and to some extent sacrifice simple consistency, we often prefer an internal compromise of this sort to an all-or-nothing kind of resolution. Therefore Kate could try to soften the dilemma by asking if Mrs Wilson would leave the room for a short while so that she could talk to Sandy alone. Kate would then have time to assess Sandy's perception of family relationships. Kate could also indicate why she would like to release herself from maintaining confidentiality so that she, Kate, could deal more openly with Mrs Wilson.

The same is possibly more dramatically true when a nurse moderates her (or his) commitment to the sanctity of life. In order to mitigate suffering and distress, the nurse compromises between two different ethical commitments: to preserve and extend life, and to relieve suffering (Brewin 1985). As Brewin (1985: 490) notes, 'It is easy to denigrate [internal] compromise of this kind. But sometimes the only alternative is to embrace one noble principle and murder another which seems even worse. So we compromise; but we hope, in a civilised and humane manner.'

Integrity is not a matter of all or none with regard to internal or intrapersonal compromise. It may not have to be a matter of all or none with regard to external or interpersonal compromise either. As individuals we may be able to engage in a certain amount of external compromise without being compromised. An outcome is not a compromise when each of the parties comes to regard its initial position as a mistake, abandons it, and embraces the same third position, which both now believe to be superior. If this new-found mutually preferred position seems somehow to split the difference between the polar positions, we will characterize it as a synthesis middle-of-the-road position – what might be described as compromise in the loose sense rather than as a compromise in the strict sense. Double-mindedness, within the context of nursing practice, in short, forces one to stop and think before one acts (Kekes 1983). It compels one to consider, yet again, the kind of healthcare professional action researcher one is going to be, the worthiness or unworthiness of our current wants and inclinations, the possibility or inconceivability of their being assimilated into our professional identities.

Thinking such as this is part of being a reflective moral agent and possibly moral carer, and has much relevance for any analysis of the concept of integrity within the context of nursing. Gilligan in her book *In a Different Voice* (1982) articulates a conception of morality that has come to be known as feminist ethics. Reacting to Kohlberg's delineation of women as morally immature – unappreciative or incapable of perceiving the force of universal reason – Gilligan characterizes women as different but not deficient moral reasoners. In so doing, she contrasts male morality – an ethic of rights or justice – with female morality – an ethic of care or responsibility. The first emphasizes separateness and individual rights, the second emphasizes attachment, the urge to care and to avoid hurt. Ultimately, Gilligan suggests, these two perspectives converge. A fully mature view would acknowledge the truth of both (1982: 165–7).

Noddings' (1984) book *Caring: A Feminine Approach to Ethics and Moral Education* has many points, central to ethical theory, that might support a concept of integrity more appropriate to healthcare practice. Perhaps most central is Noddings' shift of the source of ethical sentiment from rules to natural sentiment – especially, caring. This shift includes two elements of particular importance. First, there is a refusal to rely on principles and rules. Noddings explains how considering the particulars of a situation helps one make a decision about what to do in the situation (ibid.: 57). In short, principles don't tell us when to apply them, and in the long run they work only when we don't really need them. She argues that to accept the universalizability of principles,

> we would have to establish that human predicaments exhibit sufficient sameness, and this we cannot do without abstracting away from concrete situations those qualities that seem to reveal sameness. In doing this, we often lose the very qualities or factors that give rise to the more questions in the situation.
>
> (ibid.: 85)

This does not mean, however, that we reject principles altogether. It is just that we regard them as guidelines, not ultimate arbiters of behaviour. 'The one caring displays a characteristic variability in her actions – she acts in a non-rule bound fashion on behalf of the cared-for' (ibid.: 25).

The second aspect of Noddings' shift from rule-oriented ethics to an ethics of caring is her focus on interaction between ethical parties. Her position is that relation is ontologically basic and the caring relation is ethically basic (Noddings 1984: 3). She argues, 'Taking relation as ontologically basic simply means that we recognise human encounter and affective response as a basic fact of human existence' (ibid.: 4).

She contrasts the philosopher who begins with a supremely free consciousness, one who has an aloneness and emptiness at the heart of existence, with one who recognizes and longs for relatedness (Noddings 1984: 6). She suggests that our efforts must be 'directed to the maintenance of conditions that will permit caring to flourish' (ibid.: 5).

She emphasizes that her concern is not with the judgement or the acts, but with how we meet each other morally (Noddings 1984: 5). In particular, she introduces in caring the idea of receiving the other, of apprehending their reality (ibid.: 14). 'Caring involves stepping out of one's own personal frame of reference into the other's. When we care, we consider the other's point of view' (ibid.: 24).

Care entails attuning oneself to the needs and wants of others with whom we are in relation. Moreover, it involves doing so in a given situation. Women's thinking, that is to say, is inherently contextual. It emphasizes the particulars of a situation, the detail and texture that comes with knowledge of specific people and specific circumstances (Gilligan 1982: 101). And it insists that rather than being deduced from general principles, decisions must instead be made responsively – one considers, among other things, what is harmful to each distinctive individual and recoils from acting thus. The care perspective, in brief, involves a primary commitment to 'other persons in the wholeness and their particularity', whereas the justice perspective involves a primary commitment to 'general and abstract rules, values or principles' (Friedman 1987: 105). Furthermore, unlike men, who prize highly such notions as autonomy and independence, women's perception of self, suggests Gilligan, is much more tenaciously embedded in relationships with others. They regard themselves as selves in relations, and this orientation prompts them to try to maintain ties where possible while maintaining care and integrity of the self. Overall, women conceptualize life as a 'network of connections, a web of relationships that is sustained by a process of communication' (Gilligan 1982: 33). Kate did not, for example, conceptualize the dilemma she found herself facing as a stark choice between the principles of maintaining confidentiality and a presumption against deception. Instead she sought to reconcile these moral presumptions and thus maintain a constructive professional relationship with both Sandy and her mother. Similarly, in dealing with concrete and particular moral conflicts, healthcare professionals are doing practical ethics; that is, their reasoning and analysis focus on contexts, relationships and questions requiring more or less immediate and consequential moral choices and judgement.

Gilligan's views, particularly the empirical foundations of her claims, have been sharply criticized (Friedman 1987). And not all feminists have been sympathetic. Hoagland (1988), to name but one, points to the 'feminine' character of Gilligan's ethics and challenges the desirability of positing as ethical norms what she describes after Daly (1973) as 'virtues of subservience' – necessary survival skills women have had to learn under oppression. Criticism notwithstanding, however, researchers have noted that women readers of Gilligan's book have found it 'to resonate . . . thoroughly with their own experience' (Friedman 1987: 93). Thus, although not uncontroversial, the core perspective constitutes a central thrust in feminist research on moral theory. More importantly, it further elucidates the ethical practice of many healthcare professionals, often exhibiting a keen awareness of the context in which their practice occurs and often wanting to preserve relationships and keep the line of communication open. Doctors and nurses, as 'gendered professions', inevitably act from different values, motivations and expectations, and there is a communication gap between them. Nurses place the highest value on the 'caring perspective', which entails responsiveness and sensitivity to the patient's wishes. By contrast, doctors value above all the patients' rights and the scientific approach that implies a major concern with disease and its cure (Grundstein-Amado 1992).

Contemporary ethical issues in the practice of medicine and nursing seem, however, to have kindled a need for an ethics grounded in personal relationships and context as a complement to abstract and objective models for solving healthcare ethical issues. A context-sensitive approach to moral commitment may, for example, be the consequence of nursing education because many nursing programmes emphasize the need for contextual knowledge (as well as the application of theory and principles) in order that nurses give individualized nursing care (Benner 1991). This ethical component in nursing can be viewed from an experiential perspective, meaning that moral reflection originates in the clinical context. Similarly, Pallegrine and Tomasina (1981: 5) argue for a new conceptual framework for medical ethics that includes aspects such as 'compassion' and 'doing for another what he/she cannot do for himself/herself'. From this perspective, medicine is viewed not only as a science but also as a value-laden practice, involving personal relationships. The claim that 'health and virtue' are fundamental aspirations of human beings means that the moral enterprise of healthcare needs to develop a theory of ethics based on the realities of everyday practice – in essence, a context-sensitive conception of integrity for healthcare.

CONTEXT-SENSITIVE CONCEPTION OF INTEGRITY FOR HEALTHCARE

Articulating a feminist conception of integrity that explicitly seeks to accommodate radical change, Hoagland (1988: 286) states:

> Focusing on integrity means acknowledging ourselves. . . . It means proceeding from self-understanding . . . becoming aware of what parts of ourselves we want to change, what parts go on hold for now, what parts centre us and what part we want to develop at any given point. It means periodically assessing ourselves in terms of our values and in relation to others and their values.

The relation of question, answer and healthcare practice is an organic, unified one, and this difference within unity is characteristic of the dialectical form – as it is characteristic of ethical healthcare practice action research in the account above. When, in Plato's *Phaedrus*, Socrates is discussing the nature of dialectics, he observes that he is 'a greater lover of these methods of division and collection' that confer 'the ability to discuss unity and plurality as they exist in the nature of things' (Plato 1973). Over two thousand years later, Engels (1934), in formulating his 'laws' of dialectics, speaks of this logical form as 'the science of interconnections'. Comey (1972) also sees the way in which the dialectical form necessarily contains 'opposing elements', which, however, 'form an interrelated polarity so that they presuppose and reciprocally affect each other' (p. 10). The tensions between these elements (the contradictions, for example, that Kate perceives in her practice) 'provide the impetus for change and development; resolution of the conflict is accompanied by progression to a new stage of development' (Comey 1972).

It is precisely this kind of ongoing self-assessment that healthcare professional action researchers should be engaged in. And it is without doubt painful and frustrating. There may be a loss of unity of self and singleness of purpose. As one constantly and honestly monitors who one is and who one is becoming (Davian 1991), one is exhibiting that commitment which forms the basis of integrity – the resolution to face one's professional life in the spirit of truthfulness. Consequently, integrity-preserving compromise is in fact possible. Properly understood, not only is integrity compatible within the modern world of healthcare practice, but the preservation of integrity will occasionally require compromise of a certain sort.

CONCLUSION

Accounts of integrity often suffer from an excessively restrictive understanding of the unity entailed in the integrated healthcare professional action researcher (Callan 1992). Radical conflicts between different roles may propel a professional life into absurdity. But it does not follow that the sheer singleness of purpose of those with simple integrity is the only alternative to such absurdity. It is surely possible to live a richly variegated professional and personal life, one that combines diverse ideals and affinities, and yet maintain an overall if complicated and somewhat untidy sense of unity. Simple integrity may be one kind of integrity but it is certainly not the only kind. Indeed, one wonders if it is even conceivable in the open, and rapidly changing, healthcare systems and societies of our modern world. Furthermore, one has to ask if the unity and consistency achieved in simple integrity are worth having. The attraction of restricting oneself to a small set of coherent, closely related values and principles is that it engenders no conflict, no questioning as to preferred courses of action, no agonizing over motivation. One knows indubitably where one stands and so is enabled to act without indecision. But acting without indecision is not necessarily good. Indeed, it can very well be evil, as indubitable knowledge shades into self-righteousness, the single-mindedness transforms into simple-mindedness – 'having too few thoughts and feelings to match the world as it really is' (Williams 1973: 149). Where self-righteousness and simple-mindedness flourish, fanaticism and inhumanity swiftly follow. The comfort of unreflectiveness quickly becomes a habit, the uncomplicatedness of perceiving situations within narrow formulaic boundaries evinces an irresistible seductiveness. One might argue that within the context of healthcare practice action research, purity has a dark side, double-mindedness has a positive one.

Chapter 3

Feminist approaches to a situated ethics

Pat Usher

> The real difficulty, but also the most exciting, original project of feminist theory remains precisely this – how to theorise that experience, which is at once social and personal, and how to construct the female subject from that political and intellectual rage.
>
> (Lauretis 1984)

These words, written in 1984, encapsulate both the challenges and the tensions which feminist theory represents to male-defined ways of knowing and theorizing. Feminism has developed a critique over the past thirty-five years which has exposed the ways in which traditional philosophy has consistently suppressed women's claims to know and be heard as thinkers and moral voices. Feminist philosophers have sought to construct, through various stages of theoretical development, new approaches which allow women to have their understandings of the world recognized while at the same time revealing the particularity of men's experience, which so much traditional theory disguises as universal. Feminist ethics is one aspect of contemporary feminist social theory that 'attempts to account for gender inequality in the socially constructed relationships between power – the political – on the one hand and the knowledge of truth and reality – the epistemological – on the other' (MacKinnon 1987: 147). The traditions of Western thought, particularly since the Enlightenment, have been the history of dichotomies, hierarchical and oppositional. In its constructive project, feminism draws attention to the theoretical and practical ways in which values, politics and knowledge are intrinsically linked and seeks to redraw the boundaries between epistemology, political philosophy and ethics so that we appreciate how power and unequal hierarchies are maintained, created and re-created in research.

WHAT IS DISTINCTIVE ABOUT FEMINIST ETHICS?

Feminist philosophers who have concerned themselves with philosophy's central questions such as the nature of reality and subjectivity (ontology), knowledge and truth (epistemology), morality and the good (ethics), and rights and responsibilities (politics) have demonstrated that philosophy has never been neutral or ignorant about women (Grosz 1990; Urban Walker 1998). By studying what philosophers have said and omitted to say about women and the feminine, feminist research has revealed how philosophy is implicated in the ways in which masculine and feminine are defined, and how such definitions shape the capacities and skills of men and women. It has also critiqued the way that questions, concepts and issues that seem neutral and untouched by sexuality – like truth, reason, objectivity, virtue – are in reality coded implicitly by masculine and feminine associations. Terms such as unreason, the irrational, evil, neurotic, intuitive, chaotic are identified with the feminine and thus, by implication, position women as secondary, subservient, relational, emotional, tied to nature and incapable of higher moral reasoning.

Because critical feminism has documented the social hierarchies embedded in epistemology, ethics and politics, we need in our research enquiries a constructive scepticism about people's claim to know with certainty about not only their own lives but other people's too; not because they cannot know but because, placed in other positions, other people know life differently. Feminist ethicists insist that women's experience and moral reasoning be given space to represent their own self-images, choices and patterns of moral evaluation.

Feminist ethics challenge ethical norms that are derived from abstract ideas of a universally shared interest: such traditions do not respect either individual or social differences. Traditional ethical approaches that lay out the existence of absolute right, norms, duties and legal methods of enforcement have given people tools with which to fight oppressive relationships. But we need to be sensitive to the ways in which the same ideas can foreclose possibilities. Western moral theory has silenced the moral voices not only of women but of anyone who does not attain the abstract universal principles. Respect for differences is ethically important. Koehn makes the point, 'If we do not have discrete individuals, we lose any sense of the personal individuality that makes each of us so special and which the male ethicist would have us respect' (1998: 7).

Feminist ethicists argue that morality and subjectivity are inseparable; that we need a radically different notion of the subject from that offered by the strictly individualistic, rational, moral subject of modernist thinking. There can be no single identity for 'woman'; rather, the subject is a discursive construction and situated in all respects. The self is relational and learns to define itself through a host of voluntary and involuntary relationships.

Feminists have documented the fact that women have been assigned roles limiting them to 'private' life. Traditional theory has separated the public and private realms and defined the public sphere as the more important space, and one that men inhabit with greater legitimacy. Feminist ethics regards the separation as contestable and seeks to recast the distinction.

In this chapter, I am locating my own discussion of ethical practice within feminist approaches which believe that moral and social life are completely intertwined and that all knowledge, including moral knowledge, is situated – that we need to ask continually from where a knowledge claim derives and how it is made possible, and yet is limited by the characteristics of its location.

I am constructing a text within two modes of thinking: feminist theory and postmodern philosophy. From feminist theory I present gender as a central category of analysis in terms both of structures and of the values embedded in them. I problematize, in a postmodern perspective, those modernist assumptions that view knowledge as progressive, cumulative, holistic, universal and rational.

I challenge the modernist belief in observer-neutral, context-free knowledges; I ally my writing within those recent epistemologies that have abandoned a belief in universal truth independent of the particular characteristics of the researcher or the historical and social conditions in which the research happens. Instead of a commitment to universality and transparency in this sense, I advocate a perspectivism that is not relative to absolute judgements or knowledge but is relational and self-reflexive in judging the validity of each, and its own claims to truth-like statements. Such approaches appreciate the undecidability and the provisionality of the human condition and seek to understand the ambivalence and uncertainty of human behaviour rather than impose an illusion of order (Bauman 1991: 231–2).

My preferred feminist approach in research is one that owns up to the personal biography of the gendered researcher who speaks from a particular class, racial, cultural and ethnic position – who engages in local, small-scale theories fitted to specific issues and situations so as to ensure that definitions of reason and knowledge take account of the historical, contextual and specific conditions that produce them. The implication of such an approach is that every activity is beset with moral and ethical decisions that are contextual. People learn their own identities and understand other people through relationships that are defined by certain values. Such recognition and self-expression exists not in the abstract but through certain kinds of practice. Feminist ethics seeks to notice 'that ethics comes from somewhere and someone in particular, and that what or who ends up represented is non-accidentally related to who gets to represent us' (Urban Walker 1998: 27).

I aim in this chapter to clarify the characteristics of feminism's critique and constructive approaches in research at this moment in its development within postmodern feminisms. I will then relate this to issues of gender difference and morality, and ask how the contrasting debates about an ethics based on justice and rights and one based on care and responsibility open up the possibility of ethics that incorporate key insights from both. I will examine the implications of these debates in relation to relationships between the self and positionality within the research process, between the researcher and the researched, and examine the consequences for how we regard 'experience', 'voice' and 'authenticity'.

FEMINIST EPISTEMOLOGY AND ITS CRITIQUE

Since the 1970s there has been an increasingly sophisticated body of feminist literature published on philosophy. Looking back, it is now common for writers to track the stages in its development (Fonow and Cook 1991; Reinharz 1992). Harding's text asking whether there is a feminist method (Harding 1987b) was crucial not so much in answering her own question but in alerting feminists to the crucial relationships between epistemology – what counts as valid knowledge, who is recognized as a valid thinker; methodology – how does the conceptual framework in terms of theory and analysis exemplify the epistemological stance adopted; and method – what research techniques are adopted to gather evidence. By giving such clear definitions, Harding has helped a generation of feminists to be clear about the differences between terms which are too often used interchangeably, to understand the inevitable linkages between them, and to think more readily about feminist challenges to traditional research discourses, their epistemological assumptions and the implications for feminist research methodologies.

DISPLACING TRADITIONAL EPISTEMOLOGIES

By the mid-1980s, adherence to methodological frameworks that purported to produce observer-neutral, context-free knowledge were undermined. Belief in a transparent language that reflected pre-existent meaning was treated sceptically; rather the researcher's text was seen as shaping the way reality is perceived, and the nature of that reality was revealed as reflexive, messy, subjective, open-ended, conflictual (Denzin and Lincoln 1998: 380). The idea that qualitative research could directly present others' lived experience was undermined in favour of arguing that experience is interpreted and re-created in a text whose meaning is internally generated by the researcher. Its validity is generated from its own strategy and not from its accuracy in representing something about the nature of external reality (Flax 1990: 38).

Like feminist discourses, postmodern discourses speak many different points of view and use various methods, but all are 'deconstructive' in that they demand our scepticism about the privileged position that the Enlightenment philosophy has taken for itself. In all postmodern thinking there is an assumption that knowledge and power are co-implicated and the deconstructive method is looking at the strategy which an author uses to privilege certain concepts over others and how voices are thereby silenced by discourses that 'normalize' and dominate.

What radical feminists like Hekman (1990) and Flax (1990) have added to postmodern thinking is the insight that by deconstructing the modernist definition of rationality/irrationality and other binary dualisms associated with it – subject/object, culture/nature – one reveals its gendered character. In each of the dualisms on which modernist thought rests, masculinity is associated with the first element, femininity with the second. In each case the masculine is privileged over the feminine and maintains that position by its association with the universalizing qualities of rationality, which excludes the subjective, the emotional, the aesthetic, the natural and the feminine. What radical feminists have exposed is that women's exclusion from the creation of theory is not accidental. The subject identity of the thinker in liberal theory is not gender neutral, abstract or disembodied, but a rational, objective, masculine mind – and only such a mind is capable of discovering truth and acting as a moral subject. The dichotomous, oppositional structures which position binary terms as mutually exclusive of one another are not immutable. Distancing itself from standpoint and essentialist epistemologies which ground feminism in female experience, radical feminism examines gender as a source of power and hierarchy, and through the deconstructive method reveals that women are positioned negatively because of their association with the feminine.

This emphasis on the relationship between power, knowledge and truth is due to the influence of Foucault's work (1980). His work on the relationship between truth and power is helpful in enabling women to challenge the philosophical strategies that have created the female identity as fixed and subordinated. His arguments that power and knowledge always coexist, that what counts as truth is always constructed through discourses, that discourses create meanings and produce identities, and that it is through these categories that power relations are created and maintained – all have tremendous potential for feminists. By deconstructing the privileged hierarchies in the structure of knowledge, feminists can appreciate how patriarchal discourses are created and maintain their dominance. The response is not to attempt to reverse the binaries because that merely results in perpetuating them; rather the dualisms must be dissolved. Instead of binaries which separate and exclude – subject/object, reason/emotion, culture/nature, masculinity/femininity – the feminist project is to replace them with a plurality of perspectives that dissolve binaries into continuums and disallow categories which maintain the privileging of masculinity over the feminine. Only by following this approach can women or any other marginalized group avoid being defined as inferior against the universalizing categories of rationality, objectivity and masculinity.

In adopting a perspectival approach, feminism must accept that all claims to truth are self-interested, partial and specific. This does not imply a commitment to relativity, however: the concept of relativity exists only in relation to the concept of fundamental absolutes, both of which are discursive constructions. Perspectivism acknowledges that all discourses construct a point of view against the norms and criteria inherent in the discourse, but not all perspectives are equally valid. If a discourse is perceived to be discriminatory, it will be criticized by other discourses. What it does argue is that all knowledges are situated and are governed by the rules of those who are the knowers. Since the position of the knowers is historically variable and specific, it follows that all claims to knowledge and truth are historically specific. This implies that all knowledge claims should be self-reflexive and own up to the desire for 'power in the world, not an innocent truth' (Flax 1993: 144). In denying the right of patriarchal discourses to disguise their controlling tendencies through normalizing structures and categories, radical feminists also have to accept that their discourse does not speak a better truth. In viewing knowledge as situated and perspectival, writers like Grosz (1990) argue that all theory is relational and connected to other practices: that we must recognize the functioning of power relations within theory and the necessity of occupying a position that is political in both the public and the personal spheres of an individual's life.

If no one discourse speaks a better truth, we cannot privilege any one feminist epistemology and must be open to analysing multiple epistemologies. Postmodern theorizing creates opportunities for innovative approaches, so that instead of relying on traditional research approaches which assume homogeneity as their starting point, we develop our sensitivity to the variety of human categories; women no longer are assumed to have the same characteristics of experience as one another, and the unified category of 'woman' no longer holds. Feminist practice has been challenged to develop epistemologies which include the heterogeneous experiences of women of colour, Third World women, women in different social classes and with different sexual identities. While such an approach is deeply uncomfortable, a good feminist text in a postmodern approach would attempt to reveal how gender, race, class and other relevant categories intersect in the concrete experiences that make up the fabric of people's lives.

The implication for research practice is that there is no such thing as a feminist method; rather there are feminist perspectives which can infiltrate all disciplines and all methods, not just the qualitative (Reinharz 1992). The primary issues are epistemological ones, and once decisions are reached about perspective, then an appropriate range of methods can be used, provided the aim is always to reveal gendered hierarchies and the variety of human experience.

FEMINIST THEORY AND ETHICAL ISSUES

So far I have advocated a stance that sees research as arising out of the work of a gendered, multiculturally situated researcher approaching an investigation with a set of theoretical approaches (epistemology) that specifies a particular conceptual framework (methodology) and utilizes a set of techniques (method). Such a perspective draws attention to the relationship between the identity and positioning of the researcher and how she or he constructs the 'Other' who is studied. Embedded in this relationship and research content are a set of political and ethical issues which permeate every phase of the research process.

All feminist positions are particularly concerned with ethical questions in research because feminists have a commitment to social change and confront many dilemmas in the search for a 'better model of human behaviour that is as yet nowhere to be found' (Patai 1991:137). Feminist traditions have of necessity aligned the ethics of research with a politics of change in the name of groups whose rights and experiences have been omitted, ignored or denigrated. Feminists working in dialogue with postmodern perspectives have contributed the insight that 'any gaze is always filtered through the lens of language, gender, social class, race and ethnicity. There are no objective observations, only observations socially situated in the worlds of the observer and the observed' (Denzin and Lincoln 1998: 24).

Feminist philosophers have brought about a paradigm shift, a major re-evaluation of epistemological foundations. I do not propose to argue for or against a particular feminist position, but it is clear that the radical positions of the 1990s are an effective challenge to the history of Western thought, structured as it is around dichotomies, hierarchical and oppositional. This feminist challenge has now extended to one of the last bastions of modernist thought, that of moral theory, and there is now a very significant literature looking at alternative approaches to a feminist ethics. Denzin and Lincoln (1998: 214) remind us that all researchers must deal with ethical and political issues in their research enquiries and provide a typology of the ethical stances taken by different paradigms.

In this chapter, my discussion of feminist ethics is located within their 'constructivist' category of research enquiries. The aim of such enquiries is understanding and interpretation of how people construct their realities; values have pride of place and ethics are intrinsic in this paradigm because the values and voices of the participants are essential to the sharing of power and control between researcher and researched. The emphasis is on revelation because not to share control would destroy the aim of research which acknowledges how the dynamics of the research relationships affects the views and knowledge produced by the research.

A DISCURSIVE APPROACH TO ETHICS

Feminist ethics has challenged the universality of morality without agreeing a single feminist moral theory. There is no shortage of feminists prepared to accept traditional approaches, but here I examine those feminist positions which seek 'truths' of morality, not a single 'truth'.

Carol Gilligan's *In a Different Voice* (1982) argued that women's moral development differed significantly from men's. While for men the values of autonomy and individualism are central to their moral development, for women the values of attachment and relation are of greater significance. She argued that Kohlberg's view (1981) that the highest stage of moral development is characterized by abstraction, generalization and reality, is in fact based on a male model. As a consequence of his influential work, women who viewed moral problems in contextual, relational terms were defined as being capable only of a lower stage of moral development. Since then volumes of literature have praised and criticized her work (Larrabee 1993; Held 1995), but there is little doubt that her work raised parallel issues to those raised by feminists who challenged traditional epistemology. Her analysis gave rise to a generation of feminist theorists who advocated 'maternal thinking' (Ruddick 1989) and 'caring' (Noddings 1984) as definitions for a feminist ethics. The focus of an ethic of 'care' has been a critique of traditional ethics which prize a 'justice' perspective, with its emphasis on rights, duties, obligations and principles that can be applied to particular moral situations. By contrast, the caring perspective is characterized by responsiveness, taking responsibility in interpersonal relationships and by a context-specific mode of thought that resists abstraction.

As a result, many theorists have used Gilligan's work as grounds for a more inclusive moral theory. Complete volumes (Larrabee 1993; Held 1995; Bowden 1997) have debated the limitations of the ethical possibilities of caring and whether such ideas translate from personal interactions into the public domain. The public/private dichotomy is held to fail caring as fulfilling the fundamental requirement of a universalizable moral theory. Others see caring as fully encompassed within 'justice' theories and believe that in cases of conflict, justice always outweighs care. Other feminists emphasize the damage which women sustain in their lives from being exploited as the sex which is attentive, responsive and sensitive to the needs of others; their critique is prompted by essentialist tendencies in Gilligan's argument which preclude recognition for the enormous diversity of women's ethical experiences. What these debates illustrate is the tension between developing moral theory that is gender sensitive and includes the caring practices of women, and omitting to do so.

What is significant about these debates for me is the way that they draw attention to the dichotomous assumptions in the history of moral theory between reason and emotion, separation and relatedness, and how this leads to the privileging of a Cartesian subject: rational, autonomous, exercising moral judgement against abstract, universal rules and principles substantively concerned with justice and rights. The significance of Gilligan's work is that she suggests that there is the possibility of another constitution of moral subjectivity which challenges the dominant moral tradition. For me there are parallels in her approach with that of Foucault. Although she is coming from a very different discursive tradition, both of them are suggesting that 'the dominant moral discourse of the West, a discourse that defines only one moral truth and excludes other moral voices from the realm of the moral, is repressive' (Hekman 1995: 151).

Foucault is not offering a set of ethical positions, but his method is to both describe and critique the dominant moral tradition and to show how a particular subjectivity is constructed within discursive practices of a particular time and set of circumstances. Hekman's discussion of Foucault's approach to politics allows for a discursive approach to morality which is particularly appropriate to contemporary feminist ethics. In rejecting absolute foundations for politics and ethics, he is asking how they could effectively deal with concrete problems. Rather than seek global systemic theories, he argues that we 'analyse the specificity of mechanisms of power, to locate the connections and extensions, to build, little by little, a strategic knowledge' (1980: 145). He characterizes his method as the 'freeing of difference': 'affirmative thought whose instrument is distinction; thought of the multiple – of the nomadic and dispersed multiplicity that is not limited or confined by the constraints of similarity' (1977: 185). Radical feminists are not trying to replace one dominant theory with another but trying to win recognition that women's contexts and experiences vary widely and that to privilege any one of them is to marginalize another.

Foucault's discursive approach opens up the possibility of an ethical stance that is not based exclusively on absolutes. This does not deny the importance of ethical positions, nor does it see them as individualistic: what it does show is how to deconstruct the ethical privileging within modernist discourse and replace its gendered dichotomies with a politics of resistance that allows for the possibility of political and ethical struggles that focus on the particular situations and oppression of women. It follows that there can be no single feminist ethical position that would encompass all different situations. What we need, according to Hekman, is a discursive approach to morality, for three reasons (Hekman 1995: 159):

- a plurality of moral voices displaces the hierarchies and marginal voices created by the dominant masculinist construction of modernist moral theory; this provides for the possibility of giving 'different' voices equal standing and allows for all of them to attain the ideal of moral knowledge;
- the recognition that morality and subjectivity are inseparable and that just as there are multiple subjectivities, so there are multiple moralities. A moral voice is not an individual one but one that is located in a social, cultural, historical position and varies according to its race, class and gender;
- feminism seeks recognition for a 'politics of difference', and this must assume a reconstituted approach to moral and ethical positions. Too many institutionalized discourses about ethics portray 'women' or 'blacks' as deviant; without respect for an ethics based on contextual factors, the marginal voices are oppressed or suppressed.

Differences in experience will always explain events differently. Women who have been raped usually feel more strongly about rapists being prosecuted than those who have not. Being a victim of any violation is likely to lead to a stress on the rights of the victim. In such circumstances, a situated ethical stance does not require that individuals pretend they have no special self-interests which motivate them. Nor is it simply a case of giving everyone an equal and reciprocal right to air their feelings. Koehn warns that expressing grievances may simply lead to competitive escalation of claims as to who has been the more victimized. What she advocates is a dialogic ethic that arises out of 'consistent thoughtfulness'. Conversations where both participants admit 'that their concerns may be misconceived and that they may not understand their situation as completely as they believed [and that] they may have something to learn from their fellow citizens [make possible] the possibilities of substituting persuasion for violence' (1998: 138).

Such arguments combine to challenge modernist thought and present a paradigm shift in suggesting that meta-narratives are not the necessary grounds for either political action or an ethical position. The single identity for 'women' cannot be the foundation for a feminist ethics; what we need to document in our research texts is evidence of 'suppressed heterogeneity, discontinuity and differences' (Flax 1990: 4i). As Hekman observes, there is nothing abstract about this methodology; it must grapple with the way in which power operates in people's lives in a concrete and particular way.

THE DILEMMA OF A FEMINIST ETHICS

In this last section, I will discuss the implications for feminist research practice of adopting a discursive approach to moral issues. In traditional texts on the ethics of educational and social research, it is usual to discuss the following: the relationship between the investigator and the 'objects' of the research; negotiating with/without consent; effective means of entry and departure; the relationships between distrusting and confidence; the position of the researcher as observer or participant; commitment and betrayal; friendship and abandonment. In qualitative approaches there is a recognition that the political and ethical issues need to be resolved situationally, and quickly, without the benefit of reflection. What feminist ethics adds to these discussions are 'reflexivity, an action orientation, attention to the affective components of the research and use of the situation at hand' (Fonow and Cook 1991: 2). The degree of immersion by the feminist researcher in search of the complexity of human diversity is far deeper, but the ethical controversies are similarly all the more challenging. I illustrate this by examining a number of issues in relation to situating the identities of the researcher and the 'other', questions about voice and its account, the treatment of experience and analysis. In doing so, I refer to an essay by Jayati Lal (1996: 185), which is a self-reflexive account of a piece of ethnographic research on the working conditions of poor women working in garment factories in the slums of Delhi. Her work exemplifies the attempt to analyse her own particular location and position in the research, to acknowledge how her perspective impacted on the conduct of the research before she constructed her interpretation of the reality of the garment workers' world. Such an approach of being within the gaze of the research and analysing the multiple locations and the positionalities that made up her own identity (Third World woman in the United States, scholar and graduate student in the academy, feminist, middle-class researcher in India) is an attempt to go beyond the binary positioning of insider/outsider accepted unproblematically in most research (ibid.: 189). As such, it is suggestive of the practice-oriented intellectual work we need if we are to avoid reducing all women to one identity (Hekman 1995).

Identity of the researcher and the 'other'

In her essay 'Working the Hyphens', Michelle Fine (Denzin and Lincoln 1998: 130) discusses what she calls 'a messy series of questions about methods, ethics and epistemologies about how researchers have spoken "of" and "for" others while occluding ourselves and our own investments, burying the contradictions that percolate at the Self–Other hyphen'. If we opt to write about those who have been 'othered', we deny the hyphen: if we engage in social struggles with those who have been exploited or subordinated, we work the hyphen. She suggests that by working the hyphen, researchers must reveal how in relation to the informants, they 'create occasions to discuss what is happening between the researcher and participants, reveal whose story is being shadowed, why, for whom and with what consequence' (1998:

135). Lather's work (1991a) makes a similar point in drawing attention to the way that critical pedagogies within discourses of emancipatory education too often fail to analyse the extent to which empowerment is something done for the 'unliberated other' by those in control of emancipation. Her question is, 'How do our efforts to liberate perpetuate the relations of dominance?'

Lal's essay explores her multiple positionings during fieldwork; she simultaneously felt more of an insider with the Indian women she researched than a Westerner but also had a sense of herself as 'Other' when located as a woman of colour in the United States. When she returned to India as a researcher, her privileged, secular, upper-middle-class background positioned her as outsider in class terms since the differences between her and the garment workers were much more significant than their similarities. She was aware of confronting the Other for the first time as she crossed the class barriers into industrial manufacturing in Delhi; her own reflexivity revealed how in the actual practice of research she constantly had to negotiate between the positions of insider/outsider and take account of the power differentials and class inequalities that divided them.

With brutal honesty, she describes an instance of how her powerful position as researcher unwittingly contributed to perpetuating the inequality of the workers. A factory manager, wishing to demonstrate how he differentiated between quick workers, whom he hired, and slow ones, whom he did not, called two women in and discussed with Lal, in their presence, their traits and appearance. Irrespective of her good intentions and sympathies, she had become aligned with the management, thus revealing that her class position was of greater significance than her gender and feminist solidarity in the power hierarchy.

In analysing these painful realizations, she suggested that all researchers live in contradictory locations and that it is only by questioning where and how we are located 'that we get us out of mere reversals of the dualisms, of native/non-native, insider/outsider positionings and on to a more productive engagement with the nature of our relationships'. Her aim is 'to examine the hyphen at which Self–Other join in the politics of everyday life and to work against inscribing the Other' (Lal 1996: 200). As soon as we recognize the social contingency of race, class, gender and sexuality, then silence, lack of engagement or dismissal all pose ethical dilemmas. It is important to acknowledge that power differentials do not disappear because feminists wish it, and we must continue to confront the power in our positionality and the ethical issues that arise in the micro-dynamics of the hierarchies embedded in our enquiries. Researchers working at the interstices of radical feminism and postmodernism can no longer rely on fixed categories, or an unreflexive stance as 'do-gooder'.

Elizabeth Wheatley's discussion of Stacey's question 'how can there be a feminist ethnography?' provides a relevant example of how difficult it is to address ethical dilemmas in feminist ethnography. The crux of the difference in their approaches lies in their different epistemological stance towards the critical issue of who had ultimate authority to decide how and what to write in her ethnography (1994: 407). Stacey was concerned to write a 'realist' account that included and revealed all that she had encountered in her fieldwork even if it betrayed confidences or revealed intimate details that might cause offence to those she was writing about. Stacey had self-consciously reflected on difficult ethical and epistemological questions within a feminist perspective and had come to the conclusion that 'fully feminist ethnography' was not possible.

However, Wheatley sees the purpose of feminist work as actively seeking out and highlighting the contradictions, displacements and differences so as not to impose 'a false unity nor a false consciousness' among feminists (ibid.: 412). She advocates a 'feminist imagination' which she sees as a 'flexibility of mind that seeks to explicate the conditions and contexts that frame the contingent, localized and perspectived character of ethnographic knowledge' (ibid.: 413) All accounts for her are partial, and the ethical issues are not ones to be swept aside but are an essential part of what ethnography is. The aim is not to resolve them but to map the ambiguities and uncertainties which characterize the production of knowledge about people's lives.

Voice and its account

As I indicated earlier, one of the significant issues raised by Gilligan's work is the awareness that the moral voice is constituted rather than discovered. She emphasized the role of gender in this constitution.

Giving voice to women's experience has been a key characteristic throughout all stages of feminist theory. It evolved from the belief of qualitative researchers that they could accurately observe behaviour while at the same time express the meanings which their subjects brought to their own life experiences. However, one of the insights from postmodern perspectives which we now have is that there can be no clear window into an individual's experience: human experience is too complex and subtle in its variations and cannot be captured in a definitive account. The emphasis in radical feminism now is to build on Foucault's insight that we constitute ourselves through real practices. In constituting a moral voice, we exercise choices about how to act through the micro-practices in which power and knowledge exert their influence. Michelle Fine's work (1992, 1994) has documented the troublesome issues about the use of voices and asks researchers to be reflexive about how they use them since some methods may serve to distort and control voices. She offers three stances – ventriloquy, 'voices' and activism – from which researchers choose, knowingly or otherwise, to constitute their text. Ventriloquy relies on anonymity, with researchers omitting all references to their authority in voicing someone else's experience; recording 'voices' as if one can tell it as it is, runs the risk of omitting the multiple perspectives through which people recount the contradictions in their lives. Fine advocates activist research which lays itself open to the contradictions and conflicts within collaborative practices – be they feminist, African-American, socialist-feminist, educational or postmodern; the aim must be what Haraway (1988) refers to as 'power-sensitive conversations' (Fine 1994: 23). The characteristic of such research is that the researcher is explicit about her political and epistemological preferences; the text analyses critically the power and ideological threads within its framework and the narrative demonstrates inventive possibilities of 'what could be' (Lather 1986).

Gilligan's work can be interpreted as deconstructing the epistemological assumptions which inform modernist moral truth that it is disembodied, removed from relationships and connections in everyday life which distort moral judgements. She shows us the possibility of a different moral voice 'which speaks from the lives of connected, situated selves . . . she hears these voices because she defined morality and moral knowledge as plural and heterogeneous' (Hekman 1995: 30).

Experience and analysis

In considering the dilemma posed by how voices are heard, with what authority and in what form, radical feminists have moved on from advocating the inclusion of women's experience to highlighting the unstable nature of experience. Scott's discussion (1992: 25) of experience argued that its use is far from being an innocent concept; the idea that recounting experience is the means of self-expression ignores the social and ideological systems in which the experience was produced. As she puts it, experience 'is always already an interpretation and is in need of interpretation' (ibid.: 37). The idea in early stages of feminist theory that empowerment of voice was emancipatory arises from the egalitarian commitment of the researcher to the researched, but simultaneously it reinforces traditional humanistic psychological and *verstehen* sociology that sympathetic interviewing will provide meanings of the real person. The danger here is that without an understanding that subjectivity is produced out of discursive practices, feminist accounts merely reproduce, rather than challenge, patriarchal knowledges.

How feminists encourage participation and the recording of experience is fraught with ethical dilemma. Luke's discussion of the contradictory politics of voice when differences clash among female students of colour in her classroom alerts us to consider the power relations that define most student–teacher relationships as well as the complex differences between students. Care must be taken that in giving space for students to reveal their experiences, teachers do not 'rope some women into the Foucauldian confessional and thereby re-colonise them' (Luke 1994: 223). Her discussion of why some students of colour remain steadfastly silent can be read as their resistance to white, colonial and unaccustomed female authority rather than the common interpretation of feminine behaviours as passive, reticent and lacking assertiveness. Both she and Scott draw on Foucault's work and argue that we need to theorize how identities have been constructed within particular situations and political positions. This approach sees 'experience and identity as positionalization', 'as a mobilisation through gender, class and race . . . positions through which we move and which move through us and through each other' (Luke 1994: 224). If students and teachers understand experience in this way, they can understand how identity and experience interact to produce situated knowledges, a characteristic of all our social selves. As a teacher facing the ethical dilemma in her classroom of individuals and groups who by revealing their experiences as either white Australians or Aboriginal women created a hierarchy of oppressions, she had to confront the problems of women silencing each other. Given her own identity as teacher, white and non-Australian, she was both uneasy and unable to cope. What she had hoped to achieve through their set texts on indigenous and 'Third World' authors did not help the class theoretically or emotionally to deal with the silencing of some students. If women are to avoid divide-and-rule tactics among themselves, personal revelations need to be set in a context of strategic alliances with and among themselves.

What Luke's text signals to me is that the old ethical codes, as set out by writers like Cohen and Manion (1994), fail to engage meaningfully with the complexities of people's subjectivities, their cultural and politically structured histories. What we need to evolve are ethical understandings that relate sufficiently closely to people's lives so that we, as researchers, do not misrepresent them.

Luke's discussion illustrates the misgivings which John Caputo has about ethics: 'ethics is always already political'; for him there are complex relationships between them which 'are hard to work out; they always already bleed into each other' (1993: 124–5). But even more difficult, what he emphasizes is that there are no firm and secure foundations for the judgements we make. Choosing between evaluative judgements is a risky business, and 'one is rather more on one's own than one likes to think, than ethics would us think'. Living with the 'anxiety of undecidability' is for him a more accurate representation of the fragility of life. 'Deconstruction issues a warning that the road ahead is still under construction, that there is blasting and the danger of falling rocks. Ethics, on the other hand, hands out maps which lead us to believe that the road is finished' (ibid.: 4).

Dialogical ethics

Koehn's discussion of a dialogical ethics is an attempt to preserve the crucial insights from the ethics of caring, empathy and trust without accepting the lack, as she sees it, of checks on self-righteous projections or abusive relations. Her discussion begins with the insight that every one of us is prone to error and that sometimes the contrary of an error is not the truth but another error (1998: 18). In conducting research enquiries we need to persuade those involved that practical difficulties or disputes can be addressed in ways that are both highly specific to the circumstances and also generic by reference to ethical positions with which all who are involved in the research can engage. If persuasion is to be a possibility, it can only emerge from a shared commitment to certain principles. Such principles do not derive from a transcendental position but from critical conversations in which the dialogic ethic is sensitive to power dynamics and the likelihood that attempts will be made to dominate.

Critical conversations refrain from 'solving' ethical dilemmas. However, dialogic ethics force out into the open the issue of point of view. Ethical stances are always 'given' by someone with a point of view to someone with a point of view.

'A dialogic ethic resists any attempt to abstract away from the relevance of persons' life experiences in arriving at a description of the problem at hand' (Koehn 1998: 161). Principled dialogue is a better hope than rule-bound ethical analysis. 'Consistent thoughtfulness' is our best insurance against the manipulation and disrespect which Lal encountered in conducting her research and which Luke feared had surfaced in her classroom.

CONCLUSION

The concept of an ethics that is situated is attractive to feminists because it is central to their concerns about hegemonic, epistemological and moral traditions which define who and what may make a claim to truth and moral knowledge. I am arguing for a discursive approach to morality because modernist approaches which have dominated the construction of moral theory have marginalized and silenced diverse moral voices, not just those of women. By arguing for a politics of difference that is local, contextual and concrete, I am advocating that different values be heard in a plurality of public space so that the constitution of moral positions takes account of a diverse lived experience. To do this, we need a radically different concept of the subject from that offered by modernist epistemology – one that recognizes that subjectivity is created out of the discursive conditions in our context. Such an approach is deeply uncomfortable because it rejects absolute foundations for ethics without retreating into an individualistic approach. The challenge is to document and understand that subjectivities and moral voices are constituted from their distinctive social, cultural and historical settings; that no single morality can encompass the diversity of all the lives in our research enquiries. We need research enquiries that allow for contestation between people's description of practical issues and their competing responses to them. As Koehn suggests, we need different ears to hear those who speak in a different voice and to critically assess their claims (1998: 163).

Chapter 4

Damned if you do, damned if you don't

Ethical and political dilemmas in evaluation

Helen Simons

INTRODUCTION

Ethics in evaluation are those principles and procedures that guide right action in the field. Such a general statement of ethics cannot, of course, tell us what right action is and how we know we have exercised it. Taking action is a field decision made in relation to specific people in a specific context at a particular point in time. Underlying any such action is a complex professional judgement that is guided by ethical principles, to be sure, but also by appeal to the basic values of the researcher and his or her sensitivity to the balance that needs to be maintained in research studies between participants' 'right to privacy' and the generation and sharing of public knowledge.

In evaluation, there is a further complicating factor that influences the precise decision taken in any one context. The inherently political nature of evaluation means that politics in the site often intrude upon an evaluation research process to the point where they challenge the procedural ethics that guide the conduct and reporting of the evaluation. In such circumstances, evaluators are faced with a dilemma of how to continue to act professionally and ethically while managing conflicting political pressures without being captive to anyone's particular vested interest. This is no easy task. Evaluators have to be 'above' the politics of the site, yet themselves act strategically and politically to ensure that the evaluation stays credibly on stream. How do evaluators do this? And what issues are involved?

This chapter explores the essential interconnection of politics and ethics in conducting funded evaluation in highly politicized policy contexts. The basic argument is that the ethical act, that precise moment when a decision is taken, is a complex judgement that is both political and ethical. The political conditions in which the research is conducted and the politics of interaction in a democratic society both contribute to and constrain what it is possible to achieve and how to act ethically in achieving it. While this may be true in all forms of educational research, the inherent political nature of evaluation brings the issues centre stage.

The first part of the chapter briefly explores the political dimension of evaluation and outlines the political stance to which I aspire in conducting evaluations. The central part illustrates, through two authentic case examples, both where ethical dilemmas occurred in funded policy evaluations and how they were resolved in the specific case. The chapter concludes by revisiting the case for ethical principles and guidelines, arguing that, while necessary, they are insufficient. As the detailed examples demonstrate, the ethical act is situated in a complex socio-political context requiring the exercise of both political and professional judgement.

It is important to record and acknowledge at the outset that the two case scenarios described represent only one person's view of the evaluation dilemma – that is, the evaluator's. These are my reflections and my justifications of how I acted. Participants and stakeholders may well have experienced the dilemma differently. In the analysis of the scenarios, and particularly where there was conflict, I have tried to understand and take into account the other person's point of view. I have also tried not to take a defensive attitude to the conflict, while at the same time maintaining the evaluation's ethical stance. However, I am well aware, aspirations of impartiality notwithstanding, that the one who writes the script is likely to have a stronger voice in the text.

POLITICAL STANCE

Weiss (1975: 13) describes evaluation as a 'rational enterprise that takes place in a political context'. Political considerations are involved in evaluation, she indicates, in three major ways. First, the programmes are themselves the result of political decisions. Second, since the purpose of evaluation is to feed into decision-making, evaluation reports enter the political arena and 'compete there for attention with other factors that carry weight in the political process'. Third, and 'perhaps least recognised', evaluation itself has a political stance.

In the evaluations I have conducted over the years, I have worked with a particular set of ethical principles and procedures stemming from, and endeavouring in practice to exemplify, a liberal democratic rhetoric (see, for example, Simons 1984, 1989). These principles were first enunciated within a democratic model of evaluation (MacDonald 1974) which has as its central aspiration how to find the appropriate balance in the conduct of research and evaluation between the public's 'right to know' and an individual's 'right to privacy'.

This central problem is translated into a set of principles and procedures (embodying the democratic rhetoric) for the conduct of the evaluation. These procedures offer individuals some control over data they can be said to own, through negotiation on agreed criteria of what is to become public knowledge in the particular case. The 'right to know' is thus not an absolute right, as has sometimes been interpreted by critics of this approach, but a situated one. Who gets to know what (i.e. which audiences have a right to the knowledge generated by the evaluation) has to be established and agreed in early negotiations as significant in the particular case in question. Such deliberations need to pay due regard both to the individual partici-pants in the case (and their right to privacy) and to those beyond the case who have a right to the knowledge generated by the evaluation. The process of negotiation provides the link and the means of determining the balance between these two 'rights', which can often be in conflict, especially in the highly politicized contexts in which evaluation and research are conducted.

In a paper I wrote in 1989, I indicated how these principles and proce-dures had to be interpreted differently in different evaluations in relation to a number of factors. These include the particular problem structure of the evaluation, the informal and formal power structures within which evaluation has to operate, participant familiarity with evaluation, evaluator experience and confidence, and the socio-economic conditions of the times. I do not have time to detail here precisely how these factors led to a modi-fication in the actual procedures followed (see pp. 123–8 of Simons 1989 for one or two examples). I simply want to make the point that the guide-lines themselves are not immutable. While the general principles that underpin action remain the same, the precise procedures may alter according to the particular situation and circumstances. It is two of these situations that I now describe and reflect upon how I acted in each case.

SCENARIO 1

The first context is a national government-funded policy evaluation of a new curriculum programme that has potentially far-reaching implications for future policy development. I am the director of the evaluation and have four colleagues working with me on the task. Funded for two years, the evaluation was essentially a case study of the site that was piloting the new programme. The evaluation was acknowledged by the funders to be inde-pendent and external, and it was built into the contract that the final report would be published and disseminated to all relevant stakeholders.

The scenario concerns a telephone call I received at home one evening seven months into the evaluation from the administrator who commis-sioned the study. He asked (in an urgent tone) if I would go down to the site immediately as the students (on a particular part of the programme) had complained about the course and written a very strong letter to their union which had come through to him. He said that he needed to get some evidence straight away to reassure the minister about what was going on.

In an effort to find out what lay behind this sudden demand, I inquired about the nature of the complaint and asked whether I could see the letter. He replied that he could not send it as 'there are some very strong statements in it', but he read significant parts of the letter over the telephone and then repeated his request for me to visit the site immediately. I responded by saying that it was not the role of evaluation to intervene in what seemed like a political dispute, that I had a full schedule in the next two weeks and that we had planned, in fact, to evaluate the course in question the following year. He then asked if another member of the team could go. I reiterated that I thought it would be unwise for an evaluation to intervene in a political dispute and pointed out that we were conducting an independent, external evaluation that must be seen to be impartial to all stakeholders involved.

The administrator emphasized again the urgency of the situation, saying that the minister was pressing him for information. He then queried whether we were conducting a responsive evaluation. My reply was that we were – responsive to the issues identified by various stakeholders (we had discussed these at the outset of the evaluation and would revise them in the light of the interim report). Responsive did not mean, however, that the evaluation responded to every request from every stakeholder, especially when a visit to the site at this stage might be interpreted by other stakeholders as intervention. I said that we would need to think very carefully about the implications for the programme and the credibility of the evaluation of a visit at this stage. To be seen to be partial to any one group would destroy the possibility of conducting an independent evaluation that needed to be seen to be impartial by all the other groups involved. The administrator reiterated the urgency of the situation as he saw it, saying that the issues must be resolved down at the site.

At this point in the conversation, I thought it was important to indicate my belief in the site's ability to handle its own development and said that I expected that the key players on-site were handling the issues already. It did not require the evaluation's intervention. However, I agreed to talk with the team and see if we could forward our timetable to examine this part of the course earlier than intended, to document what had happened. We could then analyse the results in relation to the other data in the evaluation and report in the Interim Report that was due nine months later.

The administrator indicated that that would not be soon enough as he needed the information straight away to reassure the minister that the issues were being resolved. I agreed to talk with the team and get back to him.

The above is a summary of some of the issues in an hour-long telephone conversation in which the administrator was extremely pressing, to the point of trying to bully me into going to the site immediately. While at one level, and from the point of view of the administrator, the intervention sought may have seemed reasonable (it was his role to serve the minister), from the evaluation's point of view the intervention was inappropriate. It would compromise the independence of the evaluation by demonstrating partiality to one stakeholder and thereby risk losing credibility with the other stakeholders, particularly those on-site where the difficulty had arisen and on whom we were dependent for access.

An hour and a half later, that same evening, the telephone rang again. This time it was the deputy director of the evaluation, reporting to me an hour-long conversation he had just had with the same administrator. The conversation the deputy reported was practically word for word the same as the telephone call I had received earlier that evening. The tone, he said, was one of command – pressing and insistent on a site visit immediately. My deputy had resisted agreeing to this demand, offering the same reasons I had given.

I was relieved that my deputy had also upheld the agreed principles and procedures of the evaluation. Maintaining an independent stance can be extremely difficult when put under such pressure. The ethical guidelines we had drawn up at the outset and discussed with all stakeholders before begin-ning the evaluation were helpful in maintaining an independent stance but they are only statements of intent. It is one thing to have written guidelines as a principled basis for action. It is quite another to interpret them and act ethically in the moment in a situation fraught with politics, and where responding to one stakeholder's vested interest would inevitably conflict with meeting the needs of others. To respond partially to one group (and partic-ularly to give them a report on partial data), where there are multiple stake-holders involved, would undermine the credibility of the evaluation.

We resolved to handle the issue in three ways: first, to seek support from the independent evaluation consultant on our advisory committee; second, to investigate whether, given our workload and timetable constraints, we could manage to bring forward the evaluation of this part of the programme initially planned for the second year; third, to find out independently what was happening on-site.

The consultant confirmed the position we had adopted, indicating that it was not the role of the evaluation to intervene in the political dispute. However, he thought it was appropriate to document the situation and to analyse the effect of the students' dissatisfaction on the programme. With this reassurance of the role the evaluation was taking, I checked with members of the team whether they had the time to make a visit to document the situation. Two said that they could make it a fortnight later. At the same time I wrote to the chairman of the evaluation's advisory committee, informing him of the situation, the evaluation's response and reasons for it.

Arrangements were then put in hand for a short site visit by two members of the evaluation team. No sooner had this been activated than I had another long telephone call, this time from the co-ordinator of the programme on the site. He offered his view of the situation in some detail, adding that he did not think we were evaluating this part of the programme. He concluded with this health warning:

> Do not come. You will be perceived as intervening as an arm of the government. This is a union issue. It involves only a few students. We are working things out. I did not think intervention in the programme was part of the evaluation's role.

I agreed with the co-ordinator about the intervention and pointed out that this was not the purpose of the visit. Rather it was to document what events had led to the students' complaints and to see how these were being met. It was in effect just bringing forward the evaluation of this part of the programme planned for the second year. I indicated confidence in him in saying that I was sure the issues were being handled on-site. The co-ordinator was not convinced either that a visit was necessary or of the justification for it.

The evaluation here was caught in a double bind: being asked to visit by one stakeholder – the one who funded the evaluation – and being asked not to visit by another – the co-ordinator of the programme on-site, on whom we were dependent for access to the prime data for the evaluation. What to do? It seemed that we would be damned if we went (by one group) and damned if we didn't (by another).

Before the visit could take place, further extensive telephone calls were necessary: first, to another stakeholder on-site (a partner in the curriculum development) to seek his view and permission for the visit; second, to the government department, explaining the terms of the visit and the minimal feedback it would be possible to report; and third, to the co-ordinator, again explaining the terms of the visit. The co-ordinator reiterated that he thought the visit unnecessary and that credibility with site participants would be lost. He also said that the team was in danger of being used in a political game.

We decided to take the risk. The visit went ahead. However, one day before the visit, I was on the telephone practically all day, managing the compromise plan we had decided upon to keep the evaluation on track with as little damage to field relationships as possible.

Reflection on Scenario I

To me the above scenario encapsulates what happens in an evaluation when politics in the site dominate and threaten to overshadow the impartial collection and analysis of data promised by the evaluation. A strategic political decision had to be made if the evaluation was to continue. Conflicts of interest had to be managed and balanced so that each stakeholder whose interests differed got something of what they wanted out of the decision, or at least were not disadvantaged by it. Acting ethically in this context was a political as well as an ethical act.

There were a number of issues the evaluators deliberated that informed the precise decision taken. These included: how to maintain impartiality of data gathering and reporting in the light of significant threats to it; how to be responsive to the evaluation issue yet avoid becoming embroiled in the site's political problem; how to avoid being captured by the most powerful stakeholder group; how to avoid assuming the 'high moral ground' simply because the evaluation had a set of ethical principles and procedures; how to sustain empathy with all stakeholder positions irrespective of whether we agreed with their position or not; and deciding at what point it might be necessary to consider withdrawing from the evaluation. Various factors that we took into account in relation to this last point included the health of the evaluation team. This is a point that is often not written about in accounts of evaluation or research practice, but it was clearly something I considered in this case. Why should colleagues be subject to verbal bullying? How much stress was it reasonable to bear? At what point should the evaluators simply say 'the price is too high' and withdraw?

The evaluation also had to keep in mind that there were stakeholders outside of this immediate conflict to whom the evaluation needed to report – hence the need to uphold the ethical principles which were developed to underpin the independence of the evaluation and the openness of reporting. To act ethically in this context also required being responsive to issues of social justice beyond the immediate roles of participants. As House (1993) has pointed out, politics and ethics are inextricably entwined.

> There can be no ethics without politics. A theory of how individuals should act requires a theory – an ethical theory, not just an empirical one – of the institutions under which they should live: institutions which substantially determine their starting point, the choices they make, the consequences of what they do, and their relations to one another.
>
> (Nagel 1986, quoted in House 1993: 170)

The force of the issues noted above was manifest in conflicting pressures to act differently. For example, my colleagues, some of whom were doing evaluation for the first time, felt that the pressure to report partial data (as sought by the civil servant involved) compromised the conduct of comprehensive rigorous research. It was a threat to their research persona. For them, research issues took precedence over political issues. However, in this case, and in many instances in evaluation, the issue is not that clear-cut. Had I not taken a complex political decision – which in the event was a compromise with how I wanted to act – the evaluation would not have acted ethically in relation to the many stakeholders, and it might not have continued anyway. Two sides can terminate a contract.

Before we leave this scenario, it is important to mention two other crucial points. Conflicts often arise that derive from the particular people involved in the programme (including the evaluators) and the relationships that may develop between them. To principles and politics, then, we have to add people. Personalities and styles differ and have a different impact on the programme. Responses are similarly inevitably situated in, and with reference to, the complex interaction of the particular individuals and teams in the site. In this particular case the administrator with whom we negotiated the contract changed halfway through the evaluation, and relationships, even when other difficulties arose, were entirely cordial from that point. Similarly, at the site of implementation there was a role change of personnel responsible for the oversight of the programme. This also resulted in a changed relationship between those at the site of implementation and the evaluation team.

The second point is to reiterate that the scenario and the explanation and understanding of it are written by only one of the parties involved. Other parties might well have seen and explained it differently.

SCENARIO II

The second scenario concerns the negotiation of a particular part of an evaluation report of a European programme funded by the European Union. The contract, for over £200,000, was to train evaluators to evaluate educational transformation in an Eastern European country. The overall aim of the evaluation programme was to build up evaluation capacity in the country where previously there had been little experience of it, apart from performance control, regulation and inspection. I was the director of the part of the programme responsible for the evaluation training and for the oversight of the quality of case study evaluations of specific educational developments conducted by the trainee evaluators. There were twelve trainees involved – four teams of three, each led by a senior academic whose main specialism was not evaluation. That is, the four senior academics were themselves undertaking training in the field of evaluation.

As well as the provision of training and case study evaluations of impact, there was an additional requirement in the request to tender for a technical evaluation that would examine the organizational and technical processes involved in managing the development programme. Two external experienced evaluators from outside the country conducted this technical evaluation. One was an experienced independent evaluation consultant. The other was myself. The whole programme of development and evaluation was managed through a programme management unit set up within the ministry concerned and to which numerous reports had to be presented before any money was disbursed. Therein lies the crux of the problem outlined in this scenario: the structure and conditions of reporting to and through a management unit (the agent of the funding body) which was responsible and accountable for the effective management of the services and efficient disbursement of the money. The unit had to approve all reports before any money was released to participants, both in the development and in the evaluation programme. This was a staged process at different time intervals. The final 30 per cent was only paid once the Final Report had been approved. As is true of many programmes of this kind, reporting demands were excessive. In addition to an Inception, an Interim and a Final Report, the evaluation had to produce monthly and quarterly reports detailing inputs and outputs and progress. It was a highly managerial structure within which to aspire to conduct an independent external evaluation of the technical operation of the central management unit involved.

The Final Report was a composite report of the five case studies of the development programme, which constituted an impact evaluation, the technical evaluation and a chapter on self-reflection of evaluation learning based on data provided by the participants. The report was delivered to the management unit. While there were various issues to check in the case studies, it was the technical evaluation, or rather certain aspects of it, to which the management unit objected.

Before I continue with the story of the objection, it is important to note a number of features about this technical report. It was well conceptualized and structured, well written and evidence based. The lessons that needed to be learned from the report had been framed positively to facilitate acceptance and maximize learning. It was produced under severe time constraints when another European partner failed to deliver, but it was nevertheless a professional, high-quality report. The point of mentioning these features about the report is to draw attention to the kind of issues that worried those who objected to it. It was not the quality of the report to which they objected (though this later became an issue when other objections were not met). Their overriding concerns were political (about the repercussions of the report in the specific political context) and personal (in relation to their own lives and jobs), not about the details of the programme itself. It is also relevant to point out that in the terms of reference it was clearly stated that the reports had to be accepted by both the ministry and the management unit concerned. Crucially, it also said, 'The criterion of acceptance is based on the professional quality of the reports and not on the observations, recommendations or judgements contained in them.'

In the event it was the repercussions of those observations and judgements that worried the managers and which led to the prolonged negotiations which followed. Two of these negotiations were face-to-face, but further negotiations were by post, fax and telephone.

Negotiation I

The first meeting to discuss the report took over two hours, in which we went through it page by page, listening to and noting every objection the managers raised. There is no space to outline all the objections. In essence they centred on potential[1] political repercussions, potential personal consequences and, in a few instances, ethnocentric observations. No methodological objections were raised at this stage. The role we had decided to adopt was one of listening and noting. It was no part of our role to be defensive, though at certain points when we thought the text had been misread or the point misperceived, we did clarify. At the end of the meeting we agreed that we would consider the points raised and send a redraft.

Later that day, we went through each point and decided what could legitimately be changed (paying due respect to the database), what it was advisable to modify (to take account of the political context and the personal 'fears' the managers raised) and what could not be changed, as to make changes would compromise the data, misrepresent the situation and prevent others from learning important lessons about future management of programmes. The report was rewritten and forwarded again. Some quotations were omitted for balance, others were shortened. Further points were modified for tone and anonymity. Certain passages were rewritten to depersonalize an issue but not to delete it. This was based upon our judgement that the issue was an important one to record for outside audiences but that we could further disguise the origin.

The managers were still not satisfied. Some of our modifications, they intimated, had not sufficiently disguised the issue. We had rephrased the point to make it less politically problematic for them in so far as we understood their politics, but the point in our view still needed to be made. What they really wanted was to have those points eliminated. They expressed a wish to meet again.

Negotiation II

This time the meeting took place in the ministry's office with two managers. I was the only evaluator present. The meeting took one and a half hours, by which point we were only part way – less than a third – into their objections. While some of the objections were the same as before ('this must be deleted' and 'we don't like this'), others had been introduced and the ground further shifted to attack the methodology. This included the balance of quotations, the accuracy, and the extent to which facts and interpretations had been cross-corroborated from different sources.

It seemed that part of the problem in this negotiation was that one of the managers was unable to let go of a particular point and, while I was trying hard, I could not see why this point was so troublesome. The other manager was more prepared to concede on passages, even though he did not always agree with the sentiment expressed.

As the meeting had to end, and we needed a resolution, I proposed three lines of action. The first was for them to write[2] a list of the changes they would like to suggest for the evaluators to consider. The second, if we could not reach agreement on these points, was for them to write an additional account that would be added to the report. Third, if they chose not to take this route, and there were still issues they disputed, the evaluation would add a footnote to say that on this or that issue the managers had a different perspective. The managers did not like these last two suggestions. I am not sure why. Possibly it was because it might not reflect well within the ministry or on their roles. I explained that these were normal procedures to adopt where agreement could not be reached, but expressed my hope that nevertheless we could agree, as that, in my view, was the preferable route.

The managers sent a two-page list of suggested amendments. In some places omissions were suggested, in others rewording, including the rewording of some quotations. As evaluators, we considered the suggested amendments carefully and responded again, making modifications of tone in places and offering reasons for every suggested amendment that we did or did not accept. In some instances the data had been misinterpreted or not clearly understood. These points we could not change. Neither could we change quotations from interviews. These were the perspectives of particular people; while others might have disagreed with the perspective, the actual quotation could not be changed. The only change that could be made was how much of the quotation was reported, where it was placed in the text and any commentary in relation to it. A three-page response was sent.

Further negotiation – a no win, no win situation

Some of this response was accepted by the managers, but not all. There followed numerous letters, faxes and telephone calls trying to resolve the final points at issue. One telephone call towards the end of the period of negotiation was particularly urgent. It said, in effect, 'if you delete x . . ., we will approve the report'. To delete x . . . as requested would have changed the tenor of the passage and attributed blame to one group of participants (which was what was being sought). In responding I reiterated that I thought we had gone as far as we could in modifying the report to take account of their concerns. To make any further changes would misrepresent the data. Further urgent telephone calls ensued, trying to persuade me to agree to the specific final deletion requested.

It looked like stalemate, a no-win, no-win situation. The evaluators were trying to maintain an independent evaluation stance in order to report fairly and accurately on the programme to the European Union concerning the organization and disbursement of funds. The managers, whose role in this instance was to facilitate the acceptance of reports within the ministry, understandably were concerned about the perceptions that had been reported of their role and management in the evaluation and may have feared for their future. What to do? If we acceded to the managers' request we would be damned by those who provided data for the evaluation and by those expecting an independent account of the organization and management of the programme. If we did not, we would be damned by those within the management unit.

At this stage I decided that the only course of action was to add the foot-note I had suggested earlier to say that they disagreed with the perspective on that point and wrote a letter to this effect. On further reflection I did not send this letter, but another, which restated the position indicated above, that I thought sufficient account had been taken of concerns on both sides and that no further modifications could be made. The letter came back the next day with one word written at the side, 'Agreed'. (See the next section for a comment on the reason for this sudden change of view.)

Reflections on Scenario II

The ethical dilemmas in this context had a number of dimensions with a sharper edge to them than in the previous case because of the managerial position the evaluation was placed in; that is, the evaluation had to be approved by the unit that was the subject of the evaluation (and which had been criticized in the report) before the final payment was released. This structure had inbuilt potential for conflict.

Reflecting back on the situation now, it is clear that the managers in the unit had alerted the evaluators to the possibility of conflict over reporting. Quite early on in relation to a criticism which appeared in the case study of the ministry's role in one particular programme, the management unit said, 'If you say that, the report won't be approved.'

It is easy to see the problem the managers faced: having to present a report which had implicit, if not explicit, criticism of the ministry's role and practice in the programme, to ministry officials who had to approve the report. In their view, the report would have a greater chance of being accepted if there was no criticism. However, we, the evaluators, had to proceed 'without fear or favour' (Simons 1984), as we were aspiring to conduct an independent external evaluation and report to audiences beyond the immediate programme.

How to resolve: process and possible strategies

Throughout the process of these negotiations, I reflected long and hard about how to respond sensitively to the issues that concerned the managers in their political context, while at the same time aspiring to conduct an independent evaluation. Here are some of the thoughts that were going through my mind as strategies to resolve the impasse.

The first and easiest was to accede to the request to excise what the managers were not comfortable with in the report. The job would get finished. No time would be lost. The report would be approved. All concerned would get paid. Nobody would lose face. However, the evaluation would have capitulated and the 'truth' would not see the light of day.

The second was to insist that the evaluation had produced a fair and accurate report and stick to it – allowing no negotiation. In the particular context this would have delayed payment for a large number of people whose careers and livelihood in some instances were dependent upon completion. It would have destroyed goodwill. (Despite the unhelpful management structure, we were trying to work together for the good of the programme.) It would have been unhelpful. It would have privileged the evaluation over and above other concerns. Few evaluations are perfect. It is always possible to gain more data. There is always room for negotiation.

The third option was to play a more strategic game and put in the report more damning quotations (which we did indeed have) so that these could be negotiated out, leaving the essential critique, which would then be perceived as less threatening. This seemed rather Machiavellian and indirect, if not dishonest.

The fourth was to summarize the critique in the report instead of reporting direct speech. The advantage of this line of action would have been that readers could not have read who said what (even though no names, only roles, were used), and could not have guessed who said what. Most importantly, they could not scapegoat different individuals when they did not like what they had said or what they thought individuals had said in the evaluation. The disadvantage would have been that it would have lessened the opportunities for learning directly from the case with the verisimilitude that direct quotation often conveys.

The fifth option was to try to persuade the gatekeepers that it was to their advantage not to have a whitewash report when public knowledge of the programme already indicated that there were problems. The difficulty with this strategy is that the report might not have been heard by those whose role it was 'to get the reports through', if personal and political issues were causing anxiety for them in the particular context.

In aspiring to be responsive in this situation, we considered all the above options and also our difference in role. It is often said that evaluators (or researchers for that matter) have all the power in contexts such as this as they interpret the data and write the report. In this context it did not feel like that – quite the contrary, so strict and frequent were the managerial demands on the evaluation. Nevertheless, at some level those who write the report do have the last word even if it is subsequently rejected. In this context both evaluators and managers were locked in their roles. The evaluators were striving to maintain independence in a situation where they formally had none; the managers were striving to protect the description of their performance from unfair critique (in their view) while still performing their job to see that the report would get approved. It was indeed a no-win, no-win situation. Each side was dependent on the other for completion of the contract and payment to a number of people. Both positions were understandable. When the data on performance were critical, conflict was practically inevitable. As each group supported and defended their position, it almost became a 'battle of wills' to see which side would give way – the most.

Shifting the ground of the negotiations and attacking the methodology, which happened in the second face-to-face negotiation, was a way of directing attention away from the political/personal issues which disturbed those present and redressing the power imbalance in negotiation. If the negotiation did not turn out to the managers' satisfaction, they could dismiss the evaluation on methodological grounds.

In deciding not to respond with the footnote indicating that the managers disagreed with the evaluation's perspective, I avoided at the last minute playing a power game. I knew that the footnote response was not what they wanted but neither was the capitulation requested of the evaluation, i.e. 'if you delete x . . . we will approve the report'. To have responded with the footnote, a perfectly legitimate procedure in many contexts, in this situation would simply have been matching power with power: 'if you do this, I will do this'. I would have had the last word and the effect might have been stalemate or closure with loss of goodwill. My second reaction to restate the position and hope for a reasonable resolution met with agreement, though initially I was not sure why.

Post-resolution of negotiations

In the event each side gave way, probably to the satisfaction of neither. Given the prolonged negotiations, the sudden agreement and conclusion was somewhat surprising, though extremely welcome. What lay behind this sudden change of view is not exactly clear. There were a number of possibilities. Time was running out. As time passes, issues often become less significant. Completion presses. New programmes demand attention. However, one significant factor in this case was that one of the key people involved throughout the negotiations went on holiday, and shortly after this a superior gave the agreement. What seemed to be at issue here was a personal and/or political concern of a particular individual. This is a not uncommon occurrence in negotiating evaluation reports. Negotiation can take place with one person and yet someone else has to take the final decision. (See, for instance, Simons 1987: 181.) This frequently delays completion. One person agrees, yet their superior disagrees and so the issue is reopened. In this case it was the other way around. The superior agreed and so facilitated completion.

PRINCIPLES IN SITUATED PRACTICE

In the educational evaluation and research literature, we now have many ethical principles and theories to guide us, far more in fact than practical, detailed examples of how researchers and evaluators came to the ethical decisions that they did. Ethics is a situated practice and ethical principles are best discussed in concrete situations as there are a myriad of factors that can make a difference in particular contexts (House 1993: 166). I have detailed how I acted in the above situations, outlining the 'myriad of factors' involved to indicate that the ethical dilemma and indeed the ethical act in the evaluation contexts in question was a subtle, complex judgement that was at once political and ethical. While the principles and procedures we had adopted for the evaluation provided guidelines for action, these had to be interpreted in the precise socio-political contexts, taking into account not only the politics but the interaction of specific persons and relationships. I also had to act strategically politically to ensure that the evaluation stayed on stream. Such a conclusion does not mean that we can do without broad principles or codes to guide ethical decision-making. These provide an essential shared framework and reference point for checking the integrity and consistency of our actions (and those of others) and facilitating the building of trust.

In the final section of this chapter I briefly re-examine the basis and shared values of such codes of ethics. These general ethical principles have been variously stated, as House (1993: 166–7) has pointed out. In the American context, House notes that the National Commission for the Protection of Human Subjects of Biomedical and Behavioral Research identifies three underlying principles for social research: beneficence, respect and justice. Perloff and Perloff (1980) consider ethical rules under four issues: withholding the nature of evaluation research from participants or involving them without their knowledge; exposing participants to physical stress, anxiety, or acts that would diminish their self-respect; invading the privacy of participants; and withholding benefits. House (1993) himself suggests three basic principles: mutual respect, non-coercion and non-manipulation, and support for democratic values and institutions. These principles are similar to those which underpin the British Educational Research Association's code of ethics (BERA 1992).

Inherent in all these groupings of principles is a respect for persons and a respect for the dissemination of knowledge that is an essential part of a democratic society. The quotation from Nagel earlier in this chapter makes clear that we act ethically in relation to the society of which we are a part and the values that govern how individuals and groups should live and work together in that society. In his commentary on *The Ethics* of Aristotle, Thomson points out:

> Ethics is a branch of politics. That is to say, it is the duty of the statesman to create for the citizen the best possible opportunity of living the good life. It will be seen that the effect of this injunction is not to degrade morality but to moralise politics.
>
> (Thomson 1953: 26)

Ethical principles, then, are necessary to guide political action. Without them, how would we decide how to act in fair and just ways? This is not the same as saying, however, that we should follow ethical guidelines as strict rules of conduct that if rigorously implemented would guarantee fairness. This would be to treat ethical guidelines as a technical method divorced from the agency of the individuals who interpret them and disconnected from the power relationships embedded in the specific socio-political contexts in which evaluation takes place.

In both evaluations from which the above scenarios were taken, the evaluators worked with a set of ethical principles similar to those adopted in democratic evaluation that aspired to honour and respect the individuals from whom data were gathered at the same time as acknowledging the need to report publicly so that others could learn from the outcomes. The ethical dilemmas occurred when two equally appropriate principles were in conflict, what Russell has called a 'clash between right and right' (1993: 11). It is 'the balancing of such principles in concrete situations [that] is the ultimate ethical act' (House 1993: 168).

I have focused on case examples in this chapter, detailing how I acted with due respect to persons and to the dissemination of knowledge in particular situations, to offer a contribution to our understanding of the complexity and embeddedness of the ethical/political judgements we make in particular cases. I did wonder if in presenting such precise examples I might be damned. But I considered that in a book on situated ethics, I would be damned if I didn't.

NOTES

1   I have used the word 'potential' here to indicate that it was frequently not clear in the negotiations precisely what was the basis of the objection. At times it seems as though it had more to do with unspoken fears about the political context or immediate professional context than the content of the report. For further understanding of possible reasons underlying this point see Hyatt and Simons (1999).

2   The first negotiation had been verbal only, and other suggested changes had been introduced on this second negotiation. I thought a written agreement of the negotiation might prevent the ground of the objections shifting again and stop the negotiations getting into an infinite regress.

Chapter 5

'Come into my parlour'
Ethical space and the conduct of evaluation

Saville Kushner

ETHICAL CONFUSIONS

> Ethical principles are abstract and it is not always obvious how they
> should be applied in given situations. . . . Some of the most intractable
> ethical problems arise from conflicts among principles and the necessity
> of trading off one against another. The balancing of such principles in
> concrete situations is the ultimate ethical act.
>
> (House 1993: 168)

An old lady sits on her bed explaining that the doctor has told her that
she will not get any stronger. She feels fine, she says, if a little weak – but
the evaluator knows she is dying. The Mother Superior talks of her own
fears of mortality, barely allayed by her faith. Music students assemble in
the middle of a ward to recite and play music to Keats' 'Ode to a
Nightingale': 'Thou wast not born for death, immortal Bird.' All the while
the priest keeps a precise tally in his notebook of the names with dates of
those who come in and those who leave – noting that the average stay is
about two weeks. This is a hospice for the terminally ill – the atmosphere
light, positive, apparently relaxed, though portentous things happen here.
Music conservatoire students have been invited in to make music with residents as part of a project. Their evaluator takes notes, interviews, barely
suppresses his own anxieties, but unsuspectingly reads Conrad's *Heart of
Darkness* at nights before fieldwork and feels his mortal fear rise. At a workshop with those students, one woman resident recites a poem to life while
another recites hers which explains dying – they argue ideology as student
heads turn this way, then that, in confusion. One student leaves without
a thought while another stands outside in tears and yet another just gets
angry. A case study is written, rejected, redrafted, rejected again, fought
over and published against opposition from the hospice managers. These
are sensitive arenas in which to practise evaluation.

The problem is not that there are no ethical guides to conduct in such
sensitive situations – but that there are too many. More common than an

evaluator searching for an elusive ethical principle which will arbitrate in the midst of a dilemma is the evaluator struggling with two competing ethical impulses – each one exclusive of the other, both reasonable. That case study needed publishing; the concerns of the hospice managers for their privacy needed respecting; to sing 'Ode to a Nightingale' to terminally ill patients violated their right to evade the imminence of their fate; not to do so would imply submission to the frailty of fiction. Ethical principles bracket each other. They are reciprocal, commutative even; they are not hierarchical.

So the social world lays multiple ethical traps for evaluators, and demands of them that they use their judgement rather than merely apply a principle. This puts the evaluator in a significant position of power in relation to individuals, for it makes the issue of how to regulate evaluation conduct problematic. Where the evaluator sticks to a consistent principle across the contexts he or she works in, there is sufficient continuity to allow for – to use current jargon – 'sustainable' accountability. Then the evaluator can be required to show that this person was treated in the same way as another. However, this deals only with ethical consistency and is no guarantee of ethical *coherence*. There may be – usually are – grounds for treating people differently, and this case-based approach to judgement both intensifies the need for accountability and renders it highly problematic at the same time. A key consideration for contemporary evaluation is how we relate to the subject in a context which increasingly co-opts us into a programme perspective (Kushner 2000).

These are some of these traps and confusions I want to address here, drawing from evaluation experiences like those in the hospice. The evaluations I draw from throughout this chapter were all conducted under the rubric of Democratic Evaluation (MacDonald 1987). This approach (explained in Chapter 4 by Helen Simons) broadly falls within the embrace of 'pluralistic' or 'naturalistic' or 'participatory' evaluation. Later I will come back to the issue of consistency and accountability, and how these relate to an overarching concern with democracy in evaluation.

RESPONDING TO THE INSTITUTION: MISSING THE PERSONAL ETHIC

Conservatoire students visited this hospice over a period of weeks as part of an innovatory programme I was evaluating. The central idea of the hospice project was for the students, during collaborative workshops, to put to music poems written by two women residents – Alison and Jane – and, through the interactions with them, to relearn something of themselves and their relationship with their own creativity. The hospice was experimenting with the use of interactions like this to advance its mission of helping people 'to live until they die'. The intimacy and profundity of this particular interaction was a significant learning opportunity for both conservatoire and hospice.

Jane had written a poem as a celebration of life, set in a rural idyll. Alison's poem was an analysis of the self-learning required to cope with terminal cancer. The tension between the two – one arguing that there was no need to dwell on tragedy; the other that improving knowledge of these things by direct reference to them was all-important – was an unexpected and dramatic curriculum for the students. Lizzie, a 'cellist, said:

> It was so absorbing – but I was going through some strange personal thing at the time anyway – to do with my music. Alison and Jane, they'd got things together so well – they were so together. Better than me, really. It was really upsetting for me. And people looked more ill in the hospice than I'd ever seen before when I visited other hospices. But that's probably me more than them – the mood I was in – the way I was looking at them.

Artistically this was enormously demanding of the students, too. Farida had elected to play a solo taken from a Stravinsky piece during the reading of the poem about cancer.

> You normally try to understand what the composer was trying to say, and then interpret it. But here, I had to make it fit in with the cancer theme and someone dying. That was something Stravinsky didn't think about.

She too had been monitoring her reactions, unsettled by what she found:

> We sat on the bus quietly and went back to the conservatoire . . . I think we got a taxi . . . and someone was really upset and crying. I remember contrasting that someone had real feelings and I didn't feel anything. Well – I was – what was I? It was like feeling totally isolated.

Farida too had been watching the two women closely. Unlike Lizzie, she responded by discovering an absorption in the artistic challenge:

> I didn't think to imagine how Alison really felt when she found out she'd got cancer. It's like I was being incredibly objective about it all. Maybe I was protecting myself. Alison was such a wonderful and vivacious lady – I was so inspired by her.

And then there was Martine, who also felt unsettled by the hospice collaboration, and again from the artistic point of view:

I don't feel I'm even a person until I'm secure in my musical foundations. I didn't get past that phase in the hospice.

These are difficult views to represent in an evaluation account to a hospice which, perforce, has reduced social life to its simplest, most optimistic aspect – to 'live (positively) until you die'. Indeed, they came to prove controversial to hospice people who, just because they had elected to work there, were not exempt from their own feelings of insecurity and uncertainty. Such views provoked a reaction from hospice managers that the students were 'worldly-wise' – noted as a criticism, not in admiration. In so far as there was an ethical dilemma here, it impacted in at least two ways: first, on the institutional mission of the hospice, which was not rehearsed in integrating complex views of itself; second, on the personal lives and fears of hospice workers. Addressing one of these ethical dimensions did not guarantee addressing the other. Indeed, one of the difficulties for the evaluator is that, as here, people will often attribute to institutions frailties which, in fact, stem from their personal lives – denying the evaluator direct access to the ethical issue. In the hospice I spent a great deal of my resources failing to get beyond the institutional to where, I think, ethics really mattered – i.e. protecting people from their personal fears. Of course, I managed to do this very well with the students, who were not defending their institutional base – much less, they were intent on mounting a critique of the conservatoire. This itself ran the danger of irritating the hospice staff, who could see the music students free to articulate complexities about the hospice which hospice people themselves could not easily do. There was a threat to ownership here.

THE CASE CONTAMINATES THE CONTEXT

Another key problem here was that the musical experiences of the students, which were what I was contracted to evaluate, were thoroughly saturated with context; what the students said about themselves and their musical learnings intermingled with data about the hospice. Each of the statements above from the students read as, in part at least, a judgement on the hospice. I was there to evaluate the music project, but to the hospice this looked and felt like evaluating them.

Indeed, it was difficult for me as the evaluator to avoid this feeling myself. To understand musical learnings is to understand them in certain contexts of values and activities. We talk as though context and focus were conveniently separated like background and foreground, harmony and melody, mise-en-scène and dramatic action. Of course, they are. But then, they are also like scene and action in that they are continuous, seamless in their connection. We can account for context separately – for example, give an account of the hospice, then move to an account of the musical activities – but this counts for little more than convenience. When we document the students' reactions on leaving the hospice we need to offer the reader a view of what is being reacted *to*, and thereby invite the reader to make judgements about the nature and value of that reaction – was it, for example, reasonable or was it based on a misunderstanding? Now, beyond the music project *per se*, we are evaluating the hospice.

I was not there to evaluate the hospice. This was (planned as) a key experience for both project and students alike and I was obliged to document it. I was committed to publishing case studies of project interactions in community institutions and it seemed obvious to write one about these events. I used this argument to persuade the hospice staff that I was aiming to write a case study not of *them* but of the project – though, clearly, this would have to involve a *portrayal* of the hospice. In any event, I am a strong advocate of the view that case study is a process of discovering the case boundaries – that it makes no sense to announce what this is or is not a case study of. But at the personal level, which constantly surges, the intrinsic complexity of any interaction in a hospice environment was compelling in itself for the opportunity to portray what were likely to be heightened states of sensibility. I always *thought* of this as an opportunity to portray a hospice, though my primary interest throughout was to illuminate the conservatoire programme. One strategy for doing that was to immerse the evaluation in the specific contexts in which it worked. For the sake of the conservatoire programme I needed to expose the hospice – another case of mutually bracketed ethics.

EVALUATION ETHICS CAN FRUSTRATE THE ACTOR'S ETHICAL INTENT

In another evaluation, a student in a school was telling me a vivid and damning story about his mistreatment by teachers. He gave a number of examples of the school's assumption that his history of disaffection and recalcitrance persisted, whereas in fact he had changed to the point of valuing school as a life strategy for improvement. Teachers were still dismissive of him and reacted to him with the violence they (wrongly) expected of him. The story, had I published it, would have proved harmful to both him and his teachers. But when I broached this with him, he argued strongly that this was why he had told me what he had – that his teachers did not listen to him and that I was his only conduit to them; it was crucial to his mission to secure the support of the school that I publish the story, warts and all. I didn't – quite possibly because another loser might have been the evaluation, which could have been brought into disrepute by provoking such a situation. We too are stakeholders. But the key difficulty for the evaluator in such circumstances is that we are cast in a role of deciding who is to be protected and who exposed. Of course, we mitigate this so far as we can through negotiation procedures based on principles which balance participant confidentiality with the public 'right to know' – and our resolutions, it is to be hoped, are based on agreements. What my story-telling here implies is that there are important situations in which those agreements are frustrated by the impossibility of fairness. In these straits, where the legitimacy of the evaluation is brought into question by the inevitability of unfairness, we need at least to consider the viability of the exercise.

EVALUATORS CAN CONFUSE COHERENCE WITH ETHICS

I was conducting an evaluation of a community music project, and some of the work happened in a workshop with people suffering from dementia – many of them suspected Alzheimer's cases. A central issue here is clearly memory: short-term memory goes first with Alzheimer's, while long-term memory can persist. This can create distortions in the life and perceptions of the sufferer – but also in the perceptions of the observer. I undertook to interview a man, Maurice, who joined in the music workshop. He had been a successful musician before his illness took hold – a clarinettist. I asked him questions about his life and his music. He could, and attempted to, recall events and people from his past, but they came out in disjointed fashion. Figures popped up apparently out of nowhere, events were mixed up with each other, and although we exhibited all the outward signs of conversation, what passed between us was something less. So it was, indeed, with Maurice's participation in these events themselves. Though he turned up every week and helped to make up a group, in fact he arrived every week afresh, able to say that this was his first visit. There was a one-sidedness to the view that Maurice was a part of this enterprise.

Nestling within this small event are difficult dilemmas. At the most basic ethical level, could I use the interview with Maurice if I were to run the risk of humiliating this unfortunate man? But what of the fact that he would certainly lose all memory of our event, and be unable, therefore, to reflect on its accuracy and fairness? And what of the fact that his instant loss of memory might prejudice his status as *participant* in the evaluation – that is, where capacity to recall is an unspoken assumption in social enquiry as the means by which a sequence of events is sustained to create a *process*? But what intrigues and disturbs me most is that when I was looking for what it was that made this interview coherent, I had recourse only to myself and my own sense of curiosity. Maurice seemed to have moments of contentment with what he was saying, made those expressive utterances which suggested satisfaction with his constructions – a knowing smile here, a laugh there. But it was lost on me. The point, perhaps, is that were there sufficient syntactic coherence from Maurice I might easily have assumed, as I/we routinely do, an ethical basis for conducting and reporting the interview. But how often do we impose our own sense of coherence on the interview, pursue ethical principles and proceed without noticing the potential violence done to the sense of coherence of our respondents? Frequently, is my guess, and to some extent through historical legacies passed on by other disciplines. Psychology in particular has long practised those methodologies which keep respondents apart from each other, connected only by what it is (theoretically) that makes the experiment coherent. What it takes to make events and lives coherent for our respondents rarely has sufficient force to displace the theory of coherence of the social enquirer.

EVALUATORS CAN CONFUSE PRIVATE MORALITY WITH PUBLIC ETHICS

At the time I was writing the hospice case, I was – I like to think, by chance – reading a book (*Into That Darkness* by Gita Sereny) based on a series of interviews with the ex-commandant of a Nazi death camp. The parallels (*not the comparison*) were as obvious as they were horrific as they were unfair. Privately – secretly – the book and its revelations about the personal theorizing of managers around, crudely, 'people-processing' became a theoretical source of my own. Whatever else, they were influential in terms of the intellectual lenses through which I generated and conceptualized my data. Should I have included a reference to that book in my account? I did not, in fact, refer to it, knowing that it would be too threatening – and far, far too insulting to the work of hospice professionals whom I came to admire. In the event the book did prove to be influential – I still maintain that it was a valid theoretical resource – and my first case study draft was suffused with an indignant pessimism about the condition and treatment by society of terminally ill people. This nonetheless had no direct expression in the words I used. The people at the hospice felt my hostility as they read the draft but could not properly attack it because they could not pinpoint it. It was too deeply embedded, hidden behind the narrative – the evaluator's dark secret. This did, of course, handicap them in subsequent negotiations, and during those negotiations I had to wage my own struggle to disentangle my personal fears (I do dread mortality) from my ethical stance. Only having done so could I treat with any adequacy the hospice's claims that there was a positive atmosphere to the place.

ETHICS AND MORALITY COINCIDE: THERE ARE NO VICTIMLESS CRIMES

A common form of covert research is the unobtrusive observation (i.e. without consent or knowledge) which is protected by anonymizing the account. The person who was observed will never have any knowledge of it and so no harm was done. For example, in our evaluation of community music my colleague and myself were given access to a group at a drop-in centre run by the National Schizophrenia Society (NSS). The group discussed our attendance and approved of it; only then were we allowed in. My colleague tape-recorded our first visit without even my knowing. We discussed this later and quickly concluded that the tape was not usable – albeit it might prove difficult not to refer to it for purposes of checking the accuracy of the field notes. A visit the next week showed how volatile the situation was and how shaky the foundations of the consent we had been granted. During the week various things had happened and some members of the group had been under considerable stress; tolerances had shifted. And, too, there were new members of the group. Similarly, the account I have already discussed of the interview with Maurice raises questions about the nature of informed consent – usually prejudiced by something, and in his case prejudiced by the absence of memory. In this case I have chosen the contrary strategy and have elected to use the interview.

No individual stood or stands to be hurt by the use or non-use of the material I have mentioned. But this is not all the point. Wax and Cassell (1981) remind us that ethical concerns in the research literature tend to centre on the possibility of *harm* done by enquiry, but that we need also to consider the possibility of committing a *wrong* that may well do no harm – that is, we cannot assume a neat boundary between ethics and morality. We cannot plead innocence on the basis of an act that is ethically suspect but which results in no noticeable damage to persons or institutions and so wins on appeal to morality. An ethical 'wrong' does do a kind of harm – that is, to the social capital that is our sense of collective security; one of society's foundations slips fractionally.

I was reminded of this when I later spoke to the project director for the dementia sufferers. She had taken her group to the beach for an afternoon. A friend had questioned her about this – these people would forget the experience almost instantly, so what difference did it make whether they went or not? Here again memory asserts itself as a key element in the arbitration of ethical behaviour. Her response was that for the moment on the beach 'we were the same people' and that this was sufficient. The existential principle of the 'here-and-nowness' of valid experience won, over other considerations.

There are intriguing and difficult parallels to be drawn here between project and evaluation. For the dementia carer it is important to maintain a sequence and, therefore, a memory of events – a process whose continuity in memory gives it coherence. This is irrespective of its lack of meaning for the participant group. The care regime nonetheless depends upon that continuity for its validity; there is a secure and rich environment waiting for these people when they need it. An evaluation could assert the same principle – does so, in fact. For an evaluation to be meaningful it rests upon certain memory-based activities. We need to engage in iterative field-work – returning to the field to check, to negotiate, to report. But we cannot impose this as a criterion for participation on people like Maurice and that NSS group. Decisions on ethical behaviour have to be taken on a case basis and in response to the 'here-and-now' principle.

EVALUATION CREATES AN ETHICAL SPACE

I do not see these issues as disembodied from the practice and the conduct of evaluation – as though they were issues we confronted only in the office, returning from fieldwork, and in these scholarly settings. These are issues which inhabit the practice of evaluation and which present, as it were, lifestyle choices for the evaluator in its conduct. There is a particular reason for this, and it provides an explanatory framework for each of the dilemmas I have exemplified here, and which were the very creation of the evaluation. Evaluation, in fact, does something odd to the everyday sense and experience of ethics which people carry with them. Evaluation displaces everyday ethics and insists upon a new, albeit provisional, set – provisional, that is, upon their testing for effectiveness and tolerance. Evaluators can always be ejected from a setting one way or another, with ease or otherwise.

Evaluation creates an ethical space – that is, a space in which some people are invited to make novel judgements about the work of others, and in which the nature of those novel judgements can be regulated and scrutinized. It is in making relatively transparent the basis of judgement – i.e. the selection and denial of options – that we add the ethical dimension. This ethical space is often defined, in operational terms, by the principles and procedures against which evaluation operates, in so far as they govern participant rights and the obligations, of the evaluation in respect of them. When we mount an evaluation and secure agreement on rules governing its conduct, role and obligations, we establish a moral order to which participants are expected to conform. For some – for many responsive, naturalistic or democratic evaluators – this is most of what evaluations are meant to do. The moral order I tend to operate in – as a practitioner of democratic evaluation – is one in which there are mutual obligations to reflect and to share information. We might think of this, not entirely frivolously, as a redemptionist morality which rests on an assumption that we might regain a state of political 'grace' through better understanding, greater tolerance of diversity and the neutralization of pathological power structures.

The creation of that ethical space is not neutral and nor can it be impartial with respect to particular stakeholders – we can never be fair to all. This is because, as we have seen, ethical principles are mutually bracketed and confusing. But there is a root unfairness here, which is the very imposition of this ethical space through the displacement of everyday ethics. For example, as a normal working environment, the hospice could foreclose on moral issues or treat them according to its tolerances, decide what dilemmas to address and which to set aside – but in line with its own judgement. A doctor decided not to show a draft of my case study to a woman resident on health grounds – even though she was asking to see it. With an evaluation around, the hospice lost control of what to and what not to consider, for many of its options became relocated – at least, exposed – in the public, ethical space. The curtain of illusion was inexorably drawn back and a regime of authenticity imposed where, beforehand, a regime of organizational artifice was sufficient to get by.

The question of ethical space is central both to the role of evaluation (i.e. how it justifies its social warrant) and to its goals (i.e. how it serves particular needs). In relation to role, we need evaluators to be independent of the ethics of the prevailing political culture – otherwise judgement tends to be suffused with similar assumptions to those prevailing. Why, in such a case, commission an evaluation, other than to confirm the policy being implemented? Part of the structure of the ethical space created by the evaluation is made up of relations between government and people; such relations are necessarily implied by any evaluation (I am not saying that they are always made explicit). All innovations we observe in the public sector are, one way or another, paid for with public money and fall within the prevailing economic logic of government. This economic logic, as we in the United Kingdom have seen so powerfully with privatization and deregulation, is nothing more than a surrogate for a theory of the role of government – i.e. with relation to its electorate. The local management of schools, the displacement of local education authorities by private consultants, the reduction in the unit of resource in higher and further education, students' grants and nursery vouchers – all of these are motivated by a particular position on the morality of government and, therefore, on the relationship between government and people. The job of evaluation in respect of these relationships is to generate alternative ways of conceiving of them and of talking about them. This is the critical role of evaluation: to seek to stand outside prevailing political/power assumptions in such a way as to bring them under scrutiny and into question. Ethically, an evaluation cannot fail to present alternatives to prevailing social and political theory in one form or another. It is in the creation of ethical space that this can happen, for the question of how and when such alternative visions are generated is a process question; it concerns how evaluators themselves relate to government and people.

In relation to the goals of evaluation – its operational objectives – ethics plays an equally central part. End states are as suffused with ethics as are processes and procedures and, in this sense, do not exist apart from the process of arriving at them. How we journey tells us something about how we arrive and how we regard the place we have arrived at. We cannot, for example, engage in participatory evaluation and hold to the view that projects and programmes should be held to their initial objectives. Participatory evaluation defines a process which seeks to embrace plurality and is tolerant of the fact that there are alternative voices (i.e. alternative to 'official voices') which need to be heard and merit being heard. To measure the accomplishments of a project against a single set of values is to deny that same plurality, to deny that different groups within the participatory framework will bring different criteria to bear on the judgement of whether or not an enterprise was or was not worthwhile. Goals are ethical because they represent standards, and standards embody judgement. They reflect those same ethical traps I have spoken about. Into that ethical space created by the evaluation and in which we can address ethical dilemmas we must place dialogue about ends.

PRECISE TIMES, HOSTILE CONTEXTS FOR ETHICS

> This is a sharp time, now, a precise time – we live no longer in the dusky afternoon when evil mixed itself with good and befuddled the world.
>
> (Deputy Governor Danforth in Arthur Miller's *The Crucible*)

Such is our state on the cusp of the millennium. We live under what may be the most committed technocracy of the twentieth century. Prevailing political theory in the United Kingdom dictates that government withdraws from direct action. Instead its role is to conceive of policy, set criteria for realizing that policy in action and then launch inspections to ensure compliance. OFSTED, the Office for Standards in Education, is a typical example. It is the arm of a government which sees no issue in the conception of policy; but serious issues in ensuring compliance. It is in this sense that we are committed to precision, and it is such a context of command-and-control that threatens to contaminate the ethical flexibility so necessary to evaluation.

These are hostile atmospheres for democratic evaluators to breathe. It becomes increasingly difficult to bring policy into question; parliamentary majorities aside, the weight of forced consensus on the righteousness of government and official agencies creates an inertia in the struggle for access to policy realms. Alternative ways of seeing policy are virtually out of the question, such is the strength (but brittleness) of commitment to the belief in the power of government. It becomes increasingly difficult, too, to win contracts for anything other than implementation studies and studies to confirm, if not the accuracy, then the rectitude of policy. Evaluation which brings into question the way in which we understand society and its programmes is fast yielding ground to its weaker, more biddable sibling, consultancy.

At a more insidious level we are approaching a state called, by Jeremy Bentham, 'inspectability'. Bentham held a lifelong commitment to the development of the 'panopticon': the institution in which the possibility of unseen scrutiny was ever present; the institution as the 'all-seeing eye'; the inspector as the spider at the centre of the web. Bentham's favoured application (never fully realized) of the panopticon was the prison, though he found the idea from his brother, who had generated it for purposes of factory production. The aim of the panopticon was so to generate fear and a pervasive culture of inspection as to persuade those under scrutiny to modify and self-regulate their behaviour. Inspectability defines a cultural anticipation for scrutiny and a fear of judgement.

Clearly, such states are inimical to the open consideration of ethics. Both the call for compliance with 'precise' objectives and the emergence of a culture of inspectability lead to an intolerance of ethical leeway. For example, inspectability – the panopticon school system assumed by OFSTED, say – is dismissive of confidentiality and the right to professional self-determination. The British government recently had to go to the lengths of having to legislate to provide some protection for 'whistle-blowers', for people who hold openly critical views of their public-sector organization.

It is, in an obvious sense, a long way from OFSTED to a dying woman in a hospice. But, then, it is not. (The pressing need to keep patients under close observation makes of the hospice a medical panopticon, in any event.) My main argument has been that ethical decisions are made on a case-by-case basis, drawn from our experience, regulated more by context than by principle. In the balance between what we *ought* to be doing and what we *can* accomplish, ethical procedures are weighted dismayingly closer to the latter than to the former. This means that evaluators are highly vulnerable to the *zeitgeist* – to the dominant logic of the times, which defines much of what we *cannot* do and, hence, much of what we do do. OFSTED serves as a barometer of contemporary approaches to educational judgement, and it marks a cold climate. Our current flirtation with a technocratic (albeit progressive) state leaves individuals exposed. We live in a world where there is no 'Plan B', and so little room for asserting individual need.

The other implication of this policy context is that, to return to my accountability theme, strong expectations of accountability are held of evaluators – but not necessarily those which allow for responsive ethics. The command-and-control culture of policy demands of evaluators that they promote compliance and seek out non-compliance – currently an expanding role for evaluators. In such a context, our accountability is to the policy machine and to the administrative system. The consistency I spoke of earlier is given by the moral imperative of supporting the collective aims of society – for example, in social reform projects such as eradicating illiteracy. Evaluators become co-opted into means–end forms of rationality – the rationality of epidemiological vaccination. Better to calculate for a small number of casualties so as to guarantee the eradication of a pathology than to expose the whole population by protecting all of its individuals. Loss for some is justified where it guarantees gain for the collective. This utilitarian presumption is the source of a moral order which does promote a hierarchy of ethical principles and which denies the situatedness of judgement. In such a situation we may well find ourselves sacrificing ethical coherence for the sake of remaining consistent. There is an ersatz fairness to the panopticon view of society which resides in the assumption of equality of treatment; but there is a profound and authentic unfairness in its dismissal of the individual. Without access to the individual, evaluators cannot work out their ethical confusions.

As we continue to become co-opted into the policy machine, we continue to create those ethical spaces with our evaluations. These are the 'parlours' of evaluation – those entrances to novel ethical places which are characterized by uncertain gestures, nervous asides, a looking out for revealing signs of what lies beyond. Perhaps most characteristic of the parlour is a tolerance for clumsiness in both host and invited – we all know what it is like to hover on the brink of an unknown place and to invite strangers into intimacy. But what I describe is a friendly parlour, a social place, a space which is kindly to the vulnerable. There are others – and it is as well to know whose parlour we are standing in.

Chapter 6

Whose side, whose research, whose learning, whose outcomes?

Ethics, emancipatory research and unemployment

Rennie Johnston

This chapter identifies key ethical issues within the broad discourse of emancipatory research and explores and problematizes the different ethical positions that can be adopted. Through a critical analysis of a participatory action research project with unwaged adults led by the author, it sets out both to illustrate and to interrogate the ethics of emancipatory research and, through this, to illuminate and exemplify the notion of situated ethics.

Emancipatory research aims to bring about social change. It can be seen to cover a broad spectrum of research practices, variously referred to as critical research, transformative research, participatory research and radical research. It has a clear ontological starting point, namely the existence of a world characterized by socio-economic and cultural inequalities where researchers have an interest and a part to play in trying to emancipate oppressed groups, those who suffer from social and economic inequality and exclusion and a lack of social justice.

Ethical issues are clearly foregrounded within the discourse of emancipatory research; indeed, ethics is central to it. Yet its ethical position is significantly different from that of mainstream positivist and interpretive research paradigms. Following a Freirian epistemology, emancipatory research rejects both the idea of political neutrality for research and the idea that research is merely concerned with finding out about the world. Emancipatory research is about acting politically in the world.

Thus in its politics, emancipatory research has two main aims. The first is to develop a greater awareness of the relationships between power, research and social movements. The second is to help promote social action to transform the inequalities and divisions arising from the effects of poverty, racial and sexual discrimination, colonization and marginalization. In its methodology it emphasizes participation and questions of research ownership, in an explicit challenge to the epistemological dichotomy between subjects and objects, researchers and researched.

In exploring the ethics of emancipatory research, key issues to be examined in this chapter are partisanship and objectivity; research for empowerment; the interrelationship between methodology and outcomes; the ownership of the research process; researcher reflexivity; and forms of research evaluation and dissemination. However, first it is necessary to look more closely at some key ethical questions within the broad discourse of emancipatory research.

EXPLORING AND INTERROGATING THE ETHICS OF EMANCIPATORY RESEARCH

From the outline above, it can be seen that the ethics of emancipatory research is clearly situated in ideological terms, and, as such, is very differently situated from the ethics of mainstream research paradigms. This difference needs to be analysed critically. It is important to examine whether the ethics of emancipatory research still adopts a universalist, if alternative, ethical position and in what way its ethical stance is further mediated by situational factors; and to identify to what extent the discourse of emancipatory research embraces or needs to embrace a situated ethics. These questions will be explored first through an investigation and analysis of the ethical position of emancipatory research and rationale for it in the specific context of a late modern/postmodern world, and second, by relating this to one specific case study of a situated research practice with emancipatory intent.

In the light of the development of what Beck (1992) identifies as a contemporary 'risk society', typified by complexity, risk and uncertainty, where 'new areas of unpredictability are created quite often by the very attempts that seek to control them' (Beck *et al.* 1994: vii), it may be appropriate to probe and problematize the essentially modernist universalities and certainties implicit within the ethics of emancipatory research. Recent feminist and postmodernist perspectives on pedagogy and research have raised important questions about the whole idea of emancipation in the contemporary world. For example, Jennifer Gore (1992) argues that whereas an alternative set of values such as those contained in emancipatory research offers a necessary challenge to that of more conventional and mainstream approaches to research, these are still universal and, more to the point, totalizing values. She identifies the risk that, notwithstanding its clear rhetorical commitment to dialogue, emancipatory research can serve to impose yet another 'regime of truth' upon research subjects; the promise of 'speaking for oneself' can still be frustrated.

There are three main dangers here. First, in the name of emancipation, researchers (explicitly or implicitly) can impose their own meanings on situations rather than negotiate these meanings with research participants or indeed start from participants' aims. By framing the research process in terms of Freirian 'conscientization' (Freire 1972), it is possible, notwithstanding a genuine commitment to dissolving the difference between researchers and researched, to impose a top-down, overly deterministic, blanket attribution of 'false consciousness' and an alternative vision of the future which does not take proper account of (or respect for) the starting points and values of research participants. Second, in setting up a stark dichotomy between education/research for liberation versus education/ research for domestication, insufficient room is left for the specificities of local contexts and the differences and complexities which arise from, for example, an increasingly flexible, fragmented and unpredictable labour market within a complex social world. Third, such a process oversimplifies the idea of research for empowerment and the assumed central role of the emancipatory researcher as an agent of empowerment 'giving' power to the people. Such dangers may require the emancipatory researcher to focus in greater detail on the specific situatedness of the research process in question, to ponder the limits of subject agency, to re-view the power– knowledge relationship and to address the whole question of reflexivity in research.

With this critique in mind, it is now appropriate to look in greater depth at a specific case study of participatory action research led by the author as a way of situating and re-viewing the key ethical issues identified within the discourse of emancipatory research. This research is set in the context of making educational responses to the growing problem of adult unem- ployment in the UK in the mid- and late 1980s. While the historical context is now somewhat different as we move into the twenty-first century, the ethical issues identified are just as relevant today with the continuing growth of a wide range of education and training schemes to cope with the issues and problems arising out of long-term unemployment.

The Southampton Respond project was set up as a participatory action research project and began in 1984. It was one of a series of local development projects which were part of the overall Replan programme funded through the Department of Education and Science (DES). The Replan programme was the Thatcher government's first concerted, if not fully strategic, response to the dramatic increase in adult unemployment since its advent to power in 1979. It consisted of a range of national and regional initiatives which were effectively subcontracted to different organizations such as the Further Education Unit (FEU), the Manpower Services Commission (MSC) and the National Institute of Adult Continuing Education (NIACE). Its original aims, as set out by the DES, were essentially functional, with a clear focus on the increasing of employability and on skills development, linked to a fostering of coping and personal development among the unemployed – little apparent scope here for any form of emancipatory research!

NIACE, which was responsible for 'the management of a programme of local development projects through partnerships with a range of statu- tory and voluntary bodies' (NIACE 1984), is a national adult education organization with a historical commitment to a broadly based liberal adult education, which included scope and space for emancipatory aspirations and emancipatory practice within its 'broad church' perspective. With this background and some clever manoeuvring and negotiation, NIACE managed to extend and modify its part of the Replan programme brief to recognize the particularity of various subgroups of unemployed adults and to concentrate on programmes rather than curricula. This process can be seen to reflect Burgess's observation about externally funded research, that 'the funding process involves a partnership with the funding agency where researchers attempt to find scope for their aims alongside the aims of the sponsor' (Burgess 1984: 256).

NIACE identified outreach as an intrinsic feature in projects which were to be collaborative with other agencies, to use 'participative, non-authoritarian style of procedure', to show evidence of their potentiality for continuity and to be 'unequivocally *local* in scope, range and character' (NIACE 1984).

The interagency team, fronted by the University of Southampton, which put together a successful bid, already had considerable experience of working in local working-class communities and, in some cases, with unemployed groups (Fordham *et al.* 1979; Johnston 1981). Its overall approach could be viewed as being emancipatory in intent, stemming from its articulated commitment to a tradition of 'social purpose' adult education, characterized by Fieldhouse as

> providing individuals with knowledge which they can use collectively to change society if they so wish, and particularly equipping members of the working class with the intellectual tools to play a full role in a democratic society or to challenge the inequalities and injustices of society in order to bring about radical social change.
>
> (1992: 11)

With the NIACE brief in mind, the initial Southampton research approach was to frame the project in terms of participatory action research and to assert that 'Our intention is to combine action and reflection by project workers and unemployed people themselves. We are looking to involve unemployed and local people as active agents in our research process rather than as passive objects of study' (Johnston 1991: 64).

ETHICAL ISSUES IN THE RESPOND PROJECT

The particular situatedness of a research project working in the area of unemployment immediately introduces a central problem and complexity, indeed an ethical dilemma: the possibility of conducting research with emancipatory intent while being funded, albeit indirectly, by government. This dilemma becomes even more acute when this particular government could be seen to have, at least partly, created the problem of unemployment through its monetarist policies and whose main concern in addressing the growing problem of unemployment appeared to be in the realm of social control, i.e. seeing unemployment as a 'problem' to be 'managed'.

This overall political context clearly imposed certain limitations on the scope of the research and on its emancipatory intent. This is a position common to all funded research, but perhaps more especially apparent in the very political area of unemployment. For example, Shanahan and Ward (1995) start from an explicitly radical position in their adult education work in Derry, focusing unequivocally on the 'empowerment' of the 'excluded'. Notwithstanding their clear commitment to emancipation, in supporting the development of a community house funded under the 'Action for Community Employment Scheme', they also identify the self-censorship which 'inevitably' is associated with a reliance on government funding and the concomitant dangers of locking into the present socio-political status quo (Shanahan and Ward 1995: 76).

In relation to terms of *partisanship and objectivity*, the Southampton project workers were well aware of the impossibility of absolute objectivity, understood that all research reflects certain values and were clear about their own values. They wanted to make a contribution to tackling unemployment in the interests of achieving greater social equality – in Freirian terms, they were looking to develop their 'praxis', 'reflection and action upon the world in order to transform it' (Freire 1972: 28). At a local level, they wanted to make a difference in improving the situation for unemployed and unwaged adults who might become involved in the project. In terms of their attitude to research, they could all have agreed with Deshler and Selener's position on transformative research, that 'the research process should be conducted in the public interest with attention to human rights, social justice, conciliation, and preservation of environmental sustainability' (Deshler and Selener 1991: 10).

However, the ethics of the situation was still far from straightforward in the political context of unemployment. Very early on, project workers, in their contact with unemployed and unwaged adults, had to face up to the key issue of 'Whose side are you on?' Indeed, this very situation was exacerbated by being part of a process explicitly identified as 'research'.

In the introduction to his edited collection on *Ethics and Educational Research*, Burgess (1989: 2) identifies key ethical issues as follows: 'what should individuals be told about the conduct of social research? Is secret research justifiable? Is secret research desirable? What data can be collected "openly"?'

In many ways these issues were resolved by the adoption of an open commitment to participatory action research; the cards were on the table from the outset. However, in the project in question, this approach was neither a complete nor a neat ethical resolution. In the macro context of a government seen by many to be actively creating unemployment and a micro context where 'dole scroungers' were increasingly being monitored and investigated at local level, the whole idea of 'research', whether participatory or not, was viewed very sceptically and suspiciously. Furthermore, the very jobs of the project workers could be seen to be dependent, even parasitic, on the very unemployment of the unwaged project participants.

In this context the research situation was not so far away from that of the anthropologists reported by Hammersley and Atkinson as being 'frequently suspected, initially at least, as being government spies, tax inspectors, police informers etc.' (1993: 77). For example, in the early stages of the research project, the emotive term 'guinea pig' was several times used, pointedly if often in jest, by unemployed participants to describe their position in the project. Interestingly, some of those most suspicious about this aspect of research had worked quite amicably with the author in earlier activities when the work had been seen as 'adult education' rather than 'research'. So, honesty about the research process may have served to solve some longer-term ethical dilemmas but it also created some new, more immediate difficulties for project workers. In the Respond project, ultimate honesty about the research process was crucial to both the ethics and the practicalities of a participatory approach to research. In practice, however, this had to be mediated by a clear distancing from government policies and a stress on the essentially local interagency management of the project and autonomy of NIACE as project sponsors (rather than the fact that the whole Replan project was ultimately government funded) (Johnston 1991).

Indeed, this whole issue and the ethical and practical problems it raised were so problematic for the project team members that it prompted them, after considerable deliberation, to add two very explicit participatory aims to the project's initial list of predominantly educational aims:

> e) to work with unwaged people in a participatory research programme which will focus on the needs of unwaged people and ways in which an educational approach can meet these needs
> f) to involve unwaged people in the management of the project so that by the end of the funding they can continue to operate with the active support of agencies like Southampton Institute for Adult, Youth and Community Education, the University Department of Adult Education and Southampton City Council.
>
> (Johnston 1987: 7)

In the very political arena of unemployment, the answer to 'Whose side are you on?' also had its complexities. While all project workers would have identified themselves as being on the side of unemployed people in general, and seeking to empower the unwaged participants in the project in particular, further ethical issues arose from the different meanings of *research for empowerment* in this particular context. These related to a recurrent and much debated theme for the research project: the whole issue of the 'needs' of unemployed and unwaged adults, how these were constructed by the different parties to the research and how to respond to them.

Clearly, the top priority for the vast majority of the unwaged adults involved in the project was to get a paid job. This was their primary felt need and constituted their idea of empowerment. Project workers had to engage with this if they were to maintain any credibility and commitment to the agendas of research participants and to participatory action research. However, project workers, in common with some unwaged participants, were also very much aware of the wider political context of the research, and the government agenda of improving the unemployment statistics, come what may, and government's aim to 'manage' and minimize the political problem of unemployment. In fact, the author had earlier contributed to a series of 'Political Papers' written by a group of adult educators who expressly identified and opposed the dangers of becoming enmeshed in a system of social control as exemplified by a narrow vocationalism and the development of 'social and life skills' for the unemployed (Reading and Elphick 1981). As Newman had put it earlier, regarding similar work with unemployed people, 'Most of the activities in this paper have pointed the way back into employment. But if we concentrate on this are we not in danger of joining in a mass deception?' (Newman 1978: 13).

Helping unwaged people to get 'a job, any job' (as was often the demand) might be empowerment at one level but it was very far from broader ideas of emancipatory social change, identified by Beder as 'change in which the subordinated are empowered to take control of their lives and change the conditions which have caused their oppression' (1991: 4). The narrowly focused instrumental knowledge and skills that unwaged adults wanted and needed to gain access to the labour market did not easily equate to the generation of knowledge in the service of the wider kind of emancipation expressed by Beder (1991). In the project context, ideas of a polarity between research for 'liberation' versus research for 'domestication' were not helpful. Indeed, the desired 'liberation' of getting 'a job, any job' could be seen, from another standpoint, to equate only to 'domestication'. Yet it was far too simplistic, self-serving and patronizing to identify this attitude as mere 'false consciousness'.

For project workers, from a micro perspective, it was not ethical to ignore the primary identified needs of unwaged participants. Neither was it ethical, from a macro view, to engage uncritically in what might be seen as a 'mass deception'. Faced with this situated dilemma, the project had little option but to compromise in supporting unwaged participants in their plans to access the labour market but, at the same time, posing key questions about the wider social context of unemployment and how it impacted on their views of themselves and their vocational, educational and social aspirations. This linking of private problems to public issues, later identified by the author as combining 'personal empowerment: practical action' with 'contextual analysis: ideological action' (Johnston 1992), was a direct response to the ethical issues situated within this particular project context.

Another situated ethical issue and complexity was related to the project's *research methodology*. In identifying the characteristics of transformative research, Beder identifies the importance of outcomes for participants rather than adherence to methodological rules: 'Praxis is an on-going, dialectical process in which the validity of the research is assessed according to the value of its outcomes rather than by its adherence to sets of empirically derived rules' (Beder 1991: 4).

Such a privileging of outcomes over methodological principles and procedures is a dramatic departure from more conventional approaches to research and research ethics. It raises fundamental questions about the nature of research and the role of the situated researcher with an interest in and commitment to emancipation. While a focus on outcomes is completely consistent with the ethics of emancipatory research as outlined earlier, questions perhaps need to be asked as to what are the dangers and what is the ultimate effect of creating such a dichotomy between outcomes and methodology.

Project staff were certainly aware of the ethical imperative of achieving outcomes for participants. However, this did not necessarily mean a rejection of method, or of the search for more generalizable knowledge through research. One of the strengths and advantages of the project, in the politicized context of unemployment, was its university research status, which served to grant it a degree of autonomy and independence from government influence. For it to have this semi-independent status and for it to be able to call upon the research community's defence of 'academic freedom', it needed to be seen as a legitimate research process and, as such, to have an identifiable and justifiable research methodology.

Certainly, previous higher education projects which had engaged with unemployed people, such as the Leeds University Pioneer action research project (Ward and Taylor 1986), had made much of their commitment to this position. The Leeds project stressed the importance of academic rigour and the generalizability of knowledge, with a strong emphasis on the research and monitoring of provision and 'provision forming the essential empirical information upon which analyses of the most appropriate and successful models for development are based' (Taylor 1985: 104). Such an approach could easily provoke conflicting loyalties, to the more formal research process or to research participants. Indeed, this tension was clearly identified by one of the Leeds action research team, who identified conflicts between 'wishing on the one hand to adopt a critical, "objective" approach to the research' and also wanting (as a researcher with personal experience of unemployment) to identify with unemployed participants and contribute to the action in some tangible way (Fraser 1986: 57–8).

In resolving this tension between methods and outcomes for participants in the Respond project, a central part of the project strategy was to link rather than separate the two, through developing a research approach which incorporated an explicit participatory research methodology. Budd Hall identifies participatory research as being 'at the same time, an *approach* of social investigation, an *educational* process, and a *means* of taking action' (Hall 1981: 455, his emphases). A key development for the project was the setting up of the participatory research group. This group, co-ordinated by the project leader, was made up of a group of unwaged adults who had been attending a project-initiated Return to Study course called New Directions. The work of this participatory research group was crucial in the development of the project and in meeting its aims of combining 'action and reflection by project workers and unemployed people themselves' (Johnston 1991: 64). On the one hand, it served to underline the partic-ipatory nature of the research process in that unwaged adults helped to design, distribute and analyse a questionnaire to all unwaged project partic-ipants as well as carrying out follow-up interviews and disseminating and discussing findings with their unwaged colleagues. It also helped to demys-tify the whole research process and empower the research group in that they developed knowledge, skills and confidence as they carried out the research. Finally, it helped to allay some of the suspicions of others about having research 'done' to them by outsiders with their own agendas.

The work of the participatory research group served as an important inter-connection between methods and outcomes in the Respond project. At the same time, it also represented a trade-off between the more immediate and specific interests of unwaged participants and the wider research ambitions and agendas of the original project. This trade-off 'worked' for three reasons. First, the project leader realized the need to acknowledge openly his and the project's vested interest in producing research findings that were both exter-nally credible and productive of learning points beyond the predominantly localized concerns of project participants. Second, as the research work developed, some unwaged participants, through their involvement in the research process, came to take a greater interest in and ownership of the wider remit of the project. Perhaps the most important reason, however, was that as the participatory research group developed its work, the key issues and desired outcomes identified in the research process demonstrably belonged to the unwaged adults and were seen to be actively addressed by the project as a result of the group's research work.

The participatory research group played a key role in resolving the question of *research ownership* in this specific context. As a result of its work (and that of other associated participatory forums and groups within the project), the 'ownership' of the research project became more evenly dispersed and shared between project workers, unwaged adults, the project management group and NIACE, the sponsors. It provided a situated solution to the tensions of ownership and also helped to fulfil the project's original aim 'to involve unemployed and local people as active agents rather than as passive objects of study' (unpublished early project paper, January 1985).

Alan Rogers identifies an important ethical issue for adult educators working with marginalized groups in the context of development when he asks, 'Is starting with the participants' wants and moving through them . . . to our own goals, a valid process? Is it not using often very vulnerable people for our own ends?' (1992: 156). Such a charge could equally apply to research work with unwaged adults. In the Respond project context, the power relationships were complex; it could be said that the government's agenda was extended and modified by NIACE, the sponsors, whose agendas in turn were mediated by the project management group's agendas, which were further mediated by those of the project workers. The work emanating from the participatory research group was effective in avoiding much of the danger of exploitation and manipulation by building in yet another level of mediation, through connecting the wider aims and methodology of the project to the predominantly more localized and immediate concerns of unwaged participants.

In critically interrogating the conduct of research with emancipatory aspirations, Lather (1991b: 57) identifies the development of *self-reflexivity*, involving a need for reciprocity and the mutual recognition of power as providing an important bulwark against adopting a top-down and totalizing stance. While it must be admitted that the original project aims framed the whole development process, and project workers' agendas were perhaps the most influential, the participatory nature of the research process succeeded in making project workers more reflexive in their approach and so helped them in the main to avoid the ethical trap of unreflexively imposing their meanings on situations, of establishing 'regimes of truth'.

The Respond research made a contribution to a 'situated emancipation' in identifying and addressing more localized concerns and issues regarding the use and profile of the collective project base and, in some instances, helping individual unwaged adults to become 'empowered', to move on, in terms of either further education, community and voluntary work or paid employment. However, this fell well short of more rhetorical claims for research for empowerment, of fundamentally changing the lives of research participants and the conditions which caused their oppression. Indeed, this highlights a further question, posed by postmodern commentators, of the limitations of empowerment, of the extent to which power can actually be 'bestowed' upon people through the medium of education or research. The situation of unwaged adults in Southampton was so circumscribed by economic and other factors that the empowering potential of the research process was always going to be limited. Therefore, extravagant claims for the power/knowledge impact would have been unrealistic.

However, through its participatory processes, the project did contribute towards giving unwaged participants in the project a recognizable and collective 'voice', a greater opportunity to speak for themselves. Aronowitz and Giroux assert the importance of 'voice' within critical pedagogy: 'voices forged in opposition and struggle provide the crucial conditions by which subordinate individuals and groups reclaim their own memories, stories, histories as part of an ongoing attempt to challenge those power structures that attempt to silence them' (1991: 101). The context of the Respond project offered limited opportunities and identified limited ambitions to challenge power structures, in many ways reflecting Field's observation that 'Anyone who believes that the unemployed are the vanguard, or even part of the vanguard of a "new social movement" is clearly suffering from wishful thinking' (Field 1985: 5).

Nevertheless, both the possibilities and the limitations of participant 'voice' were important in the ethical conduct of the Respond project and in moving on from the 'silence' of unwaged participants. This was apparent in the participatory research group but also extended into the processes of *project evaluation* and dissemination. Key issues here were the forms of evaluation adopted and the type of language used, particularly in dissemination. As noted above, evaluation had to be, at least partly, on the terms of the unwaged participants. At an internal and day-to-day level, efforts were made to develop participatory structures such as open-ended and non-linear agendas at 'open meetings' in order most democratically to identify, articulate and address the concerns of unwaged participants and so involve as many people as possible in the ongoing evaluation and development process. In this context, language was less of a problem, although participation inevitably tended to be by the more articulate and confident members, even if they often represented the views of their less confident and less articulate colleagues. There was also a voice for unwaged participants in project management meetings, although here there was a more obvious premium on self-confidence. Some unwaged participants were enthusiastic in articulating their concerns clearly and in developing their arguments in such a context. Others, although confident in other forums, at times found these more formal and academic meetings alienating and disempowering. This situation arose partly because of their lack of confidence and experience in such settings, but also owing to the 'objectification' of unemployed people that sometimes could emerge in wider focused and more academic discussion.

A key part of the evaluation and dissemination process and an ethical imperative, especially for a short-term funded project with emancipatory aspirations, was to ensure situated outcomes for unwaged participants. For this reason, a lot of work, by project workers, the project management group and unwaged participants, went into ensuring continuing support for the project-initiated Respond Base through lobbying the local authority, making productive links with the school on whose grounds the base was located, and keying into the developing agendas of the local technical college, which was best placed to support it when the project funding ran out. It is a matter of some satisfaction for many of the people involved in the project, both waged and unwaged, that, at the time of writing, thirteen years after the end of project funding, this unwaged base still exists, albeit in a some-what different and less democratic form, as an outpost of the local college.

This was the main collective outcome identified by the unwaged partici-pants in the project. As a body, they were probably less concerned with the final project report and its *dissemination*. Once again, there emerged a form of negotiated trade-off with the research team: unwaged adults got the continuation of the base and many of its activities, and the project leader and project team got their final report, the first to be nationally published from any NIACE Replan project. Of course, in practice these outcomes were much more intertwined. Certainly, the final report incorporated and fully acknowledged much of the work done by the participatory research group, highlighted and analysed the key issues identified by unwaged participants and was subjected to review and amendment by unwaged participants in the project. The voice of participants was retained, but the language and form of the report were developed very much in line with the expected require-ments of the project sponsors, and most of the ultimate theorizing was framed by the project leader. This raises further ethical issues related to participant 'voice' in relation to the dissemination of any research with emancipatory intent: in particular, how are the research results disseminated, by whom and in what kind of form or language?

In relation to the issue of textuality, Hammersley and Atkinson (1983: 228) make the point that 'We shouldn't forever be trying to match the substance and form of an account to the expectations of a given audience. This runs the risk of simply re-producing and re-inforcing existing perspec-tives, rather than challenging them.'

Within the Respond project, the project leader and project team, in retrospect, might have attempted a more imaginative and democratic dissemination process so that the voice of unwaged participants was heard more directly and more extensively beyond the local context. Just as some emancipatory researchers have been able to generate a wide range of alter-native and ethically appropriate research methods – for example, using artistic means and photo-representations (Kirkwood and Kirkwood 1989) or people's theatre (Weiler 1996) – so, similarly, democratic and ethical forms of dissemination, such as photo novels, booklets, songs and video-tape recordings, have been developed to ensure that research findings are disseminated as democratically as possible to a wide range of participants and interested others (Hall 1981: 453).

Certainly, in the Respond project, the work of the participatory research group in linking data and theory, researcher and researched, at a micro level was not carried through into the construction (as opposed to the review) of the final report and its dissemination. This did not appear to be a major ethical issue for any of the parties to the research at the time, largely because of the expectations generated over time by the project sponsors, the project management group and the project leader who framed and wrote the final report. However, in retrospect, it can be seen to have circumscribed the participatory nature of the research in its final stages and to have limited the degree of empowerment and emancipation among participants. Perhaps alternative, and more participatory, forms of dissemination might have been developed to sustain and further participant 'voice' beyond the period of project funding.

The eventual evaluation, outcomes and dissemination process reflect one solution to different ethical tensions within a particular research situation. It was not a solution that could or did 'fit' all the ethical absolutes within the discourse of emancipatory research. However, notwithstanding these limitations, in this particular project situation there was emancipatory intent, there was a degree of unwaged 'ownership', there were outcomes for participants, there was a 'voice' for research participants but there were also limitations on these arising from the project's political and funding situatedness and from the attitudinal and experiential location of project sponsors, project staff and participants. It would thus appear to be an instructive example of an ethics where emancipatory intent was pursued and situated within particular funding and political constraints.

Chapter 7

Researching education and racialization

Virtue or validity?

Peter Figueroa

INTRODUCTION

Racism, 'race' and antiracism are among the most sensitive issues in public discourse in many parts of the world today. Recent events in Britain, in particular the Macpherson report on the inquiry into the racist killing of Stephen Lawrence (Home Department 1999) and the government's plans to make citizenship education a statutory requirement from the year 2002, have intensified discussion in Britain of racism, multiculturalism, identity and citizenship. Many of the issues are controversial, even taboo. Research, in particular educational research, in this field is fraught with problems: conceptual, ideological, methodological, political and ethical. Tensions are embedded between researcher and researched, knower and known, method and reality, validity and virtue. It is the ethical issues that this chapter primarily focuses on, although the various issues are interconnected.

The ethical issues are complex, controversial and pressing. Researchers nowadays do often raise the issue of research ethics; but is such talk often sham? Does it not often camouflage the author's own prejudices and self-interested motivations, or obscure unsustainable cultural presuppositions, structural realities and deep injustices? Furthermore, does a preoccupation with ethical issues in this field, which often translates into a crusade to liberate the culturally and 'racially' oppressed, militate against sound research and the advancement of impartial knowledge? Is the educational researcher focusing on issues of cultural diversity, inequality, racism and antiracism confronted with a choice between virtue and validity, between social justice and truth, between promoting the cause of minority ethnic people and pursuing truth conscientiously and impartially, wherever it might lead?

The very notion of ethics is difficult to unravel. Harpham in effect identifies three sets of issues, concerning the other, the ought and openness: 'Ethics is the arena in which the claims of otherness . . . are articulated and negotiated' (1995: 394). This includes the claims of the respondents and of other researchers. But it also includes the claims of the self as other (as other to others, and the me that I reflect on). In fact, several parties are involved in any educational research, and each party has rights, commitments, responsibilities and duties. The 'others' might include the researcher(s) and their assistants; low-status 'subjects', such as minority ethnic parents; high-status 'subjects', such as teachers or senior managers in a school; intermediaries, such as local education authority officers; the wider audience/consumers/citizens; the community of researchers; concerned professionals; policymakers and politicians; the respondents and the population they are drawn from; and the funders. Ethical issues arise in relation to all of these 'others'.

These issues circle around 'the one indispensable word in ethics, *"ought"'* (Harpham 1995: 395) – what ought or ought not to be done. However, Harpham also argues that 'the controversies that structure the history of ethics can never be settled. . . . Articulating perplexity, rather than guiding, is what ethics is all about' (ibid.). This means that ethical issues cannot be solved once and for all in the abstract. Nevertheless, decisions must be, and are, made in the concrete, in practice, and I would say that ethics both articulates perplexities and, as a result, offers guidance, though not clear-cut, pre-given answers. This implies the need for thoughtfulness and reflexivity, for a critical approach, for seeking to make a sustainable case.

Ethical issues relate to issues of rightness and justifiability, especially as they concern relations with others or consequences for others. The general principle may be that one should act responsibly: respecting truth, self, others and privacy; having due respect for social justice, human rights, 'reasonable' sensibilities, norms and expectations; interacting constructively; avoiding hurting or exploiting others; and, where there is conflict between various claims, values or norms, seeking balance between these, and seeking to give priority to 'higher-order' ones and to wider considerations. The trouble is the diversity of 'others', of relations and of claims. Also, the consequences can be direct or indirect, immediate or delayed, short-term, medium-term or long-term. Even more critical is that not everyone will agree on what is right or justified. Furthermore, the same action – a covert test of 'racial' discrimination, for instance, – might seem right from one point of view (to gain reliable information/knowledge/the truth) but wrong from another (deceitful). In other words, conflicts are built into ethical issues; but so is a drive towards finding some resolution.

It is within this context of conflicting demands – and of urgency – in a sensitive and controversial field that this chapter addresses the following questions:

- Is research in this area counter-productive?
- Alternatively, is it ethical *not* to focus on 'race' in educational research?
- Can research in this area be value neutral, and is truth the priority – or is social justice?
- Do the ends justify the means?

- Should the basic value be 'responsiveness to the other'?
- Where all have equal rights and diverse perspectives, can the in-built conflicts be resolved, and if so, how?

Many other important questions are implicated, but space precludes focusing on them here.

IS RESEARCH IN THIS AREA COUNTER-PRODUCTIVE?

The first question, which one still hears today, is whether it might not often be better to avoid 'stirring things up' and refrain from doing research into issues of 'race' and racism in education. A good, though early, example of this relates to 1966, when I was planning research into 'West Indian' school-leavers in London for the Survey of Race Relations. Having drawn up plans, with the assistance of a member of Her Majesty's Inspectorate, to study schools mainly in the London boroughs of Islington and Lambeth, I wrote to the Inner London Education Authority (ILEA) for permission. The reply from the Education Officer was negative: because 'schools . . . are . . . burdened with research projects', this was not 'a suitable time' to conduct such research and, finally, 'some of the questions would . . . be likely to give offence in schools' (Figueroa 1975: 495–6). A separate letter elaborated: 'asking questions in schools, specifically about racial topics, may serve to create racial problems where they did not previously exist' (ibid.: 496). When I requested clarification, the following 'confidential appreciation of the position' came back:

> We are in a transition period so far as immigrant young people are concerned. Employers have had very few young people so far who have had most of their education in this country and their attitudes tend to be affected by their impressions of earlier employees who were recruited just after they arrived here . . . therefore . . . it would not be wise to recommend the Authority to take part in a survey at a time which may not be typical of the future, or to do anything that might prejudice employers' attitudes.
>
> (Figueroa 1975: 500)

The argument, therefore, by the largest education authority in Britain with the largest minority ethnic population was that it was better not to do research so as to avoid problems. What the 'Authority' was specifically concerned about was the proposed investigation of whether 'West Indian' school-leavers were experiencing employment difficulties because of racism. As Kirp (1979) put it, the authority's notion of doing good was, it seemed, to do little.

However, was the right thing done in treating the problem as too sensitive and only temporary? In fact, how I dealt with the situation was to carry out the research, with some modifications, in an Outer London education authority that, through the intervention of E.J.B. Rose, Director of the Survey of Race Relations, was agreeable. There is no evidence that this research was prejudicial in any way, or in any way had an adverse effect on 'race' relations.

What is also remarkable is that at about the same time the ILEA (1968) undertook a study of eleven-plus transfer in schools with a high proportion of 'immigrants'. In other words, the ILEA was willing to study the achievement and ability of minority ethnic children, but not the racism of white children, teachers and employers. It is this ILEA study that Tomlinson (1983: 29) considers probably had most impact on beliefs about the 'underachievement' of minority ethnic, in particular Caribbean, children. Bagley (1968: 91) speaks of the possibility of this ILEA research having bolstered 'the ideology that coloured children are intellectually inferior'.

One of the key underlying questions here is whether it is ethical to focus research efforts on the minorities, on the 'victims', rather than on the majority, and above all rather than on the institutions and structures that may be perpetuating inequitable arrangements and systems, and indeed racism. As Mirza (1995: 165) points out, the predominantly white, middle-class, male research agenda has meant 'that the marginal, the powerless and the oppressed have been the excessive object of study'.

For such reasons, ethnic monitoring is sometimes seen as problematic, and even as racist, since it involves using 'racial' categories. There is also sometimes a concern about how this knowledge is likely to be used. Here again we have a tension: is it better not to collect the information, which could bolster equity policies – but could also be misused – rather than to 'pigeon-hole' people, inevitably perhaps in quite a crude way?

In addressing this issue, Troyna (1993) uses work by Reeves (1983) on British racial discourse, and distinguishes essentially between racist racialization and benign racialization. Implicit in this argument is also a distinction between racist deracialization and benign deracialization. Gillborn (1995) spells this out into a typology of 'race' and discourse, suggesting that there can be legitimate and spurious racialization and legitimate and spurious deracialization. According to this, racialization of discourse would, for instance, be legitimate in the case of ethnic monitoring in the service of a 'race' equality policy; but it would be spurious in a case where 'race' is not genuinely implicated in the issues concerned. In this second case, deracialization of discourse would be legitimate; but where 'race' is genuinely implicated, deracialization of discourse would be spurious.

However, there is a problem here, since this typology implies that 'race' is sometimes a legitimate concept, without clarifying what that means. Troyna himself, like many others in the field, sometimes slips into using 'race' or 'racial' as though non-problematic. For instance, he speaks of identifying 'racial inequalities in the distribution of resources' (Troyna 1993: 29). However, it is important to draw a distinction between 'race' conceived of as a natural or biological phenomenon and 'race' understood purely as a social phenomenon. As many authors (e.g. Miles 1982) have argued, 'race' under-stood as a natural phenomenon has no scientific validity. However, it is the case that people are often explicitly or implicitly differentiated in terms of a notion of 'race', and that this has real social-structural and social-interactional bases and consequences: 'race' is a social construction that, as such, has concrete reality in a racist society (Figueroa 1991). This distinc-tion is crucial for any notion of legitimate racialization and spurious de-racialization. 'Race' can be legitimately used only in the sense of socially constructed 'race', and deracialization is spurious only where there is a covert assumption of 'race' as a natural or unproblematic phenomenon.

Depending on the context, 'ethnic' monitoring can be important. However, it should not be justified on grounds of 'benign' racialization, but on grounds of combating racism and promoting equity and constructive interaction. It is racism, socially constructed 'race' and cultural pluralism that should be the focus of research and policy.

Ethical research in this field, which not only contributes to social justice, but also helps to build knowledge and understanding, is possible if the approach is critical and questioning, careful and sensitive, and committed to antiracism, social justice and individual and social well-being. This means that judgements have constantly to be made within the given context. Contrary to Hammersley's (1993) dichotomy between 'antiracist activists' and researchers, some researchers may be committed to antiracism, just as many are committed to education, or indeed to research and truth.

IS IT ETHICAL *NOT* TO FOCUS ON 'RACE' IN EDUCATIONAL RESEARCH?

A converse question arises, however: does educational research have a *duty* to focus on issues of racism and racialization? Is it ethical *not* to focus on 'race' in educational research? As with educational policy (see Troyna 1993), an 'inexplicit' approach to 'race' in research is not satisfactory. The educa-tional experience of minority ethnic children cannot be adequately understood, and social justice cannot be effectively promoted for such children, if 'race' as a social construction – that is, racism in its various forms and the process of racialization – is eschewed in research.

A relevant example here relates to a recent pilot study of parenting and the academic achievement of Caribbean-heritage children carried out by Kamala Nehaul and myself, both educationalists originally from the Caribbean, one female, one male (Figueroa and Nehaul 1999). This study was mainly interested in the question of how Caribbean-heritage parents may contribute to the progress of their children in school, and focused on eighteen Year 7 black British children in three schools, and on their parents and teachers. We certainly did not assume that these children shared certain characteristics because they belonged to a particular 'race'. However, we were sensitive to their experience of racism, to the ways in which their identities were constructed by others in 'racial' terms, as well as to gender and the concrete family and school realities, among others, and to the interaction between these. Thus, for instance, the following case of a boy in this study indicated issues of gender as well as, it would seem, of covert racism. This boy belonged to a close-knit group of five African Caribbean British boys whom (white) teachers were beginning to complain about, possibly thinking along the lines of exclusion. His form teacher, who was black, was concerned that these boys should not be excluded for minor incidents. She said:

> 'They are beginning to be in trouble. They are often late because they hang around waiting for each other. . . . They look after each other. They all stick together, support each other, if anything goes wrong. They are not naughty boys but if one's in trouble they've all got to be there.'
>
> (Figueroa and Nehaul 1999: 9)

The issue is even wider than that of research specifically on racism or equity for minority ethnic pupils. There is also an issue about educational research generally. Does it implicitly, especially when it is not focusing specifically on such issues, often – perhaps usually – tend to assume a white norm, rather than constantly being sensitive to such assumptions about the norm?

CAN RESEARCH IN THIS AREA BE VALUE NEUTRAL; IS TRUTH OR SOCIAL JUSTICE THE PRIORITY?

If it is incumbent on us to carry out educational research focusing on issues of racialization, 'race' and racism, and in general to be sensitive to taken-for-granted assumptions about the norm, can such research be value neutral? What should its primary concern be: should it be the fearless establishment of impartial, objective truth, or should it be the committed and partisan promotion of social justice? And how is this to operate in practice? Is it, for instance, important to use an interviewer/observer of the same 'race', to try to ensure reliable and valid findings, equity or the minimizing of unequal power relations between the researcher and the researched?

If the researcher's position is that racism is reprehensible, how does this affect the validity of the research being carried out? How does it affect the researcher's perceptions, approach to the research and interpretations? Moreover, what are the consequences if the researcher defines the 'problem' as being one of 'race' rather than of racism? What difference does it make how such racism is understood, and whether its definition is that of the researcher or the 'victim'? Equally, if I am committed to equality, is it really possible for me to carry out research as though I am not, as though it is of no particular importance?

Furthermore, is it unethical to study a population, situation or culture with which you cannot empathize? So as to gain any depth of understanding, the researcher needs somehow to be 'part' of the culture being studied – or, at least, to be able to relate to it somehow. On the other hand, if the researcher is immersed in that culture, the danger is that certain things will be taken for granted and perhaps passed over, or their importance for the matter in hand not appreciated; or else the issues will be seen only from one partial perspective. It might be difficult for the researcher to stand back, to look from different points of view, and so gain a fuller understanding.

In brief, there is an issue of how value positions and sensitivities affect research, in particular relating to racism, 'race', ethnicity or multiculturalism. Value commitment in some form is at the basis of all social research: in the problems that are considered worth studying, the approaches that are judged appropriate, the preferred theoretical positions, the view of society that is thought desirable, etc. To this extent, research cannot be value neutral. This is so in particularly sharp ways where multicultural and 'race'-related issues are concerned. Many people regard racism as reprehensible, while some on the right consider that antiracism is reprehensible, being, according to them, authoritarian.

However, if research cannot be value neutral, it can be – and, if it is to be ethical, it must be – value critical. It is also important that facts and analyses should not be distorted simply to fit particular value positions; that would be to undermine fatally the value of the research. A good basic step is for researchers to declare their values, though this is not sufficient. Researchers will not be fully aware of their taken-for-granteds. Values must be unearthed, clarified, questioned and balanced against other values. Central here is the question of how the knowledge claims made by the researcher relate to the researcher's values.

The debate about such issues, specifically in relation to educational inequality and racism, was sparked in the early 1990s by research by Foster in an inner-city multiethnic comprehensive. Foster claimed that no racism was found among the teachers, who 'had succeeded in creating a non-racist environment in the school' (1990: 149), and that 'within-school processes did not appear to contribute to the reproduction of racial inequality' (1992:

153). Connolly mounts a strenuous critique of Foster's research, contending that his 'claims were based upon a research design and methodology . . . determined by his own political orientation and the ethical and theoretical positions which he developed as a consequence' (Connolly 1992: 133). Although I am basically in sympathy with Connolly's position, such an argument could be turned against the critic, for might it not be retorted that *his* argument was 'determined' by his ideological position? The point is that, if questioned, a case always has to be made out for any specific claim, and that case is always in principle open to critical reason.

Indeed, Foster acknowledges, in a paper to the 1996 British Educational Research Association conference, which was published as a tribute to him shortly after he committed suicide about the New Year of 1999, that 'the truth of accounts can never be absolutely certain since researchers have no direct access to the reality they study'. However, he insists that 'research should aim to maximise the probability that accounts represent educational phenomena accurately', the main aim of educational research being 'the production of truthful accounts of educational phenomena' (Foster 1999: 25). Similarly, Foster *et al.* state that the 'overriding concern of researchers' should be 'the truth of claims, not their political or practical implications', and that 'the purpose of research' on educational inequalities 'should be to produce knowledge relevant to public debates, not to eradicate inequality' (1996: 39, 40).

Having rejected foundationalism and various alternatives, in particular relativism, these authors propose 'reflexivity' as the way of pursuing this prime objective of truth. This they see as a 'process of critical assessment of claims and evidence', within the context of the research community, based solely on 'criteria of logical consistency and empirical adequacy' – that is, on 'plausible' arguments and 'credible' processes, not on the personal or social characteristics of the researcher (Foster *et al.* 1996: 38–40). Thus, they propose a value-neutral model of research. On the contrary, however, not only is research motivated by particular values, truth itself is a value. Indeed, Foster *et al.* seem to imply that truth is an absolute, fundamental value.

Troyna takes a rather different position from Foster *et al.*, for he propounds partisan research. In one of the last papers he published before his untimely death in 1996, he argues that all research is partisan since all research 'derives from the social identity and values of the researcher' (Troyna 1995: 403). Troyna accepts 'Gouldner's imperative' (Troyna 1993: 106) that 'It is to values, not to factions, that sociologists must give their most basic commitment' (Gouldner 1975: 68). By this, Troyna means that 'the researcher's pre-eminent commitment should . . . be . . . to the fundamental principles of social justice, equality and participatory democracy' (Troyna 1993: 106). The partisan researcher is committed not just to knowing, but to transforming. Indeed, ultimately it would seem that knowing is subordinated to changing the world, to combating discrimination and oppression. Partisan researchers seek to 'go beyond . . . describing "what is going on" and explaining "why". . . . For them, unmasking oppressive structures and contributing to social and political change . . . is . . . integral to . . . research' (Troyna 1995: 398).

Thus, Troyna's argument against the postmodernists, whom he considers to be relativists, is not, unlike that of Foster *et al.*, that relativism is self-defeating, but that it leads to 'political quiescence and deference to the status quo' (Troyna 1995: 401), and therefore to inequalities – in other words, that it is conservative. His argument against Foster, Gomm and Hammersley's criteria of plausibility and credibility, and against 'mainstream research', is essentially the same: 'they are inherently conservative' (ibid.: 402). He argues that 'the avowed concern for "objectivity"' and 'approval of traditional "researcher"/ "researched" relationships in the field – provide social science's benediction to . . . inequalities' (ibid.: 397). This conservatism, he suggests, is consistent with researchers' 'blindness to the pervasiveness and institutionalisation of racism and sexism in social relations, prior to the emergence of antiracist and feminist perspectives' (ibid.: 403). For him, 'the priority for the researcher committed to "partisan" research . . . is to challenge the conventions of orthodox research by contributing towards social change in and through their research activities' (ibid.: 397).

Troyna advocates that the researcher should be *explicitly* partisan, so that the reader can 'have a clearer vision of the enterprise and can judge the analysis from an informed position' (Troyna 1995: 404). However, is it only the covert nature of value commitments that is a problem? When researchers make their value positions explicit, how does this help readers if those readers are wedded to their own value positions? Unless there is some way of deciding between value positions and/or of deciding between different truth claims, whether researchers are explicit or not about their value positions will ultimately make little difference. In fact, when Troyna speaks about judging 'the analysis from an informed position' (ibid.), he seems to be assuming both the achievability and value of truth and that readers can assess the analysis independently of their own value commitments. Otherwise, surely, either the reader has the same value commitments, the same prejudices, as the author, and so accepts the argument, or the reader has different value commitments, and so rejects the argument.

There is an issue here of what is to happen when truth/the pursuit of truth conflicts with other values, such as the promotion of social justice. Should truth prevail? Should social justice? How can one decide? There can be no simple, a priori answer to such questions. This dilemma can only be resolved, as circumstances permit, in the given situation. If, however, one is committed to both of these values, then clearly one should seek, as far as possible, a resolution that takes both into account. Foster *et al.* seem too keen to dissociate value location and value commitment from knowledge construction and evaluation, while Troyna is in danger of not being able to separate the two. But in trying to resolve such dilemmas, one has, implicitly at least, to make a number of judgements about the balance of probabilities and improbabilities and of the advantages and disadvantages. As Foster et al. say about 'sociologically interesting facts', 'it is a matter of what is and is not beyond reasonable doubt. And all of us are condemned to making *judgments* about this' (Foster et al. 1997: 422) – and we often disagree, even where values are shared. On the other hand, we can sometimes agree, even where we differ on matters of value. So, while truth and other values, and theory and practice, interrelate, there is no simple, determinate relationship between them. To make both theoretical and practical judgements, knowledge, understanding, value clarity, value commitment and a range of skills are required. It is not only judgements about matters of fact and theoretical analysis that have to be made against the background of other facts, judgements, theoretical understandings and indeed values; judgements about values and priorities must also be made against such a background. The structure of all perception (see Merleau-Ponty 1945), all knowledge, all valuing is one of figure-ground: we are always caught in a hermeneutical circle; but we can shift perspectives, and make informed, critical and illuminated judgements. Pooling such resources – the information, the understanding, the valuing – through dialogue will provide a richer basis on which a decision can be taken. Furthermore, one can reflect after the event on one's own and others' judgements and decisions to try and learn from hindsight.

In fact, both Foster et al. and Troyna seem to share a commitment to reflexivity, although the former express this only in terms of the 'assessment of claims to knowledge' (Foster et al. 1996: 40), while the latter focuses especially on making explicit 'the values which infuse the research process' (Troyna 1995: 404). Both aspects are necessary. Reflexivity implies the possibility of decentring, of questioning our beliefs, our facts, our understandings, our theories, and of transcending our value commitments. This is a key feature of knowledge: that, although it is situated and committed, yet it can question and go beyond – it is self-corrective. That is the crux of research: self-correctivity through reflexivity. Indeed, reflection – and a taking account of one's situatedness and presuppositions – and self-correction are important for all forms of human knowledge and behaviour.

There is not only the issue of how 'knowledge production' relates to value – and other – presuppositions; but also the connected question of how research may relate to subsequent policy and other practical decisions, which themselves are value based. Hammersley, having stressed the primacy of truth as the purpose of research, distinguishes 'two ways in which research may serve practical purposes': to provide relevant information on the basis of which, moreover, goals and means may be 'developed, reviewed and . . . changed'; or to serve 'a propaganda role' and to 'legitimate the goals and means adopted or to criticise those of opponents' (Hammersley 1993: 442). However, the sharp dichotomy adopted by Hammersley between 'the conventional model of research' and 'an activist conception' (ibid.: 444) is misguided. Research can provide information. It can also offer understanding, insight, theories based on evidence or a systematic process of 'testing'. Moreover, although it could be used for propaganda purposes, it can also serve to support a critical moral argument, to clarify values, or to help sort out perplexities. For instance, if research can show that a particular policy – for example, on exclusions – is more likely to cause detriment to some groups of pupils than to pupils on average, and if there is sufficient shared clarity that causing such a detriment is morally unacceptable, then such research could be seen to make a contribution to improving policies. Of course, this means that several debatable issues, which are not free-standing, need to be addressed. The main point here is that as well as 'producing truth', research may be able to make a useful contribution to the process of developing policies, although this is a political and practical matter. Indeed, it could be argued that this ought to be one of the main functions of educational research (although not the only one). The researcher could be an advocate rather than a propagandist, putting forward the evidence and arguments so that their merit can be judged (see Dockrell 1988).

A further point is that research could be conducted in such a way that the very process of the research is itself educative. At the very least, the researcher would surely want to avoid carrying out research in such a way that it significantly undermined the values which informed or motivated it. Indeed, the research process should be compatible with the broader aims informing the research. However, it is a mistake to think, with Troyna and Carrington (1989), that the research process must itself be directly educative. The immediate aims of educating or of directly combating racism and those of 'finding out' or explaining might often be incompatible.

No account of the enduring conundrums can be satisfactory which does not allow for all of the aspects of the case, all dimensions of research, all aspects of human situatedness, in particular value location and commitment, including location in and commitment to the value of knowledge and truth. While Foster et al. stress 'truth' and Troyna stresses 'goodness', both are inescapable. Merleau-Ponty (1945) said that we are condemned to meaning; in fact, we are 'condemned' both to meaning and to valuing. Knowledge and values are interrelated. To give priority to truth is to commit oneself to the value of truth; to commit oneself to the value of social justice is to have a concept of true social justice. The problem is not so much the logic of seeking 'foundations', but of seeking absolute foundations. Nor is the problem value location and value commitment, but the notion or implication that judging truth claims is in no way independent of these. Research should be orientated towards the purpose both of 'producing', or 'testing', knowledge and of eliminating inequalities. However, there is always an issue of balance, so that one purpose is not served at the expense of the other. It would be unethical, and self-defeating, to pursue truth to the exclusion of social justice, as also to pursue social justice to the exclusion of truth.

Perhaps the research project on parenting and academic success of Caribbean-heritage children referred to earlier provides a small example to illustrate some of these points, and especially the simultaneous commitment to social justice and to truth (Figueroa and Nehaul 1999). As academic researchers, we took great care in planning our data collection strategies, which were mainly qualitative. Being from the Caribbean ourselves, we were committed to social justice for the Caribbean-heritage population. Indeed, our starting point was the seemingly intractable problem of the educational 'underachievement' of Caribbean-heritage children in schools in Britain, and their disproportionate likelihood of being excluded.

One of the boys studied had sickle-cell anaemia, which meant that he missed quite a lot of school. His school was, of course, aware of his medical condition. His mother loved him, wanted him to do well in school, and was naturally concerned about his condition, which can be very painful, and even fatal. She said, 'I did get him into his books, learnt him a lot of things, alphabets . . . I used to sit him down and do a lot of work with him when he was very, very young' (Figueroa and Nehaul 1999: 7). He was a quiet-spoken boy, and was interested in chess (at least while in primary school) and soccer. His SAT scores were English, 3; Maths, 4; and Science, 4, although his CAT scores were below average. However, he quickly became disappointed with secondary school, often seemed not to be focused on the task in class, often did not hand in his homework, and even 'bunked off' school on one or two occasions. He was in set 3 (of seven sets) in English, and the class consisted of twenty-four pupils. His (white) English teacher had a very negative view of him. He had hardly been in the school two terms, and this is what I recorded in my field notes just shortly after having a chat with her in the staffroom about him:

> Her view and expectation of him is totally negative. Low concentra-
> tion span. He's stubborn and naughty. Won't do the work, homework,
> anything. Doesn't come for detention, even. I can't spend so much
> time with one child. That's real life. There are not the minutes . . .
> He didn't do the homework, like most of them . . . Next week still
> hadn't: what was his excuse? 'That was last week's homework.' As much
> as to say: you stupid woman. He's rude. Trouble quietly emanates out
> from him in the classroom. 'Stuff him'. . . . She was quite agitated.
> (Fieldnotes 17.3.98: 11–12)

A (white) Mathematics teacher, present in the staffroom at the time, also said he was 'bone lazy' – although she clearly was not as negative or dismis-sive as the English teacher.

I felt for this young black British boy. What could I do in the situation? What should I have done? Should I have tried reasoning with the English teacher? Should I have raised the matter with the boy's form tutor, or with one of the senior managers in the school?

What in fact did I do? I made as accurate a note as I could, and tried to ascertain other teachers' views about the boy. In other words, I sought the truth. But I did also try to suggest to the English teacher that maybe she should speak to his mother. I also tried to be supportive to his mother. Furthermore, according to our project, parent–child–teacher partnership meetings were to be arranged later in the year, and I hoped some action plan could be devised then to try to motivate him and improve the situation. Unfortunately, he was off school with a sickle-cell anaemia attack on the day that the partnership meeting had been arranged. The teacher who had agreed to take part, the Mathematics teacher, said she would nevertheless pursue the matter, but nothing came of it.

In other words, I did not do that much. I did not consider that, in the situation, I could. I was only a short-term visitor in the school, a researcher allowed in and with no particular influence. I hardly knew the English teacher. I did not have to teach the boy and the other children on a daily basis. How effective could any intervention I might make be, and would it be seen as inappropriate, or uninformed, or unappreciative of the realities of the situation? I had to consider trying to help him as against seeming to interfere or running the risk of prejudicing the research in the school, which at that stage was still only half-completed. Now that the research has been done, it is to be hoped that reporting such incidents may have some wider positive effect; but that won't help him individually. Besides, reporting such incidents has implications for confidentiality and anonymity.

DO THE ENDS JUSTIFY THE MEANS?

Before we pursue any consideration of responsiveness to the respondents, the question of whether the ends – be they truth or some social value such as equality – justify the means deserves some consideration. Means, to be effective, must be appropriate to the given ends. But the question here is whether any means that will achieve a given end are acceptable, or whether other criteria besides effectiveness in achieving that end must be met. Thus, if a particular strategy will give us the truth, does it matter whether it offends or reinforces prejudice? Or, alternatively, if a particular strategy will help ensure greater social justice, does it matter if it compromises the truth – or other values, such as liberty? Is deceit permissible, either in the service of true, frank responses or in the service of social justice?

The discussion here will focus on issues around three crucial aspects of the research process: the information given to, or more particularly withheld from, respondents and others involved in the project; the methods used, and in particular the legitimacy of adopting projective methods, which can be seen as a special case of covert methods; and the use of particular types of questions, such as scales or the semantic differential, which include expressions of stereotypes.

I would argue that the ends do not justify the means in the sense that it would be legitimate to use any 'effective' means irrespective of its other consequences or implications, as that would be counter-productive, offensive and even self-defeating. However, a judgement has to be made in practice about whether any particular means is counter-productive, offensive or self-defeating in the particular circumstances.

First of all, when one is researching sensitive and controversial issues such as racism, there is clearly a problem about what information the researcher gives the respondents. If the researcher is entirely honest about the project's aims, what credence can be given to the replies? But then, is informed consent possible without full information?

For instance, in the project on parenting and academic success of Caribbean-heritage pupils racism was a possible issue, and no doubt the parents, the teachers and the pupils would have been aware of this at some level; but we did not consider it necessary to highlight it. Doing so might surely have been distorting, whereas not doing so did not seem to be detrimental. Similarly, Troyna and Hatcher, in their study of racism in children's lives, told the children that 'our purpose . . . was to gather material for a book about children. We did not specify any particular interest in issues of "race"' (Troyna and Hatcher 1992: 7). In such cases it could be argued that, so long as 'adequate' information is given about the project and what the respondents are letting themselves in for, some restricting of the information given is legitimate if otherwise the research would probably be useless. Judgements have to be made about these matters in the given circumstances. In our project we explained, to parents and to school managers, that it would last a year and there would be interviews, observations and parent–teacher meetings. However, we simply stated that the project aimed 'to throw light on ways in which parents promote their children's school progress and to develop parent–teacher communication about influences on the child and ways of improving learning'. We did also point out that the Caribbean backgrounds of the two researchers might 'be helpful in understanding and clarifying any "race" and cultural issues'.

The second question may be stated thus: If indirect or covert methods are used to get accurate information, is this justified manipulation? Thus, in a study I carried out some years ago into the perceptions that student-teachers had of multicultural education and of minority ethnic people in Britain, I included some open-ended questions in the self-completion questionnaires used so as to try to get at students' taken-for-granted thinking, at their unthematized frames of reference.

Troyna and Carrington criticized the ethics of this research, claiming that 'Figueroa encouraged respondents to articulate stereotypes by completing open-ended statements such as "when I think of Asians I think ... "' (Troyna and Carrington 1989: 216). Actually, however, the whole point of using open-ended, sentence-completion questions was to *avoid* constraining respondents, and to give them the possibility of offering non-stereotypical answers. The possible answers to each of these questions would be almost limitless. For instance, 'my experience of Blacks in Britain is ...' could have been followed by any of the following, among many other possibilities: excellent; bad; nil; unusual; as for everyone else; nothing special. In fact, as I reported in the paper discussed by Troyna and Carrington, the commonest response was: 'limited' (Figueroa 1986: 7). Again, answers such as the following would have been perfectly possible to the sentence-completion questions: 'when I think of Asians/West Indians I think ... ': I wish I knew them better; they are all very different from each other; of someone I knew at school; of nothing in particular; of many different parts of the world; about the lecture last term.

The third issue, however, is perhaps more problematical: the including in the questionnaires of items that could be seen as the expression of stereotypes, which respondents are asked to agree or disagree with. Thus, in my study mentioned above of student-teachers, I used the semantic differential, as well as Lickert-type scales. Troyna and Carrington particularly criticized the use of the semantic differential:

> Figueroa's previous research had shown that when respondents were asked to rate 'White British pupils', 'West Indian pupils' and 'Asian pupils', many ... elected to use the 'can't generalize' option. As a result, the sample described in the paper under discussion was *not* provided with this option: they were *forced* into a situation where they could do nothing but stereotype. .... Surely such an approach with an incoming generation of teachers is hardly conducive to changing the *status quo* in education?
>
> (Troyna and Carrington 1989: 216)

It is certainly not accurate to say that the respondents were forced into producing stereotypes. It is actually *not* usual in the semantic differential to include an option, 'can't generalize'. However, as I explain in the paper under discussion, although I had included such an option in a similar project two years previously precisely because of my concern not to constrain respondents into producing stereotypes, I omitted it in the project under discussion. As explained there, the students still had three other options if they felt constrained by this question. They could simply not answer it, they could add a comment on it, or they could tick the mid-point of the scale. Each of these options was in fact used by some of the respondents.

Moreover, these questions need to be seen in the total context of the particular project. My paper explained that the three questionnaires used were closely related to the module on multicultural education and that the questionnaire on which the paper was mainly based was administered after an introductory lecture and before the first of two one-day conferences. These three elements, along with some optional sessions and the questionnaires, constituted the module on multicultural education. What the questionnaires did, apart from providing me with some information, and apart from helping to evaluate the module, was to raise the students' awareness of many of the key issues, and these were addressed on the module, especially through the two conferences (see Figueroa 1989).

Troyna and Carrington also criticized other researchers for supposedly 'encouraging, reinforcing or even forcing subjects to employ prevailing racial stereotypes' (1989: 213). Thus, in criticizing Brittan's (1976) survey of teachers' 'opinions about ethnic differences in pupils' and parents' responses to education, Troyna and Carrington assert that 'By inviting teachers to indicate the extent to which they agreed or disagreed with statements such as "Asian pupils are usually better behaved than English pupils" . . . Brittan . . . encouraged her respondents to employ racist . . . frames of reference' (Troyna and Carrington 1989: 213–14). This assertion is questionable precisely because the format of these questions permits the respondents to disagree with such statements. This means that the respondents are able to place the following interpretation, among others, on such statements: 'I don't think you can generalize, therefore I disagree.' Choosing the midpoint of the scale could also mean: 'I'm not sure that one can generalize', or even, 'it is not possible to generalize'.

While Troyna and Carrington have criticized researchers for being 'unethical', Troyna has himself been similarly criticized. Gomm (1993), for instance, mounted a strong critique of Troyna's article 'Underachievers or underrated?' (Troyna 1991). Among the 'illegitimate tactics' that Gomm attributed to Troyna were that 'the data . . . seem almost entirely to have been chosen to support his argument. . . . He chooses measures of pupil ability in such a way as to maximise the impression that Asian pupils are being discriminated against' (Gomm 1993: 163–4).

Some points that could be drawn from this discussion include the following:

- The researcher needs to aim at consistency between precept and practice.
- Means should be compatible with ends.
- Not any means may be used to promote the particular ends.
- The means suitable for one end may be inimical to another end.
- In the concrete situation, the researcher in determining means has to balance various considerations against each other.
- Ends and means should not be seen atomistically, but in the round, within the project as a whole.

RESPONSIVENESS TO THE OTHER

'Truth', however that is understood, is an inherent goal in carrying out research. As discussed above, other values, such as social justice, might also be significant. The research process has to take account of such varying demands. But what, more specifically, of responsiveness to the other? Is this the key value: not hurting the other, not offending the other, treating the other with respect, treating the other as an equal?

Responsiveness is usually interpreted as referring primarily to the interviewer–interviewee or, more generally, to the researcher–researched relationship. But the relationship of the researcher with all those parties implicated in the research – including colleagues – is relevant. How can one balance not only consideration for the truth against sensitivity to others, but also consideration for one set of actors (e.g. teachers) against another set of actors (e.g. pupils), or consideration for the wider community against consideration for the individual respondents?

One set of issues that figures prominently in the literature relates to confidentiality and anonymity. Does respecting anonymity and confidentiality override antiracism? Or is the researcher justified in taking action, or even required to do so, against racism – or incompetence – identified through confidential communications?

In the example given above from the parenting research, would I have been justified in bringing that English teacher's uncompromisingly negative attitudes to the attention of senior managers? Or was she within her rights as a teacher? Am I justified in reporting on these matters now? People in that school reading this would be able to identify the individuals concerned.

Moreover, in the same school, I observed teaching, by the Mathematics teacher mentioned earlier, which was unimaginative and ineffective. This was Mathematics set 5 (out of six sets), and the boy with sickle-cell anaemia was in it. It was a large classroom with fifteen desks, each large enough for two pupils, but the class consisted of only ten pupils, who were scattered in the room from the back to the front. There were three black girls, two black boys, two Asian boys and three white boys. Two boys sat at one desk, two girls at another. The other six pupils each sat at a separate desk. I sat in one corner at the back. The room was drab. A lot of time was wasted with the teacher, who was white, 'waiting for silence'. The children were constantly fidgeting and chattering. The content of the lesson was probably too unchallenging. I doubt whether anything was learned during the hour-long lesson.

Again, was there anything I could have done with that information? Would I have been acting as a spy, or would I have been breaking trust if I had spoken about this with senior management? Could I have had a discussion with the teacher? Again, apart from reporting this matter now, it did not seem appropriate for me, an outsider, not a Mathematics teacher, nor indeed a secondary school teacher, to intervene at the time.

EQUAL RIGHTS, RELATIVISM, DIVERSITY AND THE OTHER

The problem still remains in practice: where all have equal rights and diverse perspectives, how can the in-built conflicts be resolved? Neither a relativist position, nor one that says all is power-play, deals adequately with the situation. A thoroughgoing relativist position ultimately means that each position must simply be accepted on its say-so. No valid justification can be given, and dialogue is in the end pointless. But equally, if all is power-play, then reason and dialogue are pointless. Conflicts and disagreement can ultimately only be resolved through dialogue, argument and evaluation, within the given situation, if recourse to violence or other forms of compulsion is to be avoided.

The researcher in the field must constantly cock ears in different directions and step back and look questioningly at the perceptions, thoughts and understandings developing from different perspectives. Nor is it a matter of truth versus virtue, but truth *and* virtue, impartiality *and* commitment, truth *and* social justice. Although everyone has inalienable rights (which, nevertheless, *de facto* are often trampled on), no one – not the researchers, not the respondents, not the funders, not the government, not the wider community – no one has absolute rights. It is always a matter of rights relative to each other, and needing to be justified in the given situation.

CONCLUSIONS

Ethical issues are inherent in every aspect of educational research, and at every turn of a research project. They are complex, and it is not always manifest what the best decision will be. Indeed, ambiguity and ambivalence – or, rather, multivalence – are in-built and unavoidable. Matters are even less straightforward where sensitive issues, such as cultural difference, ethnicism and racism, are concerned. Or, at least, the complexities and multivalencies are more salient.

Judgements and decisions must be made in the actual lived situation, in the actual context. Questions can always be asked about how those judgements or decisions can be justified. Although a positive outcome for oneself in some sense is no doubt always important, I argue against the 'rational choice' notion that action must always involve a maximization of one's net advantage, even to the disadvantage of others (Figueroa 1991). Indeed, the priority may be a concern for a positive outcome for some other. Also, although issues of convenience and feasibility are important, they can hardly be the only considerations. The way the situation is understood, what are taken to be the facts and how they are accounted for, and key values, such as truth, social justice and mutual respect – that is, acceptance of the other in their otherness and of the self in its otherness – are also implicated.

In my own work I research racialization and racism rather than 'race', and I attempt to do this with the aims both of increasing knowledge and understanding *and* of helping to combat racism and to promote antiracism, social justice and individual as well as social well-being. Hence, several issues need to be balanced.

However, not all actors, researchers, professionals or others will share the same understandings, the same values or the same interpretation in particular situations. Furthermore, the perplexity consists also in this: that what is taken to be the basic values or basic principles can be in conflict with each other in a given concrete situation. The difficulties must be resolved in that lived situation. However, purpose and context are not sufficient: the ascertainment of the facts – as possible in the given context – and the reasoning, the clarification of the rationale – as possible in the given context – are also inherent, implicitly unavoidable. Principles, values, rationality, facts and experience are all abstractions from the realities that inhere in contingent practice.

Research must be rational *and* virtue oriented. And values too, as well as facts, theories, methodologies and procedures, must be approached critically. Nor are the claims of truth and social justice, of validity and virtue, necessarily antithetical. Researchers must be explicit about their values, assumptions and procedures. And they must be reflexive. But there are inherent limits even to being explicit and to being reflexive, and one must seek to be critically aware of these. What is needed is a double ethics, an ethics of both/and; an ethics that is a constant questioning, which has an open grasp both on self and on other.

Chapter 8

Snakes and ladders

Ethical issues in conducting
educational research in a postcolonial
context

Mary McKeever

Long, long ago in one country
There was a ladder;
It had four rungs.
The top one belonged to a white man,
Followed by his white woman.
The third one belonged to a black man,
His wife remained holding the ladder
So that others could not fall.
Once upon a time . . .

(Bila 1998: 6)

INTRODUCTION

Conducting research in a postcolonial context can be like a game of snakes and ladders. The only way to proceed is to cling to the ladders of the oppressed while trying to avoid the snakes of the colonialist past. This chapter arises from my experience of working in the progressive educational movement in South Africa under apartheid. I am Irish, was born in Belfast, grew up in the euphemistically termed 'Troubles', and come from a working-class Catholic background. I moved to South Africa in 1983, and thus in the space of a few years I moved from being one of the colonized to being identifiable, through being white in South Africa under apartheid, as one of the colonizers. I became involved in the Workers' School while working at the University of the Witwatersrand (Wits) in Johannesburg as a tutor in the Academic Support Programme. I worked alongside university manual workers, students and township youth to help set up a school – the Workers' School – on the university campus. An initial motivation came from a cleaner who had cleaned the university library for twenty years but still could not read and write. Some of the workers were illiterate and had never attended school, but the majority had been unable to complete their schooling as black children under apartheid. The school started off as a literacy project in the Sociology tearoom and was eventually given facilities of its own in a disused science laboratory on the edge of the university campus.

The Workers' School was set up in October 1988 and it closed in July 1996. Hence its life span covered the demise of apartheid and the transition to democracy, a period of truly momentous historical events. The school began its life during the fourth successive State of Emergency. This was a time of severe repression with widespread detentions and banning of progressive organizations, including student and educational bodies. My research study is thus of one small school, set up and run by black workers, caught up in this dramatic history, with the university campus being the site of riots, disturbances, protests and strikes throughout this period. I worked at the school on a voluntary basis for four years and taught English. I was also an elected member of the School Steering Committee, acted as secretary and fund-raiser and was involved in facilitator training. It was only after leaving South Africa and enrolling for a PhD in England that I chose the Workers' School as my research topic. I decided to trace the shifting relationship between power and knowledge in this school, at this university, as South Africa moved from apartheid to democracy. My specific interest is in power, knowledge and social change.[1]

There are certain general questions which I think any researcher trying to act ethically in a postcolonial context will need to address. In my opinion the first step must be to attempt to understand the specific historical context. Every postcolonial society will be different and the ravages and legacies of colonialism will vary from country to country, complicated by the history of the country prior to colonialism. Not only will the history vary from place to place but colonialism will also have affected different sectors of the society in very different ways. It is important therefore not to see the postcolonial society as monolithic. Second, the researcher will need to study the systems that were developed to resist colonialism and the various forms this resistance took. Ethical systems will have evolved in the resistance movement and these will need to be taken into account. For example, in a country such as South Africa where there is a strong ethic of non-racialism, an emphasis on cultural diversity could be viewed as divisive, if not as a hangover from apartheid, which rigidly divided the society along racial and ethnic lines. So the first step must be to learn about the history of colonialism and resistance to it. In this chapter I will illustrate this general issue with reference to South Africa and then go on to discuss three specific ethical issues which have arisen in my research.

I have selected three issues which I think will resonate in other postcolonial or neocolonial contexts. The first question is whether I, as a white person, have any right to research black experience. The second concerns the conflict that arises between traditional methods of knowing, learning and teaching and those imported to Africa by the colonial powers. The latter are now institutionalized in certified state educational programmes, with the resulting naturalization of these foreign educational practices and the demise of traditional practices. This will be explored with reference to my research into the teaching of English at the Workers' School. The third question focuses upon the ethics of knowledge production in a country that has experienced colonization and the dangers of conducting research that perpetuates a colonialist ethics, and I will look at this with specific reference to my own research in South Africa. However, before addressing these issues I will give a little of the contextual background of my study.

THE COLONIAL UNIVERSITY

When I was employed at Wits University I did not, at first, question its origins. It felt as though it had always been there, and at that time I did not know that the history of the university was tied up with the history of gold mining. South Africa was first colonized in 1652 but it was the discovery of gold in the Transvaal region that gave birth to Johannesburg, or i-Goli, city of gold. The history of Wits may be traced back to the transfer of staff and students from the South African School of Mines at Kimberley to what in 1904 was called the Transvaal Technical Institute in Johannesburg (Stimie and Geggus 1972: 65). The close links between the university and the Chamber of Mines remain to the present day, with the mines being the university's biggest financial benefactor. In line with racial segregation in South African society, the university went to considerable lengths to avoid admitting black students. In fact, in 1926 the university council appointed a committee 'to ascertain what procedure is necessary to empower the university to exclude students on grounds of colour' (Murray 1988: 298). The attitude of the university is best summarized by Professor Raikes at a Wits Students' Representative Council dinner in 1933: 'We should endeavour to maintain our ascendancy, but reaching out always for the further development of the native at the same time' (Murray 1988: 310). In 1939 there were four black students at the university, a figure which had risen to eighty-seven in 1945, and by 1953 4.9 per cent of the student population were non-European (ibid.: 229). The contradiction between the university's public non-racial stand and racist practice is evident in the conditions that black students and members of staff had to endure. Black students were segregated on campus and the first black academic staff member was refused a lectureship and employed as a language assistant (*Perceptions of Wits* 1987: 4).

However, in 1953, when the apartheid government announced its intention to establish separate universities for students of different races, the university protested against this as an attack on its academic freedom. In response, the South African Institute of Race Relations sponsored a symposium entitled 'The Idea of the University' in 1954. Professor Harris of Wits opened the meeting with a discussion about the fundamental role of the university:

> Let us consider a little more in detail what is involved in learning or the pursuit of knowledge. In the first place it involves a single-minded and unselfish devotion to an ideal ... the paramount virtue of the scholar is honesty – intellectual honesty, which is the source of every other sort of honesty.
>
> (Harris 1954: 5)

It is interesting to speculate how the university establishment was able to retain the ideal of honesty as an overwhelmingly white institution, benefiting from apartheid and serving the needs of the mining industry in a colonized African country. The principal of the University of Cape Town took up the idea of the university and provides an insight into how white academics viewed themselves and African society:

> surely it is desirable that those who can benefit from the superior culture of the white man should not be denied the blessings of these contacts which alone can raise him from the primitive and barbaric. To restrict him to an education system based on his own African culture is to deprive him of his chances of intellectual and spiritual salvation.
>
> (Davie 1954: 11)

There is little doubt that many in the university hierarchy saw their role as a civilizing one. Rather than relating to the African society in which they were located, they believed their roots to be in Britain and in the international research community. Wits University, as an educational institution, was modelled on the lines of Western universities from the architecture to the curriculum, a gatekeeper for the professions and a confirming instance of Foucault's power–knowledge formation. It was in a pivotal position as an employer and trainer of the almost exclusively white élite and the employer of almost exclusively black manual labour. The link between the iron fist of colonial expansion and the velvet glove of colonial intellectual and cultural production appears to have been severed in the minds of the university hierarchy, who define their 'civilizing' mission in the most altruistic of terms. However, the implication of the university in the power structures and in the prejudices of South African society is in contradiction to the university's self-image as an independent agent at the cutting edge of the most advanced thought of the society and engaged in the disinterested pursuit of the truth.

The fact that generations of the most liberal and the most highly educated section of South African society could campaign for academic freedom, while remaining seemingly oblivious to the fact that the majority of the population in South Africa were living in what amounted to open-air concentration camps, points to the danger of separating a university off from the society in which it is located. It also raises the intricacy of ethics in this context. In their lives as white academics under apartheid, one can only assume that the majority of academics at Wits led ethical lives, that they did not falsify their research results or act unethically in their personal dealings with others. Yet to work as a white person, with all its attendant privileges, teaching white students at a white university under apartheid could be viewed as completely unethical, if one were to move from a perspective that locates ethical responsibility with the individual to one that would see it as involving a responsibility to the wider society. This is further complicated by the fact that the ethics of the Western academy are considerably more individualistic than those of South African society, where there is a strong community ethics. Thus researchers can find themselves embroiled in different and at times incompatible ethical systems. However, in general it would seem advisable for the researcher to trace the history of any institution connected with the research and to see whether it was involved in colonialism, and if so, to what extent. It is also important to question the seeming neutrality of universities and to be critical of the conceptual resources they offer. Hence not only the university, but the research methodology that it advocates, is itself researchable and was developed by people to meet specific needs, and this may or may not be appropriate in a postcolonial context.

BANTU EDUCATION

To return to South Africa under apartheid. Whereas the white population had access to a wealth of educational resources, things were rather different for the black population. While racial segregation was being enforced at university level, the Bantu Education Act was passed in 1953. This effectively enshrined the apartheid education system, which alongside the Land Act, the Population Registration Act, the Immorality Act, the Group Areas Act and the Mixed Amenities Act, constituted the apartheid regime. In the words of Dr Verwoerd (1953):

> we can see to it that education will be suitable for those who will become the industrial workers in the country. ... What is the use in teaching the Bantu mathematics when it cannot use it in practice? that is quite absurd. ... Education is after all not something that hangs in the air. Education must train and teach according to the spheres in which they live ... I just want to remind honourable members that if the native in South Africa today in any kind of school in existence is

being taught to expect that he will live his adult life under a policy of equal rights, he is making a big mistake.

In the end, the apartheid regime set up four different education authorities, one for Africans, one for Indians, one for 'coloureds' and one for whites. From nursery school to university level there was strict segregation on racial lines and expenditure was strictly in accordance with race. For example, in 1976 the per capita educational expenditure on every white child was fourteen times that spent on every African child (Christie 1994: 110). Thus the gross violation of human rights on racial grounds was accompanied by an inferior and unequal educational system designed to create a docile workforce. It is hardly surprising that it was an educational issue that sparked the first major uprising against apartheid in Soweto in 1976. The Soweto Students Representative Council declared, 'We shall reject the whole system of Bantu education, whose aim is to reduce us, mentally and physically, into "hewers of wood and drawers of water"' (Tomaselli 1989: 140). It also puts the decision by the workers at Wits into a different light. In the words of one of them, the school was set up 'because in that place there was no schooling for the workers. When the worker comes there he is just a worker . . . he should get some schooling because Wits is a schooling place' (WSI, TN/D 1996: 150). At this time in South Africa, black people were transgressing many boundaries to enter facilities previously reserved for whites, such as schools, public transport, housing, beaches and swimming pools. The workers' decision that they were no longer content to merely clean the floors of the university, but wanted to share in the learning, can be understood as part of this national trend.

PEOPLE'S EDUCATION

South Africa is unusual in that the struggle for power and the struggle for education are explicitly interlinked. This can be partly understood in terms of the history of Bantu education, which rendered visible the role of education in perpetuating the apartheid regime and also by the fact that, as previously mentioned, it was school students who led the first major challenge to apartheid, a challenge that was taken up by ever-growing sections of the population throughout the 1980s. By 1985 schooling had broken down in many areas of South Africa, the army was occupying the townships, thousands of black activists were in detention and youths were coming into ever-increasing conflict with the police and army. A group of parents in Soweto decided to step in and try to negotiate with the Education Authority on the youths' behalf. Within three months the parents called a National Consultative Conference on Education out of which People's Education developed and won the support of the mass democratic movement. People's Education was a rejection of apartheid education, but more importantly it was also an attempt to transform the educational system from within, with a view to youth, parents, teachers, community groups, trade unions, church and political groups all working together to bring about the end of Bantu education and its replacement with People's Education. Mkatshwa defined People's Education as follows:

> ... when we speak of people's education, we mean one that prepares people for total human liberation; one which helps people to be creative, to develop a critical mind, to help people to analyse; one that prepares people for full participation in all social, political or cultural spheres of society. Education based on values of consumerism or affluence, of military adventurism and aggression and on racism is certainly not our ideal type of education.
>
> (Mkatshwa 1985: 7)

People's Education inspired widespread debate about the fundamentals of education, and by 1988, when the Workers' School was set up, its leaders had been detained and all its teaching materials banned from school premises. However, in terms of research ethics, representatives of community groups involved in People's Education in Soweto had this to say:

> There is a unanimous feeling that Wits should move its research priorities from narrowly technical considerations towards a greater responsiveness to community concerns. As with community work, this should be planned in consultation with the relevant community organizations. Academics need however to be sensitive and meticulous about their research methodology and care should be taken not to misrepresent community positions. Also research should not just depend on the requirements of a higher degree, ceasing when the qualification has been obtained. The period of research and the information should be attuned to the needs of the community and made available to the community.
>
> (*Perceptions of Wits* 1987: 24)

It will be seen from the above that it is important and it can be very helpful for researchers to investigate the history of the resistance movement under colonialism and their perceptions of issues relevant to the research. Having presented some of the historical background to issues researchers need to be aware of in conducting educational research in postcolonial contexts, I now turn to the three specific ethical issues that have arisen in my research.

'WHITE' RESEARCHERS AND 'BLACK' EXPERIENCE

There have been several criticisms of white people researching black experience. In Britain black researchers at the Centre for Contemporary Cultural
Studies in Birmingham attacked the ethnocentrism of various white sociologists in *The Empire Strikes Back* (Centre for Contemporary Cultural
Studies 1982). Their major criticisms were, first, that white researchers
cannot elicit meaningful data from black respondents because of status and
power differentials between them; second, that the data elicited by white
researchers are often interpreted in ways which pathologize black communities; and third, that white researchers can unwittingly enable the state
to increase control over black communities (Troyna and Carrington 1989:
209). I think that these are all very important issues to consider and it
certainly would be a valid question if any member of the school were to
ask me how I could possibly know what it was like to be black in South
Africa under apartheid. Parekh complains, 'Most researchers in the field
are white. They have no experience of what it means to be black, and
lack an intuitive understanding of the complex mental processes and social
structures of black communities' (1986: 24).

This was certainly true in my case before I lived and worked in South
Africa, and my understanding of African life is limited to the eleven years
I spent in that country. Nevertheless, working on a daily basis as a participant in a democratically run school has given me some understanding of
what life was like for black workers, students and academics at a historically white university. Still concerned that I would not be able adequately
to represent black experience, I wrote to a member of the school about
this issue. He replied:

> you are concerned about research ethics in respect of your work on the
> Workers' School. I sincerely feel that you should be free to do what-
> ever is necessary to tell our story about the school. It is also your story,
> you are part of it, and you should ask permission of no one to tell it.
> The fact that you are in England and doing it for a Ph.D. should not
> make us lose the main point: telling the world about what we tried to
> build with workers in apartheid society.
>
> (WSD 1997: 2)

I think that this response raises an important point. I am in a position to
record the history of the Workers' School, and the disadvantages of my
whiteness need to be weighed against the advantages of having this aspect
of black South African working-class educational history recorded and
analysed. Incidentally, nobody in the school has questioned my suitability.
I am voicing concerns which have arisen in my reading of the literature

on race and research. Moreover, although it takes time to develop trust and understanding, it is possible to build honest relationships across race, class, gender and culture. This can be facilitated by working together on a jointly defined task. It is also possible to build safeguards into educational research so as to cross-check the reliability of the data. I conducted interviews myself, but also have interviews conducted by a black worker and by a black intellectual, to try to get a more balanced picture. Also, I think it is a mistake to assume that even under apartheid race is always the primary frame of reference or that it is a category that people accept passively. In fact I was able to use my position as a white employee of the university to raise money for the school and to negotiate with the university authorities. Given these circumstances, my colour on occasion became an asset rather than a liability. Indeed, when analysing the data, I was made aware of the incipient dangers of contributing to the construction of a racist frame of reference (Figueroa 1991). While I assumed that the workers saw themselves as black workers at a white university, it seems that the following man, a cleaner at the university, saw himself as a person employed at a university, rather than as a *black worker* at a *white* university:

> You know before, we were not even having that broad mind of this is a white school in Africa. We know that this is a university. We were not thinking of that white oppression or something. We were thinking that even if the professors around and the lecturers around were white too much, we were thinking that maybe they will get interested in helping the school with what we were doing. But you know in that sense of Africa, a white school in Africa we didn't even, I mean, when you in the place you just see yourselves there, you think that you belong there yeah?
>
> (WSI, TN/D 1996: 161)

The point that I would like to emphasize is that there does seem to be a real danger of perpetuating racism when researching it and of making assumptions about how the research respondents see the world – and that applies to any researcher, whether researching their own or another culture. There will always be blind spots and difficulties and strengths and weaknesses in the position of the researcher. It is important to foreground these as much as possible so that the reader can make a judgement about how these may affect the research.

EXISTING PATTERNS OF KNOWLEDGE AND ACKNOWLEDGING PATTERNS OF EXISTENCE

One of the most devastating effects of colonialism was the destruction of local patterns of existence which had been developed through trial and error so as to make a living within a given environment. Environment, knowledge and culture were all intertwined. A primary ethical consideration in a postcolonial context must be to avoid riding roughshod over local traditions. The researcher will need to be sensitive to local knowledge but also to the patterns of knowledge introduced by colonialism and the often bizarre juxtapositions of the two. The researcher at the Western power–knowledge institution is given access to all that the colonial system has produced by way of intellectual resources, and the knowledge systems of the colonized, if they appear at all, are rewritten into the text of Western science or literature. It is also important to keep in mind that central to colonialism was the appropriation of local knowledge systems, which were claimed to have been 'discovered', and these were often absorbed or rewritten into Western classificatory grids. This has many implications for how we regard knowledge. For example, Harding states 'thus the distinctive patterns of knowledge and ignorance characteristic of modern sciences are in significant part products of both the needs and resources provided by European expansion' (1997: 55). If knowledge were not the fuel for European expansion very different patterns might have arisen. As Goonatilake argues,

> The socially structured knowledge tree has thus explored only certain partial aspects of physical reality, explorations that correspond to the particular historical unfolding of the civilization within which the knowledge emerged. Thus entirely different knowledge systems corresponding to different historical unfoldings in different civilization settings become possible. . . . Thus an entirely new set of 'universal' but socially determined natural science laws are possible.
>
> (quoted in Harding 1997: 63)

It is possible to look at research as the 'means (academic practices) by which the discourses of one culture (the observed) are recorded, described and understood by another (the observers') culture' (Tomaselli 1996: 41). Just as it is no longer regarded as acceptable to go to another country and claim it for your own, so it is no longer acceptable to annex or totally rewrite other peoples' discourses. On these grounds it is possible to look at research techniques as the tools by which the history of the Workers' School is transformed so that it becomes palatable to the university.

> Academia has, in many instances, become the myth making process where factories called universities shape scientific explanations and descriptions in terms of dominant scientific paradigms. . . . The paradigms, as social and public texts, are really Western forms of myth. As such, they encode sets of ideas, assumptions and conclusions which

basically reflect a broader social and political consensus on the way people process events, conditions and situations to be understood during particular historical conjunctures.

(ibid.: 94)

So how does an educational researcher work to avoid such exploitation? On the one hand, there is the awareness of the limitations of the knowledge systems based on colonial expansion and on the other, the exploitative basis of much existing official knowledge. Researchers in Africa have argued, 'The European Same has not engaged with the African Other. When it has, it tends to mirror it in a parallel world (language, film, writing) which like trains that pass in the night, pass, rather than intersect, the other ... the differences relevant here are those of ontology and cosmology' (Tomaselli 1996: 140). The differences can thus be fundamental in that there can be profound differences in how the world is viewed and understood.

I was made aware of these differences at the Workers' School. In one of my English classes the workers said that they thought that somebody had sent 'lightning' to the school, or that the Nkanyamba was coming. The Nkanyamba is a mythical snake that is like a whirlwind and when it comes, it destroys everything in its path. I recorded the mythical explanation as given by the workers in class from memory and returned it to the group as a reading in the next lesson:

> it is a giant snake that destroys everything in its path. The sky turns black, black so you can't see anything. ... If it sees a white roof it will jump into it thinking it is water. The Nkanyamba lives in the lakes and sometimes it goes to find a new home and it is then you have a tornado. If anybody comes, like the whites who like to research, and takes the Nkanyamba's baby, then it will follow that baby until it finds it, even to Lesotho or even into the labs at Wits.

(WSD 1991: 1)

This mythical figure of the Nkanyamba was later taken up by a member of the school in a poem, a section of which is reproduced here:

I am a lion
My roar is
Revolution

I am the Messiah
My heaven is
Society without classes

I am God Almighty
My command is
Be ready to die for the struggle.
                    (WSD 1991: 17)

As a researcher, how am I to respond to these data? I understand this as arising from a different ontology. As a researcher I operate within my own ontological system, and my understanding of the nuances and the significance of another system will be limited. Researchers in Africa have argued that 'The history constructed by one section of society will refer to a world not the same as that constructed by someone from another part' (Tomaselli 1996: 142). There is the argument that African languages are based on a different ontological system, that of interacting forces rather than discrete subjects and objects (Tempels 1959; Tomaselli et al. 1995). Others argue that European dualism is 'incapable of understanding the extra-ordinarily complex, multi-directional and multi-layered signification generated by the languages of oral cultures' (Tomaselli 1996: 143). However, I think that the section of the poem quoted above gives an indication of the reasons for respecting local ways of understanding phenomena. What I find interesting is the way the Nkanyamba is not just a mythical figure confined to the past, but a dynamic figure that changes and absorbs different belief systems, from Christianity to Marxism, while remaining the Nkanyamba. To dismiss or replace the old explanation would be to take away a dynamic vehicle for connecting the present with the past and one which is accessible to all who have shared or encountered these changing belief systems.

DIFFERENT WAYS OF LEARNING

The third question I wish to explore concerns the conflict that arises between traditional methods of knowing, learning and teaching and those imported to Africa by the colonial powers. The latter are now institution-alized in certified state educational and research programmes. Again, by way of illustrating this point, I will draw on data arising out of my Standard 8 English examination class at the Workers' School. In our set text there was a story, 'Tselane and the the Giant'. I was completely taken aback by the contrast between the discussions about this story and the other stories in the book. In discussing 'Tselane and the Giant' everybody suddenly brightened up. The discussion became animated and developed into a deeply philosophical discussion about crime and punishment. Once again, I recorded the discussion from memory and returned it to the group as a reading for the next English lesson. Here is a short extract from the data:

Some people thought that the story taught children obedience. Tselane refused to obey her mother and she got into great danger herself and caused her mother to suffer. The lesson of the story is that Tselane should have obeyed her mother and gone with all the other people.

But other people said no. Tselane liked her place. It was a lovely place with a sunken lake and flowers and trees. The place suited her. The giant came to disturb her and it was right for her to stay and fight the giant. Because she stayed the giant died and all the people were able to come back to their nice place again. The lesson of the story is that you don't run away when something comes to disturb you but you stay and fight the thing that disturbs you.

(WSD 1992: 1)

The recorded text is full of arguments and counter-arguments about what the teaching of the story was. What was striking about the discussion was that all the various and contradictory interpretations were allowed to coexist. I had to prepare the group for the Standard 8 examinations and so had to set a comprehension exercise along the lines What was the giant's name? Where did the giant live? Why did the people hate him so much? It could be said that the inclusion of an African myth in an English literature set text was a progressive thing, and it was seen as such by many people. However, the type of knowledge that 'comprehension' exercises are testing is factual recall, which is the equivalent of using a limousine as a rubbish truck: it is the wrong vehicle for the job and it gets destroyed when used for purposes different from those for which it was designed. The inclusion of an African myth in an English literature textbook raises many ethical questions. First, it could be seen as appropriation of indigenous educational resources. Second, the fact that it appears as an English story could confuse those who had grown up with it from childhood. It is possible that people with a deep appreciation of their own culture could be failed in an English exam for giving the 'wrong' answer to what seem to be meaningless questions about it. I see this as an example of the destruction of traditional ways of learning through their incorporation into an alien pedagogy. It worries me in my own research project that the use of an alien research methodology could similarly destroy the Wits workers' understanding of their school.

PRODUCING KNOWLEDGE AND THE KNOWLEDGE PRODUCTION BUSINESS

This brings me to the question of knowledge production, with its parallel in imperialist production practices. The novice researcher is initiated into the ritual expectations of the Western academy, which are linked to the more macho masculine attitude that you can only acquire 'true' knowledge and status as the expert once you have bloodied yourself in the field. This involves taking and demarcating your territory as if fieldwork is a military campaign.

(Jones 1996: 12)

The parallels with the voyages of discovery are obvious, with the university being the motherland that sends the researcher out to collect riches which are then brought back, analysed, named and categorized. So coming back from 'the field', do I hitch a ride on the 'post express', with postmodernism chugging out in front, followed by post-structuralism, postfeminism, post-history, post-apartheid, find the postcolonial carriage and put my name on the door? There is the question of location and power.

Second, who is my audience? The traditional audience for research is the international academic community, but this 'natural' audience would be questioned by members of the Workers' School, whose primary audience would be people like themselves. Researchers can thus find themselves with two very different, if not completely incompatible, audiences. While it is true that, in general, people are beginning to resist becoming subjects of enquiry in research that will be of little or no benefit to them, most research is still carried out for the researcher's purpose rather than for that of the researched. It is also the case that much research is conducted by students as part of higher degrees. The competitive and individualistic structure means that I go to Africa and interview people about their lives and experiences, and under normal circumstances this would come out as part of my published research. What I did in this case, as indicated earlier, was to catalogue all the materials as Workers' School documents, rather than subsuming them all under my name. This raises a related and more general issue of the ethics of research in subsistence communities and questions of ownership of the knowledge produced and also questions of payment. In South Africa some progressive video producers did not take out copyright of their work on the grounds that it concerned 'the struggle' and thus belonged to 'the people' (Tomaselli 1996: 118). The point here is that the knowledge produced should be not only accessible to but attributed to 'the people'. It would be difficult to know how to go about getting the people's consent or approval, and the term is obviously open to abuse if authors or film-makers are not accountable for the work that they produce. However, it would seem that a primary ethical concern of research in a postcolonial context is how to organize it so that the credit and benefits accrue to the researched. In this case I have decided to produce two texts – one for the university in my name and another, co-authored with the workers, to be sold for their benefit.

To conclude, in this chapter I have addressed some of the ethical issues that have arisen in my research into a school for black workers at a white university under apartheid. I have stressed the importance of understanding the history of colonialism and of resistance to it. Using South Africa as an example, I have also examined the implication of seemingly neutral institutions such as universities in the economic and power structures of the society in which they are located. I have also looked at how traditional ways of knowing and learning can be destroyed when incorporated into foreign pedagogy, and stressed the parallels between imperialist practices and knowledge production. This leads me to a final question of how a researcher is to proceed ethically in this context. I take my lead from the community groups in the People's Education movement in South Africa, who argue that research should serve the interests of the community or the dispossessed. If researchers can work *with* rather than *for* communities, and conduct research with them into initiatives that they themselves have taken to try to address some of their problems, then I think that research may be able to play a truly progressive role. The researcher must recognize that the conceptual resources that they bring with them from the university are ways of producing knowledge that have been tried and tested in other spheres and for specific purposes. However, it may be possible to use these research methods in an imaginative and sensitive way so as to enhance rather than detract from local knowledge systems and for the benefit of local people. The primary ethical consideration must be to avoid research which exploits the researched, a situation described by South African worker Alfred Themba Qabula:

> Although you don't know us, we know ourselves:
> We are the movable ladders that take people up towards the skies
> Left out in the open for the rain.
> Left with memories of tear gas, panting for breath.
>
> (Qabula 1995: 14)

NOTE

1   In the course of the research I coded Workers' School interviews and Workers' School documents as WSI and WSD respectively to indicate that the ownership of the data belonged to the Workers' School. See the section 'Producing knowledge and the knowledge production business' (pp. 113–15) for discussion of this point.

Chapter 9

The moral maze of image ethics

Jon Prosser

INTRODUCTION

Visually orientated educational research, relative to orthodox educational research, is a 'newcomer' to the qualitative research field. As such it lacks a history of accepted ethical practice or a range of theoretical positions on which to base ethical judgements. This chapter does not focus on a general set of ethical principles that are the benchmark for 'wordsmiths' but instead considers common ethical predicaments that result from applying an image-based approach to qualitative research. Those involved who make and use images in a research context are ethically obligated to their subjects. There are moral and political reasons for this. Future visual researchers require access to images and image-making possibilities if image-based research is to make a significant contribution to qualitative research. To gain and maintain that access, to stay in potentially stimulating visual contexts, there is a need to secure the *confidence* of respondents and fellow researchers. Establishing respondents' confidence means assuring them that they will not be 'damaged', misrepresented or prejudiced in any way; in terms of researchers' confidence it means agreeing ethical procedures that protect respondents yet ensure the trustworthiness of findings. Image-based research, being a relative newcomer to interpretative studies, needs theoretical and methodological tenets on which to base its credentials. However, confidence in image-based investigations will be generated only when ethical principles are agreed between researchers and researched, and within the research community, and adhered to by visual researchers across a range of visual contexts.

Identifying what constitutes an appropriate ethical practice, as the title of the chapter suggests, is not easy. In order to explore the twists and turns of the ethical maze this chapter is divided into two parts. The first part considers *still photography* and provides examples from my own work to illustrate ethical dilemmas that face practitioners of image-based research. The second part considers *moving images*, and emphasis is placed on documentary-type film and video. This is an artificial division, as many issues, for example those of access, political pressures and aesthetics, discussed within the *still photography* subheading, are equally applicable to *moving images*, and the converse is also true. Hence, ethical issues should be considered as operating across this divide and encompassed by the more general term 'image-based research'.

IMAGE-BASED RESEARCH

Image-based research is comprised of moving images in the form of film and video, and still images, for example, photographs, cartoons, and drawings. It thus does not form a homogeneous set of technologies, techniques or practices. This divergence is compounded by different analytical procedures and differently generated data used for different ends. Researchers using images may draw on a diverse range of disciplines which, potentially at least, apply a different set of ethical practices. The diversity of theory and practice within image-based research does not suggest a particular field of educational research which constructs and applies its own set of ethics. What makes image-based research differently situated as compared with other forms of research lies in the obvious: visual images are quite different in nature from words in their allusion to 'reality', and participants see themselves and can be seen by others.

Image-based research is often perceived by academics and practitioners alike as having a lower status (Prosser 1998) and operating on the margins of qualitative research. Orthodox, word-orientated researchers relate, methodologically and ethically, to their respective disciplines of sociology, history and psychology. Image-based researchers, on the other hand, derive their methodological and ethical inspiration from visual sociology and visual anthropology. However, with this alignment comes a new set of problems, especially for film-makers and photographers. Although photographs, for example, were used in early sociological journals, their use damaged any hope of academic integrity. Riis and Hine, for example, the most prominent protagonists in the use of photography to bring about social change, were seen by many as 'muck-raking' (Stasz 1979: 134). Equally, documentary photographers of this period such as August Sander's portraits of German social types (Sander 1986) and Eugène Atget's survey of Paris (Atget 1992) were perceived as lacking a methodological framework. Hence not only did early practice undercut the acceptability of image-based research in the eyes of social scientists, more importantly it failed to provide an initial ethical framework. Indeed, visual sociology emerged as a subdiscipline only around 1970. Consequently, few role models of acceptable ethical practice have been debated, let alone established for others to follow. All this has repercussions for image-based educational researchers and ethical practice who rely on visual sociology, visual anthropology, films of the documentary genre or media reportage for methodological models. Given the matrix of adoption and the paucity of role models for those educational researchers using images, there is little in the way of ethical consensus.

STILL PHOTOGRAPHY

Photographs have numerous uses in educational research and at different phases of the research process different ethical principles come to bear. The period prior to making images, the act of constructing images, and issues arising after they are made, each carry discrete ethical implications. (This also holds for moving images.) In practice the process begins by negotiating access for image-making. This means negotiating with the head of an educational institution – as prime 'gatekeeper' – what can and cannot be photographed, how photography is to take place, and how resultant images are to be used. Of course both researcher and 'gatekeeper' have reasons for seeking permission or agreeing (or otherwise) that photography may occur. The researchers have their agenda: to add to sociological knowledge, to increase career prospects; and the 'gatekeepers' too have their agendas: to be treated fairly and to use the research activity to their own advantage. Becker (1988: xv) reminds us that contracts with a visual locus are rarely based on philanthropy but rather on some potential usefulness to both parties:

> Remember that the heads of . . . institutions such as hospitals, jails or schools, who need not participate in having films of themselves made, generally think there is something in it for them: perhaps a chance at reform, perhaps some public relations benefit. They may well think they are smarter than the film-maker or researcher. Is it unethical for image workers to pretend to be dumber than they are to take advantage of that arrogance? Others, less powerful, also have their own reasons for co-operating with image-makers, so the bargain is seldom one-sided.

There is no straightforward answer to Becker's question. Balanced against the possibility of unbridled researcher deception is the potential for participants to behave 'unnaturally' if the focus of the study is made explicit. But implicit in Becker's statement is another ethical dilemma: that 'gatekeepers', during negotiations for access to schools, may set parameters or limitations on the research enterprise. The headteacher, being in a position of power, can influence how staff and students are portrayed by controlling access to him- or herself and therefore images (by, for example, insisting on photographing in 'formal settings' or 'staged' shooting), while allowing and directing access to those less powerful. This is borne out in the paucity of visual studies of powerful leaders of institutions and organizations as compared with the multitude of studies of less powerful groups such as teachers and schoolchildren. During negotiations for access, general guidelines have the potential to be made specific and formal or non-specific and informal. However, the underlying ethical issues are the degree to which the aims of the project are made clear and the extent to which academic freedoms are curtailed by censorship.

Stereotypically, a photojournalist appears in Hollywood films as 'standing on the hood of a tank as it lumbers into battle through enemy fire, making images of war as he risks his life' (Becker 1998: 85). Photographers seeking to document events in educational institutions need to be more wily in their approach. The introduction of a camera to participants can take place on the first day as a 'can opener' (Collier and Collier 1986) or over a period of time using a 'softly softly' approach (Prosser 1992: 398). The 'softly softly' approach entails walking around an institution with the camera in an 'out of the case over the shoulder like a piece of jewellery' mode, followed by 'safe' photography of buildings or positive publicity-type images suitable for inclusion in the institution's prospectus. Only much later is 'serious' photography normally attempted. There is a delicate dividing line here between being sly, deceitful and furtive, and being sensitive and judicious. The final arbiters of ethical decisions may lie not with the visual researcher, nor the research profession who are not in a position to know, but with participants who, in accepting or rejecting the investigator, signal their response.

Images can be obtained openly or covertly. To act covertly, for example, would be to hide from the subject, use a telephoto lens that allows recording of a scene from a distant position, or to use a 'snooper' which allows the photographer to point their cameras in one direction while actually taking a photograph at right angles to the apparent angle of shooting. Such techniques are rarely practised in educational contexts. Nonetheless, since cameras may incite suspicion and discourage naturalistic behaviour, disputable tactics are used, such as shooting 'from the hip' or setting a camera on 'auto' to give the impression the camera is not functioning, when it is. Visual sociologists would justify this practice by arguing that if permission to take photographs had been granted, emphasis shifts to applying techniques that are appropriate to obtaining trustworthy data, and this may entail shooting when subjects are unaware. Nevertheless, few image-orientated educational researchers would countenance outright covert or clandestine photography, as it more often reveals researchers' discomfort with their own photographic activity than it does insights into the daily lives of their subjects.

During the opening phase prudent photographers identify no-go areas and those participants not previously excluded by the 'gatekeeper' who do not want their photograph taken. This is a question of privacy made ambiguous by territory, motive and consequence. Educational establishments are neither private nor public places, making the legal position even more unclear than is normally the case (the law on privacy and intrusion with regard to photography in public and private places is vague in the United Kingdom). Besides, teachers and managers feel 'ownership' of their spaces that comes from a deep sense of professional autonomy. To assume they are not 'private' places would be a mistake on the part of the photographer. Of course, the most dramatic, even sensational, images may be of those not wanting their photographs taken, but that is no reason for taking photographs. Such actions are not only dishonest, but also counter-productive to the enhancement of sociological knowledge. Ultimately the reason for not taking photographs of participants if they are hostile to the idea is not a matter of privacy or morality but the likelihood of such action compromising rapport – a necessity for any researcher hoping to remain in the field.

Although access provides initial ethical problems, these can normally be anticipated. Any problems at this stage are precursors to more substantial dilemmas, anticipated and unforeseen, that attend the photographic activity that follows. Given that all photographs are constructions, it is important to know something of the context of creating an image if the implied promise of truthfulness to the subject, the audience and the research profession is to be upheld. I will use examples of weaknesses in my own work to illustrate how the serendipitous nature of photography can compromise not only the face validity and the veracity of images but also the ethical status of the photographer.

Figure 9.1 'The Ritual of Knock and Wait' Photo by Jon Prosser

Figure 9.1, 'The Ritual of Knock and Wait', used in a study of school culture, shows a teacher knocking at the headteacher's door, bending, listening for a response from within. The objective – to illustrate a taken-for-granted ritual – was planned and drew on the work of Cartier-Bresson (1952) in isolating a 'decisive moment' for its visual arrangement. The context of taking the photograph is interesting because it highlights a range of ethical issues. The first is the possibility of misrepresentation stemming from the polysemic nature of images, for even a single image has many legitimate interpretations. My intended meaning of the photograph was simply 'this is the everyday ritual of knocking and waiting'. However, the aesthetic device (more on this later), the inclusion in the frame of a visual clue (the painting on the left), potentially implies a 'Big Brother is watching you' relationship between the teacher outside and the headteacher inside. This would be one interpretation, but a misrepresentation, since observations and interviews showed that such an implication would be quite unfounded. The aesthetic device, used to make a more dynamic, and implicit but consequential statement, detracts from the original objective of the image. It demonstrates the importance of using images in conjunction with words to project an intended meaning. Equally, it illustrates that while the researcher-created images may be attributed a meaning by others, their intended meaning is best signalled in relation to the socio-political context of how and why the image was made.

The second ethical issue is concerned with fabrication. The first time Figure 9.1 was taken, the film was damaged in processing and could not be printed. When I came to repeat the photograph, the lens, film, time of day, angle of shooting and the scene were the same but the painting (it having been returned to the pupil who painted it) and the teacher were missing. The pupil agreed to bring the painting into the school for one day – the day the head was away from the school. Teachers, aware that he was away, did not knock on his door. After I had waited for two hours a teacher, out of sympathy for my plight, pretended to knock and I got my picture. The second image replicated the first in many respects, but is nonetheless artificial, a 'set-up' with little in the way of the naturalism so central to documentary photography and qualitative research. The photograph, used as an illustration, was included in reporting the findings of the study without mention of the context of taking.

Is all deceit morally equal and to be equally condemned? My feeling is 'no'. It depends, for example, on the mode of communication. Would it be considered deceitful if, during an interview, a tape recorder failed and the interview were repeated? Probably not. However, as the mode of communication in the case of 'The Ritual of Knock and Wait' is a photograph, there is a stronger case to argue that deceit has taken place. Image-based researchers frequently state that photographs are not and will never be an objective witness of reality or a 'window on the world'.

Nevertheless, many audiences expect an unrealistically high level of 'objectivity' and 'truthfulness' of photographs, more so than would be expected of verbal or written forms of communication. The problem of photographs being perceived by audiences as 'telling us what the world is really like' (Beloff 1985: 100) is long-standing, as Gross *et al.* (1988: 4) point out:

> The 'marriage of conviction' between our faith in the truthfulness of the photographic image and our belief in the possibility of objective reporting has lasted nearly a century and a half, and has been strengthened by the invention of motion pictures and television. Although both partners in this marriage have come under growing suspicion, undermined by our growing awareness of the inevitability of subjectivity in the selection, framing, contextualisation, and presentation of images and reports, their continuing acceptance in public discourse and belief testifies to their resilience.

Therefore, because image-based researchers are aware of the inherent problem stemming from the 'marriage of conviction', it is their moral responsibility to pass on information relating to the context of making which tends to support the so-called trustfulness of the photographic image (more on this later). Consequently, what makes 'The Ritual of Knock and Wait' ethically indefensible is that the context of taking was not revealed, denying audiences informed interpretation and further enhancing the possibility of a false sense of trust in the photograph.

Figure 9.2, 'Pupil on Walkabout', illustrates a quite different ethical problem. One person's representation may be another's misrepresentation, and in photography aesthetic considerations are one way of shaping a truth. Aesthetic devices are important in documentary photography and are used in constructing powerful images which in turn encourage 'readers' not only to look but also to accept a particular meaning of an image. However, this is a two-edged sword since aesthetic qualities, knowingly or otherwise, can distract or disproportionately influence the photographer's meaning and the 'reader's' interpretation. 'Pupil on Walkabout' is an example of this problem. The boy was regularly found on a Friday afternoon hiding in the school's fuel storage area or in the cloakroom (usually under a mound of coats). He explained how each Friday the physics teacher told him to 'get lost', so he did. The photograph was taken to illustrate his predicament.

Two issues arise from the use made of this photograph in a research context. There is a dynamic relationship between words and images. Edward Weston, a famous American photographer, in discussing the relationship between photographs and titles, said, 'a poet can write a few words under it [a photograph] which will change how you see it. In this case words and picture will affect each other, they enlarge each other' (Danziger and Conrad

Figure 9.2 'Pupil on Walkabout' Photo by Jon Prosser

1984: 30). In the case of Figure 9.2 neither the title nor the text used in the report (Prosser 1989) support my intended meaning of the image.

A second and more significant failing compounds this weakness. In the past, documentary photographers, for example Sander (1986), have developed what can be described as 'pseudo-objective' photography. They used standard lenses without filters, emphasized frontality of the subject and flatness of space, recorded people in their natural environment, and printed their negatives full frame to produce an aesthetic style known as 'standers and sitters'. This style was used in Figure 9.2 and raises a number of general ethical questions. As stated earlier, one ethical responsibility of researchers is to report conceptions and procedures on which a research report is based. However, given that photographs are constructions, to what extent is it possible for photographers to account reflexively for the influence of aesthetic considerations? I was aware that using the 'standers and sitters' style, coupled with chiaroscuro lighting, would produce an 'arty' image. Equally, I was aware that the central positioning of the boy, the pathos of the figure and the gloominess of the place would evoke an overly emotional response in the viewer. In conveying a sense of isolation and depression I was representing an interpretation that was unsupported by data and had no substantive basis. This was not a case of incompetence (I knew what I was doing), more a case of the artistic style, drama and sensationalism of an image being given priority over academic integrity. Limitations resulting from lack of reflection show ineptitude; limitations resulting from failing to act on reflexivity constitute unethical behaviour.

MOVING IMAGES

Although there are technical and procedural differences between moving and still imagery, in terms of ethical dilemmas there are many similarities. There are similarities between photographs and moving images as a result of similar technologies and modes of communication. The still camera and the movie camera each in their own way are technological devices that replicate accurately what is set before them. However, importantly, they do so at our bidding. Both are 'visual' but, being different in their mode of recording and presentation, pose different ethical dilemmas. Their similarity gives rise to similar ethical questions, and in the same way their differences give rise to a different set of ethical issues. Therefore, despite their interchangeable ethical problems, a contrast will be drawn between moving and still images.

The most marked differences between still and moving images are pointed out by Beloff (1985: 104), quoting Hopkinson:

> A newsreel has movement, but the still photograph has permanence. It is a moment of time frozen. The famous picture of the South Vietnam general shooting a terrorist with his own hand in a Saigon street would have meant little flashing by on television screens. As a still picture it stands forever – an accusation of mankind.

An alternative distinction is provided by Adelman (1998: 156), quoting Berger:

> The fact that a film camera works with time instead of across it affects every one of its images on both a technical and metaphysical level. . . . Most important of all, the eye behind the film camera is looking for development not conjuncture.

The implication that single images without accompanying words to provide context rarely fulfil the reflexive and internal validity afforded by moving images is an important one. Despite these critical distinctions, there are many interchangeable ethical dilemmas facing both still and moving image-makers.

Perhaps the most common ethical debate focuses on notions of the truth and veracity of still and moving images. Our belief in the capacity of photography to provide evidence of the external world is reflected in the saying 'the camera never lies'. We know this has never been the case. Shortly after photography was patented at the Academy of Sciences in Paris in 1839, for example, the inventor, Louis Jacques Daguerre, was experimenting by retouching photographs. Winston (1998) catalogues a large number of manipulations of the photographic image ranging from Gardner's rearrangement of bodies after the battle of Gettysburg (dragging them about forty metres and changing their clothes) to Robert Doisneau's famous picture 'The Kiss' in which the main protagonists were not photographed in the act of spontaneous gesture of affection but were a specially commissioned actor and his girlfriend. Kane (1994) provides an inventory of digital manipulation including *National Geographic Magazine*'s moving two pyramids closer together for aesthetic reasons. Yet since we know that photography was never objective, why do we hold on to the authenticity of the photograph? Kane (1994: 10) suggests a reason:

> Even when photo-images are faked, they only confirm the essential power of the photographic. When Stalin infamously removed Trotsky from the picture of Lenin in Red Square, or when surrealists and avant-gardists fiddled with exposures and turned the photo into a phantasm, both parties were exploiting – for political and artistic purposes – our fundamental trust in the camera. We believe the camera's eye can bring us truth, whether subjective (the snapshot of a loved one, the performance of a great actor) or objective (pictures of weather forecasts, police suspects, lab experiments). The photographic is the way we moderns test that reality is *out there*: we rely on its veracity more than we readily admit.

Given that we invest images with an integrity 'more than we readily admit', how can we best stand outside of ourselves to judge them? To begin with, the trustworthiness of moving and still images depends on their contextual validity. In terms of the context in which images are *made*, transparency of the process is central; in terms of the context in which images are *viewed*, their mode of representation and the cultural and pictorial codes of their reception are central. Judgements and claims of contextual validity are best made essentially via *reflexive accounts* but also through their *representation*. Reflexive accounts attempt to render explicit the process by which data and findings were produced, and are the 'Achilles heel' of all film genres claiming academic integrity. It is clear that until recently anthropological film, for example, has been insufficiently reflexive or integrated. (Usually, reflexive accounts, where they do exist, are provided as an adjunct to the film.) Nonetheless, even in the case of a reflexive documentary account the academic community will find fundamental faults since there is a widely held belief that 'reality' is distorted by directors' beliefs, sponsors' needs, artistic convention and for artistic reasons (Winston 1995). This argument is also applied to all forms of the realist mode of communication, including the 'photographic essay' and 'documentary photography'.

INFORMED CONSENT

The above concerns are not abstractions, of interest only to academia. The problems resulting from the social and political milieu that are part and parcel of any film-making show themselves in a series of moral and ethical dilemmas. Consider the scenario of making a documentary film of a school. The relationship between the film-makers and their subjects is initiated within a framework of *informed consent*. This customarily means that subjects are free of coercion or deception; have an understanding of the process by which a film is to be made, the outcomes, and the uses to be made of the film; and, as individuals or groups, have the capacity and competence to consent (Anderson and Benson 1988). Even a cursory reflection on these criteria applied in an educational setting would pick up potential discrepancies. The hierarchy of the school, on understanding the potential advantages of making the film, could entice or inveigle the subjects (teachers, administrators and students) to take part for the school's common good. This would have direct repercussions since the subjects, not steeped in filmic knowledge, would be unaware of the techniques and ploys of directors going about their art. Moreover, as with any case study the outcomes of filming cannot be preordained. Only in editing can the final 'story' be told, which means that ultimate control lies with the film-makers, not the subjects. Also, pupils (minors requiring parental consent) and parents may be given only cursory information about the film and rarely have the luxury of 'opting out'. Finally, since the effects of the film on actors and audience can rarely be predicted by the film-maker, there can be no guarantees of negative repercussions on subjects.

These points exemplify how easy it is for ethical ideals to be subverted in practice. It should be borne in mind that 'informed consent' is more often a matter of individual conscience and rarely takes the form of a contract identifying particularities. Without acquiescence and the participation of teachers and pupils, observational films in educational settings would not exist. If truly informed consent were absent or lacking, the films' ethical integrity would be impaired. If directorial freedom were confined, constructive and artistic integrity would be limited. Clearly, for directors there is a tension between needing actors' co-operation during filming and wanting complete autonomy during editing. The view of participants, as cited by Becker (1988: xiii), highlights the irreconcilable ethical dilemma:

> I ought not to be able to sign away my rights to be treated, when someone collects images, in an ethical fashion, whether I want to or not. . . . I cannot give my consent unless I am truly informed, and that I know at least as much about the process of making photographs and films (or doing social research) as the people doing the work.

RECURRING THEMES

Generally, situated ethics constitute a set of dilemmas for film-makers that are not easily resolved. Where they are resolved, it is only by setting aside one set of values in preference for another. This is most obvious in the Griersonian documentary film tradition applied in the past to studies of education, health, welfare and housing. Directors used their creations for social reform, to expose bad or evil, and to bring about desirable change. However, in taking up the cause of social improvement by documenting social victimization, they put to one side any consideration of improving the lots of the subjects of their films. In paying little attention to the moral rights of participants they provide evidence for claims that 'most documentary film-makers have relatively little commitment to the subjects of their films' (Beauchamp and Klaidman 1988: 138). Moreover, in the past, the popularity of such films led to a recurrence of themes commonly termed 'victim documentaries' (Winston 1995). Brian Winston (1988: 34), in quoting a comment made by Basil Wright in 1974, exemplifies the recurring 'victim documentary' theme:

> You know this film (*Children at School*) was made in 1937. The other thing is that this film shows up the appalling conditions in the schools in Britain in 1937 which are identical with the ones which came out on television the night before last: overcrowded classes, schoolrooms falling down, and so on. It's the same story. That is really terrible, isn't it?

What Winston implies is that 'overcrowded classes, schoolrooms falling down' is a recurring 'victim'-type documentary that had media currency in 1937, 1974 and 1988. Given the combination of pressures from sponsors, the public's need for exposé, and the enhancement of career prospects of the film-maker, it is little wonder that films of the less powerful in society are repetitious while case studies of the powerful are significant by their absence. Direct cinema, when aiming to show everyday comprehensive schooling, tends, at least in part, to focus on poorly performing or over-whelmed teachers. Not surprisingly, those in the 'spotlight' are unhappy when they view the film for the first time – usually much later, when screened on national television. This view is common in documentary work:

> how rare it is that image-makers show us to others as we would like to be seen, and, moreover, put in question the assumption that the image makers' perspective is more objective or valid than that of their (willing or unwilling) subjects.
>
> (Gross *et al.* 1988: viii)

Directors willing to discuss interpretation of their work are rare. One of the few is Roger Graef, well known for his series of films in the early 1970s, 'The

Space between Words' – essentially about communication but encompassing comprehensive schooling. He accepts that his filming threw up unpredictable issues, that teachers are not committed to accepting outcomes and should be in a position to respond to both the record and the director's interpretation:

> my solution . . . is to provide as part of my rules for filming, a guaranteed viewing during the editing stage to all the key participants, with a firm promise to change anything that can be pointed out to be *factually inaccurate*. That extends to re-editing for *emphasis* as well [original emphasis].
>
> (Graef 1980: 171)

Graef has developed a set of procedures (Graef 1980: 175) to explain and guide his ethical practice, though, as he himself points out, these do not themselves guarantee ethical practice or fair treatment of participants. Nevertheless, his position represents the 'high water mark' of ethical practice in observational filming of educational institutions.

It is the director who has responsibility for the interpretation of data and the presentation of findings. However, it is clear that a distinction should be drawn between observational film that is governed by principles that underpin research and documentary films which are shaped by the vagaries of mass audiences. The ultimate ethical concern in documentary films, shared by Beauchamp and Klaidman (1988: 183), is that truths are distorted: 'The search for "truth" fades and becomes a search for a preconceived moment, a biased hypothesis that captures the "essence of truth" in the mind of the documentary maker.'

The pressures on the makers of docu-soaps (often referred to as 'bubble gum for the eyes') and documentaries, as a result of the need to please audiences of 10 million or more, are significant. It is clear from the extent of documentary frauds at present that such 'investigative' films have major ethical implications concerning how they treat people and how they represent or misrepresent the 'truth' of a situation. Contemporary documentary films about education, although methodologically and ethically flawed, are viewed by mass audiences as evidence of the decline of schooling.

VIDEO-BASED CLASSROOM RESEARCH

The use of camcorders by researchers to record classroom interaction is far removed from the pressure of documentary and journalistic enterprise and their compulsion for dramatic narrative. Video-based classroom research enhances the possibility of researcher–practitioner co-operation, decreases the theory–practice divide, and, where there is mutual 'close reading' of visual data (Mitchell and Weber 1998), provides respondent insight and validity. It is a particularly pure form of vérité, being without commentary and focusing on observational method. The resulting visual records provide extra-somatic 'memory'. The camera's reproductive and mimetic qualities can be used to systematically record visual detail with emphasis on reproducing objects, events, places, signs and symbols, or behavioural interactions. The ability of the camera to record visual detail without fatigue, to be organized, catalogued and analysed at a later date, is useful to fieldworkers.

Filming in classrooms necessitates a close working relationship being established between the participants and the researcher. The issue of ownership and control is central since disconcertingly, and unlike in word-orientated research, not only do participants have the opportunity to see themselves interacting with each other, but so too do others. Those who claim ownership, excluding the researcher, are not necessarily the actors themselves. Certainly the 'gatekeepers' who hold power have claim, as do governors and the heads who are responsible for their schools' good name. There are examples (Graef 1989: 1) of observational film benefiting those in positions of power yet 'blighting' the career of subordinate actors. This is because problems commonly occur when observational films and videos are shown to outside audiences (that is, outside the immediate circle of researcher and actors). Graef (ibid.: 2) believes that 'Vérité brings out that viewers are very nosey about details of other people's lives, but disapprove of that noseyness in themselves and transfer this disapproval into disapproval of what they are looking at.'

The problem of judgemental audiences of video recordings is picked up by Busher and Clarke (1990: 121):

> It is perplexing why audiences rush to judgement about aspects of action, approaches to teaching and personality when viewing a video of a teacher in action. Video-extracts of lessons are void of all but immediate information about the action of the scenes on view while yet appearing to offer an adequate basis for the exercise of judgement by viewers. In this sense videos can be dangerous in easily causing a false sense of understanding of the truth of things as can glimpses of lessons snatched while walking down a corridor.

Since it is very difficult to predict outside audiences' reaction to observational film of classrooms, participants' awareness of potential hazards of external interpretation is integral to informed consent, and as important as who owns and controls the data is how data are to be used.

Videos of classroom interaction necessitate shots of the largest group in the frame: pupils. Not only is their performance most visible, but without their co-operation filming could not take place. Teachers in whose classroom video recordings are made usually tell their pupils that filming will take place but rarely discuss its meaning – perhaps because of the scale of the consensus-seeking exercise, which is more difficult to achieve as pupils' age decreases. This raises the common ethical question of 'How much information do subjects need to give "informed consent"?' (Graef 1980: 163), and signals a less frequently asked but important question: what about minors' rights? Pupils' 'voices' are absent and their disempowerment is complete if they (and their parents) are not invited to view their 'performance'. Busher and Clarke (1990: 144) make an additional point that 'some children seem to attract more attention in the classroom than do others', and that consequently the visual record 'is likely to be skewed both to over-display, and to overemphasise the importance of the attractive children'. This, coupled with Calderwood's findings (1988) that videos of classroom interaction incite colleagues' curiosity more than other forms of record-keeping, and the unpredictability of audience reaction, makes empowerment of pupils an important ethical issue.

CONTEMPORARY CLASSROOM VIDEO RECORDING

The ethics of educational research has undergone modifications over the past decade, as a result of increasing complexity in the research process and challenges posed by critical theorists and postmodernism. Latterly, post-modern and narrative influences have brought a new meaning to reflexive accounts. Hence, depending on the stance taken, discussion of contemporary visual ethics ranges from privacy, ownership, informed consent, to truth, transparency, reflexivity and realism. Modern documentary films can be viewed as the quintessential postmodernist media in that they attempt to depict reality, champion relativism and set little store by objective standards of truth. Winston (1995), in *Claiming the Real*, examines the continuum of principles, ethics, epistemology and practices of documentary work, offering an important insight into the essential differences between film as documentary, and the documentary as fiction. The issues of relative but conflicting ethics, of representing different 'voices' contrasted with notions of fictions and realism, are central in this type of work.

The postmodern and narrative approaches are also beginning to impinge on classroom video recordings. This is clearly illustrated through the work of Weber and Mitchell (1995) and Mitchell and Weber (1999), who use photographs and videos of themselves and colleagues as tools for narrating auto/biography of their professional lives and as an aid to help practising teachers examine their professional identity. Ethical obligations now take a different turn. To what extent should the sensitivities of participants be taken account of when film-makers turn their cameras on their own schools, own colleagues and own classes, whose agreement and trust they may take for granted?

These questions are not easily answered. There is the difficult reflexive question of procedural reactivity. Are film-makers sufficiently sensitive to predict the outcome of recording and, more importantly, replaying recordings of the taken-for-granted act of teaching? Video-based research allows participants to see themselves and reflect on their practice *but* it also has the potential to displace previously established self-images. This makes video-based research different from still-image research and quite different from word-orientated ethical considerations. Self-initiation or initiating others into video recording of classroom practice are acts that carry responsibilities. Teachers' initiating of colleagues into video recording of the relatively private intimacy of their classrooms is to confront them with a camera's unfaltering stare, to be caught 'looking in the mirror', requiring the teachers to open themselves to the public. Mitchell and Weber (1999: 199–200) and Busher and Clarke (1990: 120–2) both illustrate the potential pain from self-analysis to teachers as a result of unsupported or insensitive use of video recording.

Finally, autobiographical film and video are capable of going further by telling the stories of the repressed and under-represented, whose 'voices' are rarely heard in classroom documentaries. However, the degree of trust, confidence, faith and intimacy, so essential for this type of work, also brings with it particular moral issues. Katz and Katz (1988) describe how the ethics of autobiographical films, where close associates may be drawn in alongside the biographer to form a special relationship, differs from an orthodox ethical code. A strength of autobiographical studies and studies made from within communities as distinct from external agencies lies in their ability to act as an antidote to what Winston (1995) terms 'victim documentaries'. Victim documentaries are the focus by the powerful on the private and everyday lives of the less powerful. Rather than rely on pervading values of bodies that often fund documentaries, 'in-house' films and videos have the opportunity to give 'voice' to ethnic, religious and sexual groups that are external or peripheral to mainstream beliefs.

A WAY THROUGH THE MORAL MAZE?

There are innumerable examples of poor ethical practice by image-based researchers. This ethical 'black hole' is sustained because few experienced visual researchers have established a consistent set of ethical procedures and few image-based research students are taught ethics. As a result, important ethical issues are rarely debated and ethical knowledge seldom disseminated. There are additional reasons for the moral complexity of image-based research. It is a subdiscipline that is applied across a range of disciplines including sociology, anthropology and psychology. Ethics are situated differently according to each discipline's 'slant' on what comprises befitting moral behaviour. Add to this the relative newness of visual studies and the multiplicity of image-based research in terms of technology used and processes followed, and we begin to recognize the complexity of the moral maze within which it is situated. The ethics of visual research is in its infancy and, metaphorically speaking, located near the centre of a complex moral maze. There are many false avenues to explore before escape from an ethical 'wilderness' is possible.

More established subdisciplines, such as educational psychology, have established a code of practice that in the past has acted as a focal point of debate and, potentially at least, consensus-based action. Image-based research lacks guidelines and codes of practice in its evolution. Of course guidelines and codes of practice in themselves do not amount to good practice, but they are important arenas of debate on the road to realization of moral behaviour in visual research. Consequently – and this may sound at odds with the views of other contributors to this book – visual researchers need to take a backward step, to reach a consensus on what constitute the principal ethical dilemmas of image-based research. The establishment of a 'checklist' of moral dilemmas is important because it will reflect the different nature of image-based research relative to other styles of research. The 'checklist' is a necessary evil that will act as a springboard to attaining ethical practices that are situated in image-based research as opposed to, for example, word-based research. Recognition of the distinctive ethical dilemmas posed by visual research is the first and most significant step in escaping the moral maze. What is important is that practitioners of visual research reflect on and report back their experiences in order to ground their situated ethics in actuality. It is difficult to avoid prescription at this point, but it seems clear that case studies of situated ethics should be widely disseminated to students of image-based research and those under the gaze of visual researchers. The situatedness of differing research styles is central to establishing enhanced ethical practice. It is equally important that situated ethics becomes a matter of public knowledge rather than remaining the domain of implicit professional knowledge.

Chapter 10

Dancing with the devil

Ethics and research in educational markets

Nick Foskett

RESEARCHING EDUCATIONAL MARKETS

Among the rapidly changing landscape of education policy and practice of the past two decades, an important focus of research has been the nature, impact and operation of centrally imposed quasi-markets (Le Grand and Bartlett 1993). Marketization of the educational environment has characterized many states during this period (Power *et al.* 1997), resulting in a wide range of market forms, and transforming the operational environment of many schools, colleges and education authorities (Waslander and Thrupp 1996; Lumby and Foskett 1999).

Marketization has impacted on the research of all those working in the fields of educational policy and management, and not just those interested specifically in educational markets and marketing. It may be argued that most current educational research requires a market perspective to be built into its analysis. Issues of quality assurance and external accountability, for example, permeate all aspects of curriculum and institutional management. However, the focus of this chapter is on the ethical issues raised by research into educational markets. This includes research on:

- *demand-side* issues such as institutional choice or education/training pathway decision-making;
- *supply-side* issues such as environmental analysis, institutional strategy and operational approaches; and
- the *interaction* between the demand and supply sides, which is the market in operation.

Research output in these areas grew substantially during the 1990s, but has been dominated by, on the demand side, research into parental (?) choice of secondary schools (e.g. Adler and Raab 1988; Carroll and Walford 1997; Gorard 1999), on the supply side by research into the management responses of schools and colleges (e.g. Gewirtz *et al.* 1995; Foskett 1998), and, in terms of supply–demand interaction, on relationships between parents and

schools (Glatter *et al.* 1996; Woods *et al.* 1998). Research into the operation of markets in post-compulsory education has only recently started to
emerge (Smith *et al.* 1995; Foskett and Hesketh 1997), but is recognized
as being essential to understanding the implementation of government
policy agendas in areas such as lifelong learning and widening participation
(Kennedy 1998; Woodrow *et al.* 1998).

The researching of educational markets provides new ethical challenges
to educational researchers. While some of these challenges are common
to all educational research which focuses on real people and real lives, in
the context of educational markets a further specific ethical arena needs
to be taken into account: the inherent nature of markets and the market
sensitivity of the processes being researched. The essence of a market is
competition, and within a competitive environment knowledge of many
components of the market can provide a distinct market advantage. Data
are sensitive and knowledge can have real financial market value. As a
consequence, secrecy is a frequent response from institutions to requests to
participate in research or release information and data, risking the generation of only partial insights from the research process. *In extremis*,
disinformation processes may be seen as a legitimate tactic by players in
the marketplace. The conflict between the objectivity of research and the
development of public-domain understanding of process and practice on
the one hand, and the market needs of institutions on the other, may
provide a real research problem. This in turn generates a number of key
ethical issues that must be addressed as part of the planning of research
programmes in the context of educational markets. These include:

- gaining access for research;
- the researcher's intervention in the market;
- inequitable benefits from research into markets; and
- ethical issues in researching life decisions.

GAINING ACCESS FOR RESEARCH

Gaining access is an important first stage in planning any educational
research, and its ethical dimensions have been explored at length elsewhere
(e.g. Simons 1987; Johnson 1994). Negotiation is normally underpinned
by the key principle of informed consent, and the negotiation of ground
rules for access to and the use of data. These include confidentiality and
publication agreements. Gaining access to undertake market-based studies,
however, raises particular practical ethical issues, including important
considerations about the use of deception.

'Markets' and 'marketing' are not neutral terms from a values perspective for most working in educational environments. The concepts have traditionally been 'alien' (Foskett 1996) and not within the experience of many working in public-sector environments, which were traditionally 'domesticated' (Carlson 1975), with institutional survival assured and only professional, as opposed to political or market, accountabilities. The terms were also a condensation symbol (Edelman 1977) on which to target fears and concern about changing accountability in education. As such they may represent significant barriers to the negotiation of research access, which depends initially on the researchers 'being able to demonstrate that they are worthy, as researchers and as human beings, of being accorded the facilities to carry out their investigations' (Cohen and Manion 1994: 354). Two perspectives may make it difficult to negotiate access in this context.

First, *a priori* assumptions of those working in schools mean that the researcher may be seen as actively promoting the notion of markets and marketing to a degree that is in conflict with the moral and ideological standpoint of the staff in the institution. Ethical objections to the establishment of a market culture in education have been extensively explored in the literature (e.g. Jonathan 1990), and concerns about equity issues in the context of markets may be projected on to the intending researcher. As Bowe *et al.* (1992) have suggested in the context of developing market ideas within schools, seeking access to research markets may become the 'site as well as the stake' of ideological conflict. The researcher may be perceived as guilty of 'dancing with the devil' that is the marketplace in operation.

This perceptual coin has two faces, however. The growing presence of a marketing culture in schools (Foskett 1998) and colleges (Smith *et al.* 1995) can lead to researchers being perceived as possessing a strongly 'anti-market' stance with an *a priori* prejudice and a research agenda focused on a critique of market processes. Such assumptions have been the focus of debate in the literature between, *inter alia*, Tooley and Ball (see Ball and Gewirtz 1997). Alternatively, the researcher may be regarded as promoting the ideology of the market, on the assumption that any individual who is actively interested in marketing must be pro-markets in their personal philosophy. Bowe *et al.* (1994: 63), for example, accuse some of the early researchers into parental choice of being 'captured by the discourse' of markets.

Such debates are reworked at the point of negotiation of access for research. A negative view of the impact of markets on equity in education may be compounded by a negative view of the ethics of marketing processes. Marketing itself is often portrayed as having many unethical practices, perhaps based on traditional images of selling in business environments. Chonko (1995) cites ten common accusations against marketing, including the belief that those engaged in it are guilty of manipulation of customer choice, misrepresentation of goods and services, distortion of data, and exaggerated performance claims. If these are projected on to the researcher and the proposed research there would seem to be little chance of access to schools and colleges.

Taking an impartial view in the debate about the place of markets in education may seem initially to be an appropriate philosophical stance, and the reports of research frequently feel the need to counter the accusations explicitly by emphasizing the researcher's objective position. Jephcote *et al.* (1996: 36), for example, in reporting research into the responses of further education college principals to the growing market culture, stress that 'the purpose of this paper is not to argue that a shift towards a market culture is necessarily a bad thing!'. Despite such a declaration, though, the researcher may still find assumptions about the likely perspective of researchers in this field attributed to them. Since no position on the place of markets is neutral, what stance should the researcher adopt? Should this be tailored to the approach deemed most likely to encourage access? If so, then two key ethical questions emerge:

- How ethical is the presentation of an ideological standpoint that may not be a truthful statement of the researcher's position?
- How can this standpoint be identified without seeking pre-access information from third parties, and how ethical would this be?

Both are essentially questions about how honest the researcher should be about the focus of the research. While avoiding the use of 'markets or marketing' in the title or the description of the work may be feasible, can this extend to presenting an emphasis which is not truthful about the intended outcomes or focus of the research? The use of deception in establishing access has been extensively discussed (see, for example, Aronson *et al.* 1990). Cohen and Manion (1994) point out that deception may be inevitable at times to ensure that the research target group have no knowledge of the research aims that would forewarn them, enable them to think issues through and hence be different from a 'normal' sample for the purposes of the research. Indeed, they suggest that most research participants will accept the necessity for deception when it is explained *post hoc*. Kelman (1967) argues that deception is acceptable provided it is minimized, is entirely justified by the pursuit of 'objective' outcomes, is used only in the absence of alternative research approaches, and is explained and justified to participants at the end of the research.

Foskett and Hemsley-Brown (1999) discuss the issue of deception in relation to a study of the role of teachers in providing careers information to children in primary and secondary schools. Previous research (Foskett and Hesketh 1997) had demonstrated the importance of class teachers in influencing the perceptions young people formed of specific careers, but had suggested that the knowledge and understanding teachers held were themselves based on perceptions, stereotypes and misinformation. A research programme was designed to investigate what knowledge teachers had about specific careers. It was recognized that negotiating access to schools to 'test' the knowledge, and potentially reveal the ignorance, of teachers in this area would be very difficult. The research was remodelled, therefore, for the purpose of negotiating access, to emphasize one of the sub-aims of the work rather than the primary aim. This sub-aim was to identify what alternative sources of information could be developed to inform teachers in their role in careers education. Following data collection, the primary aim was revealed to teachers and headteachers, through whom access had been negotiated. All accepted the necessity for the deception, all confirmed that access would have been withheld if the primary research aim had been known, yet all confirmed that the research was of importance and value to their work in schools.

While this example illustrates the possible benefits of deception, it does not necessarily provide a benchmark for ethical standards. The distinctiveness of each individual situation means that the precise ethical action needs to be considered in relation to the specific context. Ethics is often a contingent concept in relation to some areas and an absolute concept in relation to others. What is clear is that embarking on research into education markets may challenge the ethical basis of research right from the point of seeking to negotiate access.

INTERVENTION IN THE MARKET

A second ethical issue relates to the impact of the researcher and the research on the 'system' that is being investigated. Important to understanding ethical issues in this field is the distinction between commercial marketing research and academic research into markets and marketing.

Professionals in education are familiar with the idea of research investigating traditional issues of teaching, learning and assessment, and studies of policy change and management processes have become more familiar in the past two decades. Markets and marketing are familiar to most in education, however, through their experiences as 'consumers' in their everyday lives, and discussion of research in markets will resonate with the familiar notion of 'market research'. In reality, market research is only one component of the commercial arena of 'marketing research' – it is research into the nature of the market itself through, for example, attempts to measure the location or size of the market for a particular product or service. The broader concept of marketing research also includes investigations of consumer behaviour, measurements of customer satisfaction with products, or product research seeking to identify the needs and wants of potential customers. A common assumption of those asked to participate in research into education markets, therefore, is that this is simply marketing research in action. Indeed, such research may use some of the techniques and tools of marketing research, but it is crucially different in its aims and its intended use of findings.

Marketing research has as its primary aim the provision of information which will enhance sales and market performance for a particular supply-side organization or business in the market. It seeks to advantage one market participant over another, and is the realm of research by organizations for their own purposes or by external commercial organizations contracted to work solely for the benefit of the sponsor. It is unilateral in origin and involves a closed and inaccessible link between the commercial sponsor and the market. It is an attempt to intervene in and change market processes by enhancing the understanding of one market player.

Academic research into markets and marketing, in contrast, is an objective social science process, seeking better understanding of specific social and economic systems. Its intention is to provide public-domain information accessible to all with interests in the operation of these systems, but in itself not to interfere with the operation of the market under study. It is thus typified by research by public bodies and research institutions, or by research undertaken by commercial organizations on behalf of such bodies. Such research may be termed 'academic marketing research' in contrast to 'commercial marketing research'. The distinction between the two ideas is important, and may be a real one to social science researchers. However, it may be argued that all research into educational markets is commercial marketing research to at least some of the participants, despite the researcher's best intentions, so the guise of objective educational research into markets may be illusory rather than real.

The assumption by potential participants about the motives for the research in these terms may further complicate the negotiation of access considered earlier. If the only perspective of potential respondents is that research is commercial marketing research, then the fear that an initiative from outside the institution is inevitably marketing research for a third party will certainly discourage the granting of access. Not using 'markets' or 'marketing' in the research title may prove helpful in avoiding this issue, but may in itself raise ethical questions of deception. The only way for a researcher to deal with this matter is to be persistent and consistent about the motivation for the research, the source of its funding and the use of the data.

If the constraint of assumed third-party gain can be overcome, there are still a number of further ethical issues to consider, relating to the potential impact of the research on the market and its processes. These relate to the use of data from the research and the impact of not considering the ideological underpinnings of particular research methods. Six aspects of these issues will be examined here:

- market advantage through information gain;
- data ownership;
- data release;
- market advantage through participation in the research process;
- the use of disadvantaging data; and
- the impact of methodological choice.

Market advantage through information gain

Schools, colleges or other organizations may see their participation in a project as a means of undertaking marketing research for themselves under the guise of objective social science, to gain commercial or market advantage from the process. A traditional payoff for participation in educational research has been access to the data and the findings for the institution's own use. Where the gain is in terms of improved experiences and outcomes for pupils, through, for example, change in teaching and learning approaches, there is no substantive ethical issue involved. Where the gain is a market advantage for the organization, with a consequent market disadvantage for other organizations, there are real ethical questions for the researcher. Should the research proceed, for example, if there are to be disadvantages to other participants in the market, perhaps without their knowledge? Should those other participants be informed about the research and its findings? In most market studies in education the tradition of giving data to participant organizations has been sustained as the price of the research. However, the market value of the data raises other ethical questions, which are examined below.

Data ownership

An important question to resolve is 'whose data are they?'. Where the research has been examining components of the external environment of the institution, for example factors influencing choices of post-16 institution in a locality, it is reasonable to argue that the data are in the public domain, and that the organization has no prior claim on that information. Where the data relate to an internal aspect of the institution, issues are more complex. If data have been obtained through interviewing pupils, students, parents or teachers in a particular institution, it may be argued that they are in many ways the property of the organization, since they are an aspect of those currently employed by or served by the school or college. Furthermore, they would not be available to the researcher without the co-operation of the institution, so it could be argued that the data are in some ways a product of the institution. While the ownership of personal ideas and perspectives clearly rests with the individuals surveyed and not the organization, there is a relationship that goes beyond employer–employee or provider–customer that imposes a moral obligation for aggregated (rather than individual) perceptions to be made available to the organization. The issue of the protection of the rights of individuals will be discussed later in this chapter.

Data release

If the data are to be given to participant organizations, when should they be made available? The issue of advantaging an organization by making data available to it may be resolved in part by negotiating simultaneous release of data to the institution and to the public domain, perhaps by providing data at the time a final research report is published. Simultaneous data release may be justified through the assertion that the full meaning and value of any data are apparent only at the end of the research when the synergy of different components of data collection, analysis and evaluation has been achieved. Pressure for early access to findings may need to be resisted, but this may be more difficult where the issue of ownership of 'internal' data discussed above is raised.

Market advantage through participation in the research process

Market advantage may accrue to an organization simply by participation in the research, and irrespective of the findings. The opportunity to engage in reflection about markets and marketing, and to draw a wide range of staff into the process of analysis, may in effect constitute 'internal marketing'. Robinson and Long (1987) describe internal marketing as the process of sharing vision and ideas across the staff to ensure a committed and coherent interaction, subsequently, with the outside marketplace. The researcher may be the catalyst for internal marketing, and this may be unavoidable as part of an informal process. However, the formalization of that role may constitute a problem for the researcher in attempting to maintain an objective standpoint within the research project.

The use of disadvantaging data

A common ethical concern in educational research is the use of data that are critical or negative about participants. This issue is enhanced in considering data that would disadvantage the participants commercially or competitively if they were known in the public domain. Marketing research in commercial terms is not only about obtaining positive perspectives on the organization and its operation. The identification of negative perspectives or destructive forces in the market is advantageous since they can be countered and responded to. Such data will normally remain confidential in a commercial marketing research relationship between organization and researcher, but may raise important ethical issues in social science research. Kemmis and McTaggart suggest that an important ethical principle of research is retaining the right to report the work:

> Provided that those involved are satisfied with the fairness, accuracy and relevance of accounts which pertain to them, and that the accounts do not unnecessarily expose or embarrass those involved, then accounts should not be subject to veto or be sheltered by prohibitions of confidentiality.
>
> (1981: 62)

For the researcher this raises the need to discuss with potential participant organizations how such issues may be dealt with. Preservation of anonymity in research reports is one important component of resolving this issue. Where single institutions are the focus of research through case study, or where a larger study means that no organizations operating in the same marketplace as each other are included, there may be little difficulty with this issue. An absence of overlap between markets of researched institutions may indeed be a benchmark for making decisions on data release. However, where the operation of specific local markets or micro-markets is the focus of research and several players in that market have participated, confidentiality in the final research report may be almost impossible to preserve between the research participants. A researcher cannot impose a no-use limit on data collected for objective research but published in the public domain, and cannot be a guarantor of the promises of participants on such issues. For this reason it is essential that such ethical issues are discussed openly during the negotiation of access, and that a procedure is established that enables emerging issues to be discussed during the research and publication process.

The impact of methodological choice

An important arena of ethical debate in relation to intervention in the market relates to the position of the researcher and the methodological requirement to pursue objectivity and to seek to identify the potential for bias. This emerges from the recognition that decisions to impose any specific system of social provision such as education are ideologically derived. They are based on a view from politicians about how the world works or should work. Research which employs methodologies underpinned by sociological assumptions that match those of the ideological stance of the policy-makers might, therefore, inevitably produce findings which reinforce the policy perspective. This raises ethical questions for researchers, who need to be appropriately critical of the underpinning assumptions in their methodology to protect themselves from accusations of promoting, perhaps inadvertently, particular ideological standpoints.

Bowe *et al.* (1994), Gewirtz *et al.* (1995) and Gorard (1997) illustrate this issue in their critique of factor analysis research into parental choice of secondary school. Their contention is that approaches to parental choice which focus on parents' prioritization of lists of choice factors emphasize the rationality of choice and minimize the complexity and social embeddedness of the choice processes at work. Gewirtz *et al.* (1995: 6) assert that such methodologies are 'sociologically and politically naïve . . . [since] the view that factors and reasons form the basis for human behaviour bears a strong resemblance to the assumptions that underlie economists' abstract accounts of market behaviour (especially the individual rational calculus of classical economics)'.

Put simply, their contention is that such a research approach promotes the notion of rational choice, and in its findings supports its existence. It ignores the contentiousness of such a perspective, and in so doing is not ideologically neutral. In effect it promotes the virtues and values of the market as a resource allocation mechanism. As Bowe *et al.* indicate (1994: 64):

> we should not be limited by . . . a 'policy science' approach, the testing of government claims, we must also consider parental choice politically and sociologically, as a matter of 'policy scholarship'. . . . It needs to separate out the simplicities and misrepresentations of 'choosing' in political debates from the complexity of the choice making process in real social contexts.

For researchers into educational markets, recognizing the ideological implications of their research methodology is of prime importance, since an ethical issue that must be addressed is the potential impact of promoting or refuting the role of the market as a resource allocation system in education. This issue is examined in the next section.

INEQUITABLE BENEFITS FROM RESEARCH INTO MARKETS AND MARKETING

The impact of markets on social equity is one of the important issues raised by those opposed to the development of social markets (e.g. Warnock 1991). If research into markets and marketing risks enhancing the inequities they may produce, this is a serious outcome of the research. It was identified earlier that all research into markets is commercial marketing research for some of the participants, in that they may gain competitive advantage from the data or findings generated or from the process of the research. Any new perspective on their own organization or on the micro-market within which they operate will be advantageous to educational managers. At a macro scale, however, there are distinct advantages to schools and colleges from gaining a better understanding of markets in general. Research outside their own market may help an understanding of their own position and future development. For researchers this raises a broad ethical question relating to the general impact of research. If markets and competition produce 'winners' and 'losers', does improving the understanding of decision-making and market processes risk negative effects on some supply-side organizations and some parents, pupils and students who are participants in the market?

Foskett (1996) has introduced the concept of *institutional cultural capital* in the context of market participation. Cultural capital (Bourdieu and Wacquant 1992) is the concept of the possession of social skills, knowledge and status that gives individuals advantage in social markets. For example, affluent, university-educated, middle-class parents not only may possess the knowledge of school application systems, and the confidence to access them, and the resources to undertake vigilant information-gathering about schools to facilitate their choice, but may also have the status to make themselves and their children attractive to over-subscribed schools. *Institutional cultural capital* is the equivalent for organizations. Some schools and colleges will be advantaged by their natural catchment areas such that their achievements make them attractive in the marketplace. However, this effect may be enhanced or diminished by their ability to capitalize on that advantage by their knowledge and understanding of markets, market systems and marketing processes. An important component of this will be their use of the findings of both commercial marketing research and academic research into markets and marketing.

Part of the advantage gained lies in the understanding of the interaction of pupil/parent choices and the promotional messages and pathways used by schools or colleges. Providing the 'right' information at the 'right' time may be highly influential in choice (Foskett and Hesketh 1996); indeed, the aim of promotional strategies by organizations is to do just that! Hemsley-Brown (1996) has shown how the promotional messages of colleges are used as *post hoc* justification of choice by new entrants. If the modelling of the market and its processes is improved, then the effectiveness of supply-side organizations in influencing choice may be enhanced. This suggests that by enhancing the knowledge of market processes that institutions hold, their ability to influence choice among potential customers is enhanced. This raises ethical questions about the rights of individuals in the choice process and their protection from manipulation by organizations that understand the process well. Similarly, there are issues about the rights of other organizations in the market, which may be able to compete less well in the absence of information, with resulting reduction in resources, quality of provision and viability. Researching markets and marketing, and increasing understanding of the processes in operation, may promote the inequities that are the product of markets in operation, and from this perspective researchers should be wary of schools, colleges or individuals that are very enthusiastic about participation in the research, for they may have distinct commercial motivations.

An important dimension of this arises where data are collected from individuals which provide, as an end product of the research, insights into market processes that enable institutions to have more influence over their choice, and perhaps achieve social aims that are not congruent with the aims and needs of individuals. The researcher's moral responsibility to the individuals who consent to participate in the research is significant. Is this ethical in relation to the researcher's relationship with and moral obligation to the respondents? By researching markets are we in fact enhancing the effectiveness of the market as a mechanism of social control and reinforcing social selection? Such questions are fundamental ethical debates for all researchers in the social sciences, for the process of research itself contributes to change in the system, through both its process and its outcomes.

ETHICAL ISSUES IN RESEARCHING LIFE DECISIONS

Research into the process of choice in education markets has in recent years moved strongly away from investigating 'respondents' responses' to lists of potential influencing factors towards studying choice as a product of people's social existence. Research into school choice by Ball and colleagues (summarized in Gewirtz *et al.* 1995), Carroll and Walford (1997), David (1997) and Gorard (1999), into post-16 choice (Foskett and Hesketh 1997; Ball *et al.* 1998) and into choice processes in vocational training markets (e.g. Hodkinson 1995) has adopted a perspective rooted in Bourdieu's notion of *habitus*. This suggests that

> individual action, belief and, therefore, choice, must always be culturally and socially situated, for we are all born into a social setting. We cannot, therefore, act or think other than as a person of a particular gender, race, class, nation etc. living in a particular period of time. The 'dispositions' that make up individual subjective perceptions are located within objective 'positions' or social structures.
>
> (Hodkinson *et al.* 1996: 146)

Choice is therefore dependent on personal histories, experiences, perceptions and interpretations of the influence of explicit and implicit socio-economic and cultural pressures. It is 'pragmatically rational' (Hodkinson *et al.* 1996), and is situated in 'the partly unpredictable pattern of turning points and routines that make up the life course' (Hodkinson and Sparkes 1997: 43).

Against such a perspective, research into demand-side processes in educational markets is much more complex and exploratory, working with individuals over periods of time and observing the development and emergence of choice outcomes. Beyond the normal ethical issues of working with individuals, such as confidentiality, freedom to withdraw from the research and the minimization of intrusion into the individual's life, the wish to facilitate individuals in reconstructing complex historical processes may place pressure on researchers to overstep key ethical boundaries. The researcher clearly has no 'rights' of access to intimate personal histories or life accounts, and can only encourage their emergence with the full co-operation of the individual concerned. Not only is pressure unethical, but it may also lead to distortion of the individual's perception of reality as they seek to account for decisions in rational terms. The sensitivities required to explore these issues are akin to the skills of counselling, in which the individual is encouraged to explore their perceptions and ideas themselves. But two ethical questions emerge from this notion, too.

The first is, how ethical is it to use such approaches to discover personal histories that will be used in public-domain findings, irrespective of assurances of confidentiality? The second is, how ethical is it to push respondents to relive experiences and choices that may have strong negative feelings emanating from the decision point itself or from post-decision negative consequences? Research by Hemsley-Brown and Foskett (1999) on the choice process of young people taking up modern apprenticeships, for example, shows how the research process was at times personally challenging for those recalling negative experiences both of schooling and of training. Clearly these ethical issues can be addressed by the fully informed consent of participants, the retention of ownership of ideas with the respondent, and the option to discontinue at any point. However, this implies a veto on dissemination from individuals that we have already suggested should not, ultimately, exist for organizations.

Working with individuals also raises issues of independence and non-involvement in the choice processes of parents and young people. Carroll and Walford (1997) demonstrate how parents across the full range of social backgrounds are aware of their ability to exercise choice. As a consequence, they may see the opportunity to engage with research into choice as a means of gaining enhanced information on the processes in the market – for example, through access to privileged information about the requirements of schools and colleges. The researcher provides a ready vehicle for such information, yet providing it, knowingly or unknowingly, distorts the operation of the choice process, renders invalid the research into the process of choice, and advantages those parents or other young people at the expense of others. Distinguishing the role of consultant and researcher is essential, therefore, both methodologically and ethically.

CONCLUSION

Education markets are ethical battlegrounds at a number of levels. As Bowe *et al.* (1992) have suggested, at the level of operational activities they are the 'site and stake' of conflict, with strong debate about the ethical issues in the establishment of a market system in the public sector, and about 'winners' and 'losers' at the level of individuals and institutions. At the level of research, the need to gain a clearer and more refined understanding of how such systems work in practice raises ethical questions that researchers must address in relation to negotiating access, intentional and unintentional intervention in the market, concern for the inequitable benefit from the research, and the ethics of researching real lives and autobiographies. Researching markets and marketing is not an ethically neutral activity, and those seeking to contribute to debate and development must consider their stance on key issues before setting foot into the marketplace. Since research is a competitive arena in itself, with the payoff being the recognition of making a leading contribution to understanding, those researchers into markets and marketing who fail to address the ethical issues raised here may find themselves excluded from substantive future research, and hence losers in the education marketing research marketplace!

Chapter 11

A regrettable oversight or a significant omission?

Ethical considerations in quantitative research in education

Keith Jones

Policy decisions about the teaching of school subjects such as literacy and mathematics are increasingly becoming intensely political. At the centre of these debates are often the findings of quantitative research in education, particularly the results of national and international surveys of pupil achievement. For example, McQuillan (1998) has attempted to debunk what he identifies as common myths about levels of literacy in the United States of America, such as the claim that students in the United States are among the worst readers in the world. In terms of mathematics teaching, Brown (1998) has revealed the manipulation of international comparisons for political ends, particularly the data from the Third International Mathematics and Science Study (TIMSS), a survey which claims to be the largest and most ambitious international comparative study of student achievement yet undertaken. Indeed, the debate about mathematics teaching in the United States has come to be dubbed the 'Math Wars'. Such has been the ferocity of these 'Math Wars' that the US Secretary of Education has requested a 'cease-fire', saying that there is a need

> to bring an end to the shortsighted, politicized, and harmful bickering over the teaching and learning of mathematics. I will tell you that if we continue down this road of infighting, we will only negate the gains we have already made – and the real losers will be the students of America.
>
> (Riley 1998)

These are strong words and convey a clear message. It seems that some of the fallout from the TIMSS study, and similarly, perhaps, from studies of literacy standards, could be harming the educational chances of some of the very students the studies sought to benefit. This goes to the heart of ethical issues in educational research, whether quantitative or qualitative. Yet in examining, for instance, the TIMSS technical reports (Martin and Kelly 1996, 1997), the TIMSS Quality Assurance in Data Collection report (Martin and Mullis 1996) and the monograph detailing the research questions and the study design (Robitaille and Garden 1996), there appears to be no explicit consideration of ethical issues. The question this chapter addresses is how the treatment of ethical concerns within the field of quantitative research is constructed and practised, and whether this apparent lack of attention to research ethics is a regrettable oversight or a significant omission.

The chapter begins by reviewing a range of standard texts on quantitative research in education, to show the consideration such texts give to ethical issues in the research process. This is followed by a review of the key ethical considerations inherent in quantitative approaches to educational research. Finally, this range of issues is used to examine a number of reports of quantitative-based research in education, including research on gender differences in achievement, teaching methods, intelligence testing and school effectiveness. The overall aim of the chapter is to reveal the situated nature of research ethics and how they are practised in quantitative research in the field of education.

ETHICAL CONSIDERATIONS IN RESEARCH TEXTS IN EDUCATION AND THE SOCIAL SCIENCES

There is no doubt that an awareness of ethical issues within educational research has grown in recent years, and this is reflected in the prominence given to such concerns within standard texts on educational research methods (for a review see Dockrell 1988). For example, in her book *Research Methods in Education and Psychology*, Mertens places ethical considerations in chapter 1, suggesting that such issues are 'an integral part of the research planning and implementation process, not viewed as an afterthought or a burden' (Mertens 1998: 23). While such contemporary general texts address ethical issues in the research process, the situation is quite different if we turn to texts that contain a reference to statistics in their title. For example, none of the following popular texts has any explicit mention of ethics even in its index:

Agresti and Finlay, *Statistical Methods for the Social Sciences* (Agresti and Finlay 1997, 3rd edition)
Glass and Hopkins, *Statistical Methods in Education and Psychology* (Glass and Hopkins 1996, 3rd edition)
Healey, *Statistics: A Tool for Social Research* (Healey 1996, 4th edition)
Howell, *Statistical Methods for Psychology* (Howell 1997, 4th edition)
Pagano, *Understanding Statistics in the Behavioral Sciences* (Pagano 1994, 4th edition)

Of course, these are revised editions of earlier texts, and so ethical issues might not yet have emerged at the time earlier editions were written. Yet even newly published texts on research methods in the social sciences that contain a reference to statistics in their title have no explicit mention of ethics even in their indexes. Some examples are:

Bartholomew, *The Statistical Approach to Social Measurement* (Bartholomew 1996)
Hinton, *Statistics Explained: A Guide for Social Science Students* (Hinton 1995)
Peers, *Statistical Analysis for Education and Psychology* (Peers 1996)
Plewis, *Statistics in Education* (Plewis 1997)

The only book on research methods in the social sciences, as revealed by the small-scale survey carried out in preparation for this chapter, that has statistics in its title and that explicitly mentions ethical issues seems to be Coolican's *Research Methods and Statistics in Psychology* (1994). Even then, the coverage of ethical issues is within the last chapter and is more concerned with general issues, such as confidentiality, deception, stress and discomfort, than with the particular consideration of statistical techniques.

Where texts are designed to promote particular quantitative approaches to educational research, such as Neuman and McCormick's *Single-Subject Experimental Research: Applications for Literacy* (1995), explicit ethical considerations are again notable by their absence. Furthermore, in Creswell's general text on qualitative and quantitative approaches to research design, the only mention of research ethics in the index is for 'ethical issues in qualitative study' (Creswell 1994: 148).

In contrast to this situation in educational research, practice in other fields employing quantitative research methods is gradually being informed by ethical considerations given to statistical approaches. An example from medicine is Kadane's *Bayesian Methods and Ethics in Clinical Trial Design* (1996), which presents a methodology for clinical trials that claims to accommodate both ethical and scientific imperatives.

The above review, though based only on a small-scale survey, appears to reveal that while contemporary general texts on educational research methods explicitly address ethical issues, such considerations do not extend to texts that cover statistical procedures. Of course, no text can cover everything, yet the contrast in coverage revealed here is quite striking. It also accords with the apparent omission of explicit ethical considerations within the TIMSS study. This evidence suggests that while texts on statistical techniques employed in quantitative research in education usually emphasize the importance of using such approaches appropriately, they do not devote much space to discussing what 'appropriate' means. Such a discussion would entail a consideration of 'appropriate for whom', who gets to benefit, and the potential utility and consequences of the findings or of the results. The implication is that the use of such quantitative techniques is possibly seen as ethically neutral, and so an ethical consideration of them can be omitted.

The purpose of this section is not to repeat the debate about the appropriateness of quantitative approaches to educational research at the general level. Such issues are more than adequately dealt with elsewhere (for example in chapter 9 of Hammersley 1992, or, in relation to research ethics, in Sammons 1989). Rather, the aim here is to reveal how, in the practice of quantitative research in education, ethical issues are located in the practice of such research. After all, quantitative approaches account for a sizeable proportion of published research in education. For example, an analysis of 2,882 published education research articles showed that a third of them could be classified as quantitative (Weiner 1998).

Such articles of the type identified by Weiner provide the empirical site for an examination of what situated ethics means within quantitative research in education and how ethics work in practice. What the articles do not necessarily do is provide the framework for revealing their ethical practices.

ETHICAL CONSIDERATIONS IN CONDUCTING AND REPORTING QUANTITATIVE RESEARCH IN EDUCATION

Sackett (1979) identified fifty-six possible 'biases' that may arise in what he refers to as 'analytic research'. Over two-thirds of these biases relate to aspects of study design and execution.

Table 11.1 Sites of possible bias in the research process

Stage in research process	Number of possible biases
Planning	5
Design	22
Execution/data collection	18
Data processing	–
Data analysis	5
Presentation	–
Interpretation	6
Publication	–

Source: Data from Sackett (1979) as displayed by Altman (1980), reproduced by kind permission of the *British Medical Journal*.

Altman reveals, in a series of articles published in the early 1980s in the *British Medical Journal* (Altman 1980, 1981), that the distribution of 'biases' suggested by Sackett reflects, to a close degree, the relative seriousness of statistical errors at each stage of the research process, and indicates where there is greatest need for statistical expertise: in the design of quantitative research. Errors in analysis or interpretation can usually be rectified, if detected in time (for example, before publication), but deficiencies in design are nearly always irremediable. Altman reports that various analyses of quantitative-based articles published in medical journals during the 1970s found that between 44 per cent and 72 per cent of such articles had statistical errors or important errors of omission (Altman 1981: 45). Such errors impact on people, both those who are subjects and those affected as a outcome of the research. No wonder that Altman demonstrates, and the medical profession concludes, that the misuse of statistics is unethical.

The review that follows of the ethical issues pertinent at each stage of the quantitative research process is informed by the 'Declaration on Professional Ethics' of the International Statistical Institute (1986), which, among other things, advises that quantitative researchers and statisticians

- should consider the likely consequences of collecting and disseminating various types of data and should guard against predictable misinterpretations or misuse;
- should not exaggerate the accuracy or explanatory power of their data;
- should alert potential users of their data to the limits of their reliability and applicability.

This review is also informed by the *Ethical Guidelines for Statistical Practice* of the American Statistical Association (1998), which states that quantitative researchers and statisticians should

- present their findings and interpretations honestly and objectively;
- avoid untrue, deceptive or undocumented statements;
- collect only the data needed for the purpose of their enquiry;
- be prepared to document data sources used in an enquiry; known inaccuracies in the data; and steps taken to correct or to refine the data, statistical procedures applied to the data, and the assumptions required for their application.

Further issues of ethical concern are taken from articles by Altman (1980, 1981), Herrera (1996), Krenz and Sax (1986), Kromrey (1993), Sammons (1989) and Sax (1986). The following sections cover the main categories of ethical consideration in the process of conducting and reporting quantitative research in education.

Research design and sampling

Research design encompasses all the structural aspects of a study. In quantitative research in particular, this can include the nature of the study sample, the sample size, the type of statistical design, the form of quantification employed, and so on. The stage is quite critical to the success of a research study as no amount of sophisticated analysis will later be able to compensate for major design flaws. The major areas of ethical concern at this stage are defining those who are eligible to be studied, and ensuring randomization. In the latter case, the main ethical problem arises when attempting to balance the welfare of those being studied against potential benefit for them or future groups.

A crucial aspect of quantitative research design is the process of quantifying (or measuring) phenomena. The complexities involved in quantification are considerable and can easily be underestimated. Bradley and Schaefer (1998), for example, document the limitations of the process of quantification, including the problems associated with defining variables and with methods of measurement.

In terms of sampling procedure, Altman (1980: 1336) suggests that ethical issues arise in two ways. First, if the sample is too large, this entails the unnecessary involvement of additional people, wasting people's time and causing possible harm through, for instance, unnecessary testing, not to mention incurring additional costs. Second, if too small a sample is chosen, the study may well be unable to detect results of practical importance, and so be a complete waste of time, resources and possibly goodwill. A particular fault in some quantitative research, Altman suggests, is the omission of proper consideration of the statistical power of the test being used, and the lack of use of this in calculating sample size. Such an omission can mean that studies looking for differences can miss effects of practical importance. This may well have different consequences for different groups of people.

Data collection, processing and analysis

When processing data, it is necessary to check that all records of numerical data are within reasonable limits. Particular consideration needs to be given to questions of how to deal with outliers (data values that are very different from virtually all other values), particularly if these are to be excluded from analysis, and when dealing with missing values. Picking and choosing data just to make the results look better is unethical. The removal of any records from the collection of data requires careful thought and justification.

The incorrect analysis of data, Altman (1980) claims, is probably the best-known misuse of statistical methods. Such misuse can apply to most of the standard techniques. For example, with the t-test, problems usually relate to the fact that the data being analysed fail to comply with the assumptions underlying the test: that the two sets of data come from populations that are statistically normal and have the same variance. With the chi-squared test, the problem can be too few observations. Correlations can be spurious, while with tests of significance, which are based on the assumption of joint normality of two variables, a decision has to be made about which variable is independent. In regression, problems have several sources. For instance, the underlying assumption is that the dependent variable is normally distributed with the same variance for each value of the independent variable. Problems with regression also come from making predictions outside the known range (this is referred to as extrapolation), with linear regression applied to non-linear data, and with the use of simple regression rather than analysis of variance. The ethical impact of any of these misuses of quantitative procedures can be to exaggerate the accuracy or explanatory power of the data, or even to derive conclusions that are deceptive or untrue.

Ethical issues also arise when selecting which data to analyse. The basic principle should be to analyse according to the original design. Other results that look as though they may be interesting should really be used only as pointers to further research. The situation is different in some qualitative research, where the data collected may be rich enough to allow unexpected outcomes to be investigated with confidence and integrity. The nature of quantitative research, however, is such that the measures employed may have been designed for quite specific purposes, with the consequence that it is unlikely to be appropriate to use them for purposes other than those for which they were designed.

Data presentation and interpretation

The presentation of data and results is open to unethical practice in at least two ways. For example, well-known instances when care is needed include the choice of scale for graphs, and adding a regression line to scattergraphs for no legitimate reason. Quantitative indicators also need to be used in an ethical manner. An example might be choosing to quote the standard error of the mean as a measure of variability, rather than the variance, just because the standard error is always much smaller.

It is ethically (and vitally) important that valid interpretation is presented of the results of any study, since misleading conclusions can falsely influence practice and further research. For, example, assuming causal relationships can be tempting, even in the absence of any supporting evidence. Yet many associations are not causal; and misleading associations can occur when each variable is actually correlated with a third, 'hidden' variable.

As is the case with a number of terms used in quantitative research, the term 'significant' is perhaps an ill-chosen one. By definition, one in twenty comparisons of equally effective treatments will, in the long run, be 'significant' at the 5 per cent level. So, accepting all statistically significant results as 'real' is quite unwise. While the issues of ethical concern raised above may appear to be of a technical nature, quantitative-based research in education has had, and continues to have, a considerable impact on both policy and practice.

ETHICAL ISSUES IN REPORTS OF QUANTITATIVE-BASED RESEARCH IN EDUCATION

The ethical guidelines of research associations usually include statements of the form 'educational researchers should aim to avoid ... misrepresentation of evidence, data, findings, or conclusions' (British Educational Research Association 1992). In terms of quantitative research, the declaration on professional ethics by the International Statistical Institute (ISI 1986) states that

> one of the most important but difficult responsibilities of the statistician is that of alerting potential users of their data to the limits of their reliability and applicability. The twin dangers of either overstating or understating the validity or generalisability of data are nearly always present. No general guidelines can be drawn except for a counsel of caution. Confidence in statistical findings depends critically on their faithful representation. Attempts by statisticians to cover up errors (see Ryten 1981), or to invite over-interpretation, may not only rebound on the statisticians concerned but also on the reputation of statistics in general.

In this section, the range of issues identified in the previous section concerning quantitative research is used to examine a number of reports of quantitative-based research in education. These examples comprise research on intelligence and schooling, gender differences in achievement, teaching methods and school effectiveness. A return will also be made to research on international comparisons. These examples have been chosen because of their impact on educational policy and practice. Through such examples, the intention is to reveal the situated nature of ethical principles in the practice of quantitative research in education.

Intelligence and schooling

No study of the ethics of quantitative research in education could be complete without some mention of the mountain of research carried out into the study of intelligence and schooling. Indeed, the study of intelligence has been intimately involved with the development of statistical techniques. Unfortunately, one of the most infamous cases of fraud accusation has also occurred within research on intelligence. This is the case of the work of the eminent educational psychologist Sir Cyril Burt, who, after his death, was claimed to have 'faked' at least some of his data. Such accusations have been rebutted by others. For a full discussion of the case see, for example, MacKintosh (1995).

Research in intelligence and schooling continues to court controversy. When it was first published in 1994, Herrnstein and Murray's book *The Bell Curve* sparked intense public debate. The book claims that it is intelligence levels, not lack of education, environmental circumstances or poverty, that are at the root of many social problems, and that race–ethnicity and social class differences in intelligence are for the most part determined hereditarily. Such claims of genetic inferiority of certain ethnic and social groups set off what has been called a 'firestorm' of controversy about the assertions, methodology and conclusions of the book. It became a best-seller, selling out its first print run of 125,000 copies.

In their book Herrnstein and Murray make extensive use of statistical analyses to support their position. A number of texts (for example, Devlin 1997; Fischer 1996; Fraser 1995; Kincheloe 1996) provide critical examination of many of the statistical and measurement aspects of *The Bell Curve*, raising concerns about, for instance, the appropriateness of the causal inferences, aspects of model specification (most notably the absence of measures of education from the models), model fit, and the validity of IQ and socioeconomic status measures.

Particular problems have been identified with Herrnstein and Murray's repeated misuse of the concept of heritability as if it were an absolute number (for instance, when they 'estimate' that the heritability of IQ is about 60 per cent). It is, in fact, meaningless to talk about heritability as if it were a number; heritability is defined as a ratio (the ratio of genetically determined variance in a population to the total variance). On top of that, Herrnstein and Murray then use measures of heritability *within* groups to make assertions regarding the differences *between* groups. Herrnstein and Murray also present regression curves but do not show the scatter of variation around the curves, an essential element of proper statistical presentation. This means that the graphs do not show anything about the strength of the relationships between variables.

Most education researchers would consider education to be an intervening variable in the chain that runs from child background to adult outcomes. Yet Herrnstein and Murray omit any measure of education as a conditioning variable in their basic analysis. On pages 124–5, for instance, they write that 'the role of education versus IQ as calculated by a regression equation is tricky to interpret'. Yet considerable research (documented in

Devlin 1997; Kincheloe 1996) points to the fact that education makes a profound difference in attainment such that when students have equal access to high-quality curricula, teachers and school resources, disparities in achievement narrow sharply.

In medical research and in the professional practice of statisticians, consideration of research ethics extends to the design and analysis of research studies. In 'research' such as that by Herrnstein and Murray, such considerations are notable by their absence. The emphasis that Herrnstein and Murray place on differences, and their attempt to argue that such differences are due to hereditary factors, has played a part in education research into gender differences in education outcomes. It is to this topic that I turn next.

Research on gender differences in achievement

There is a substantial body of educational research into gender differences in achievement. While some early research (around the turn of the twentieth century) now appears to have been designed solely to demonstrate an apparent intellectual inferiority of women compared to men, the consensus from some current research (for a recent review see Arnot 1998) seems to be that females have a slight advantage on average in verbal and literary abilities and males have a slight advantage on average in mathematics, and perhaps science. This has led to recent interest in the apparent relative low achievement of boys in language and literacy. The apparent relative low achievement of girls in mathematics continues to be a focus for research (see, for example, the special edition of *Educational Researcher*, June–July 1998), with the differential effects of socialization being seen as the causal factor (for example, see Campbell and Beaudry 1998). Yet such research, in that it frequently uses so-called standardized tests to measure achievement, may often have what Walden and Walkerdine (1985: 23) call 'hidden problems'. Indeed, MacIntyre (1997) refers to this area of work as 'a minefield of research issues' because of its 'politicisation, the proliferation of studies without adequate methodologies, and a number of biases'.

Recent analyses reveal that not only are gender differences in the means and variances of achievement scores very small, but they are of only minor practical significance (Tate 1997; Nowell and Hedges 1998). As Walden and Walkerdine (1985) explain, the focus on gender differences, usually differences that can be quantified and then stated to be real using statistical techniques, has two important consequences. First, similarities are treated as failures to show differences and hence become non-results. Yet similarities may be of more practical importance than differences. Second, such research can tend to emphasize even trivial differences. In large-scale surveys, for example, the close link between sample size and statistical power (the probability that a statistical test will detect a difference) means that trivially small differences can emerge as statistically highly significant. The practical significance of such differences may as a result be over-emphasized.

While it might suit some to continue to emphasize the apparent low achievement of girls in mathematics, or to demand more resources for boys in literacy, better theoretically informed and more methodologically sound research is needed, particularly if it can inform policy decisions. As noted by MacIntyre in a phrase already quoted, the 'proliferation of studies without adequate methodologies' appears to indicate the omission of any proper consideration of the main categories of ethical consideration in the process of conducting and reporting quantitative research in education.

Teaching methods

The ways in which the actions of the teacher impact on the learning of the students in their class are reasonably well documented, at least in general terms (see Brophy 1986 or Sylva 1994 for reviews). One study that made a substantial impact at the time is that by Bennett and colleagues into the relationship between teaching styles and pupil progress (Bennett 1976). This study claimed to show that pupils taught in a 'traditional way' as a whole class made significantly more progress than pupils taught using 'progressive' teaching methods. It may be that the study continues to influence policy in education, given that an expectation of whole-class teaching has recently emerged in the United Kingdom in advice from government and school inspection officials (and see Francis and Grindle 1998). Indeed, this re-emphasis on 'traditional' teaching may well be another consequence of the United Kingdom's apparently poor performance in international comparisons such as TIMSS, mentioned at the start of this chapter. Yet Bennett and colleagues subsequently reanalysed their data (following critiques by, for instance, Gray and Satterly 1976) and completely changed their conclusions, indicating instead that the 'significance of the differences was reduced' (Aitken *et al.* 1981). This re-evaluation of the findings is summarized by Gray and Satterly (1981) as follows:

- Differences between teachers within teaching styles were far greater than differences between styles.
- Differences between teaching styles were so small as to be overwhelmed by differences between other systematic effects.
- The direction of differences between styles did not consistently favour one style over another.

The original publication by Bennett caused a media storm and is said to have sold more than 10,000 copies on the first day of UK sale alone (Shipman 1997: 31), something relatively unusual for a book reporting education research. However, it was not primarily a research report. It was written in a non-technical style and presented as if in an attempt to resolve a popular controversy (McIntyre 1976). For a piece of quantitative research, the criticism of its use of statistical techniques was wide-ranging, although probably the most telling was for its use of analysis of covariance rather than, for instance, multiple regression, a technique which, by comparison, leads to more ambiguous results. The riposte from Bennett (Bennett and Entwistle 1977) was that at the time of the research there was no consensus concerning the most appropriate statistical analysis, and that they had received conflicting advice from statisticians. Bennett's later reanalysis (Aitken *et al.* 1981), which appeared in a scholarly journal without the publicity that surrounded the original publication, was prompted by the 'rapid developments in the statistical methods available for the analysis of complex data'. As Shipman (1997: 31) remarks, the most significant findings of the reanalysis were 'the recognition of the difficulties in defining teaching styles and establishing how they were linked to pupil progress'.

While Bennett's work was carried out over twenty years ago, research into school (and teacher) effectiveness has been a characteristic of much recent education research, usually taking a quantitative approach. It is to that research I turn next.

Research into 'school effectiveness'

In recent years research into 'school effectiveness' has come to have a profound influence on education policy in many countries. Yet Slee and Weiner (1998: 2) argue that, while the aim that all schools should be as effective as possible seems to be common-sense, 'school effectiveness' is, in their view, 'epistemologically problematic and politically promiscuous and malleable'. They claim that 'while purporting to be inclusive and comprehensive, school effectiveness research is riddled with errors' (p. 5). They suggest that school effectiveness research is discriminatory in excluding 'children with special needs, black boys, so-called clever girls', is normative and regulatory by operating mainly within narrow sets of (quantifiable) performance indicators, and is bureaucratic and disempowering.

As Goldstein (1997) explains, 'school effectiveness' has come to describe educational research concerned with exploring differences within and between schools. Much effort in 'school effectiveness' research has gone into developing 'performance indicators', yet difficulties associated with performance indicators are well known. Goldstein suggests that such difficulties are twofold. First, the use of performance indicators tends to be very narrowly focused on the task of *ranking* schools rather than on that of establishing factors which could *explain* school differences. Second, as Goldstein relates, a number of studies have now demonstrated that there are serious and *inherent* limitations to the usefulness of such performance indicators for providing reliable judgements about institutions. Goldstein maintains that much of the existing school effectiveness research is methodologically weak, so that strong conclusions about why schools become 'effective' or, conversely, 'fail' are difficult to sustain.

A number of the methodological weaknesses with school effectiveness research are described by Rowe and Hill (1995). They point to the failure of many studies to account for the inherently hierarchical or multilevel sampling structure of the data. Clustering poses special problems such as aggregation bias, undetected heterogeneity of regression, misestimated parameter estimates, and so on. Such problems lead to an increased probability of making Type 1 errors, falsely rejecting the null hypothesis in tests of statistical significance. Rowe and Hill point to a crucial requirement in quantitative research, that of ensuring that the statistical models used are commensurate with the sampling structure of the data to which the models are applied.

The work of Goldstein and others suggests that, even with the use of the best currently available statistical techniques, most classes and schools cannot be reliably separated for purposes of comparison. Yet the publication of lists of 'effective schools' and 'failing schools' continues, with such publication being either seriously misleading or potentially harmful. As a result, Goldstein and Myers (1996) have proposed the development of a code of ethics for performance indicators. The aims of such a code would be to combine avoidance of unwarranted harm, a core ethical issue, with the right to information.

International comparisons of educational achievement

In this section I return, briefly, to the issue of international comparisons of educational achievement with which we began this chapter. As in the case of school effectiveness research, Brown (1998: 33) argues that 'the information in international league tables is often too technically flawed to serve as an accurate measure of national effectiveness'. Brown also illustrates how recent events have demonstrated how international comparisons have been manipulated for political ends. For example, the results of the Third International Mathematics and Science Study (TIMSS) assessment of the performance of 13-year-olds in mathematics and science were known in May 1996, but a delay in the publication until November 1996 was agreed internationally so that it did not affect the outcome of the American presidential elections due to take place in the first week of November that year. One country broke the internationally agreed embargo, the United Kingdom. The reason, according to Brown, was that UK government ministers wanted to announce, in June 1996, the inclusion of mental arithmetic and no-calculator papers in UK national tests at 11 and 14. Unfavourable international comparisons appeared to provide a legitimate reason for doing so.

The methodological weaknesses in international comparisons include recurring problems with the definition of the sample, curriculum match, the development of suitable tests and the forms of reporting. As Brown concludes, international comparisons 'have been seized on as providing a perfect justification of whatever moves government, the media, or others have decided need immediate implementation'. In a similar vein, Keitel and Kilpatrick (1999: 254) argue that 'TIMSS threatens to poison for some time the waters of educational policy, as politicians and researchers scramble to take advantage of what TIMSS allegedly says about teaching and learning mathematics in their country'. They suggest that unwarranted inferences are being made concerning the link between selected views of teaching and fallible indicators of performance. They conclude that studies such as TIMSS 'rest on the shakiest of foundations ... [and] assume that the mantel of science can cover all the weaknesses in design, incongruous data and errors of interpretation'. As noted earlier, methodological weaknesses can appear to be solely a technical issue, yet following TIMSS there has been intense policy activity in a number of countries which could be harming different groups of pupils and their life chances.

FINAL COMMENTS

What all the above studies in quantitative research in education demon-strate is the complex and subtle nature of ethical issues encountered in educational research (see Cohen and Manion 1994: 347ff.). The strength of quantitative approaches to research in education lies in the clarity and rigour of the standard procedures, the clear definitions and control of vari-ables, the opportunity for replications and comparison across different studies and sites. However, one of the weaknesses of quantitative approaches is that they cannot reveal deep meanings or, as yet, cope with the full complexity of teaching and learning in all its settings. Even in qualitative research, the concept of arriving at external 'truths' has come under intense scrutiny as interest has grown in the situated nature of meanings and inter-pretations of events that are given by the participants in the research context. The consideration given to the particular studies chosen in the previous section is not meant to demonstrate that ethical guidelines were deliberately flouted in carrying out the research. Rather, as Vaughn and Lyon (1994) suggest, 'the overriding question ... is at what point does the researcher go astray to such a marked degree that the ethics of his/her research procedures and findings are in question?'.

All information, whether systematically collected or not, is subject to misuse. No information is devoid of possible harm to one interest or another. Researchers are not, in general, in a position to prevent action based on interpretations of their data. Indeed, to guard against the use of their findings would be to disparage the very purpose of much educational inquiry, which is to improve public discourse and understanding. Quantitative research in education is seductive in its claim to objectivity, clarity and rigour of established procedures, and techniques to manipulate large samples and a wide range of variables. With such a methodology it is perhaps easy to see how ethical issues may be buried. Yet in some fields – in medical research and in the work of professional statisticians, for example – what appear to be technical issues of design, analysis and presentation are considered to have important ethical dimensions. The lack of an explicit consideration of ethical issues in quantitative research in education may once have seemed like a regrettable oversight (Cohen and Manion 1994: xxi). Currently, it looks more like a significant omission.

Chapter 12

Deconstructive happening, ethical moment

Robin Usher

In this chapter I will attempt to argue that there is an ethical moment in the research process, an immanent ethics that is not purely a function of the application of ethical codes of practice and ethical 'principles' for the doing of research. These codes and principles have their place but that place is in the domain of method. My concern rather is with the condition of possibility of that domain; what, in other words, *precedes* method – a condition of possibility which, I shall argue, is the immanent ethical moment in the research process. I shall further argue that deconstruction, or the deconstructive happening, reveals that moment because deconstruction *is* an ethics – albeit not an ethics as ethics would be conventionally understood (which itself is an aspect of the problematic that informs my argument). I shall therefore first discuss deconstruction in terms of presenting an attempt to explicate some relevant concepts drawn from the complex work of Jacques Derrida, its most famous (and perhaps notorious) exponent. This will be followed by two examples of research texts which embody deconstructive readings, where I shall show how deconstruction works in order to introduce my argument about the immanent ethical moment in the research process. The final part of the chapter will then attempt to explicate more fully what I mean by this, and will 'dip into' the work of Emmanuel Levinas as a crucial point of departure for my argument. I will end with some thoughts about rethinking the research process anew in the light of this notion of an immanent ethical moment.

BOUNDARIES AND CERTAINTIES

> Derrida's philosophy is one of a contingent world and contingent knowledge; one in which the dividing line between the world and knowledge is no longer clear or wished to be clear. With that dividing line go all other sacred boundaries.
>
> (Bauman 1992: 130)

The setting of boundaries and the fixing of what legitimately falls within those boundaries, and thus what must be excluded, is perhaps one of the most fundamental aspects of Western thought. Derrida refers to this as 'logocentrism'. This logocentrism is the basis of a totalizing impulse which reduces heterogeneity to homogeneity, difference to an economy of the same, the contingent to the determinate, and the flux to the stable and the given. In particular, this impulse takes the form of an attempt to enclose and 'master' language, a closure of the disseminative power of language or the inherent tendency of signs to refer to other signs *ad infinitum*. But as Lemert (1997: 106) points out:

> Language is that one social thing that, when it is made the centre of things, disrupts everything, including the possibility of a centre of things . . . when language is taken seriously for what it is . . . it is no longer possible to view the world as internally and necessarily coherent. To take language seriously . . . is to decentre the world, to eviscerate it of grand organising principles (God, natural law, truth, beauty, subjectivity, Man, etc.) that mask the most fundamental truth of human life, differences.

By questioning logocentrism and foregrounding the place of language as a signifying system that works through difference and absence, Derrida, the coiner of the term 'deconstruction', thus challenges the very activity of boundary setting and excluding.

Logocentrism implies that interpretation, the finding of meaning, is about finding the source, origin or centre that brings interpretation to an end – that which absolutely is and which provides the one definitive and final meaning of a text. Derrida on the contrary argues that interpretation is not about finding a source or origin which ends interpretation since what is at work in texts is a logic of supplementarity rather than a logic of closure – a logic which makes the task of interpretation that of creating another text in a process which is potentially infinite. In effect, there is potentially no end to interpretation, no limit to ways in which texts can be read and thus no 'natural' and necessary boundaries (i.e. boundaries found in nature rather than culture) which can necessarily define and exclude. It is not therefore a matter of finding a foundation in a definitive or final meaning but, by remaining open to the disseminative power and multiple meanings of a text, a matter of recognizing the absence of any such foundation.

Derrida sees this refusal of language as a particular kind of metaphysics, a metaphysics of 'presence'. By this he means to refer to the notion of a grounding or foundation for theories, knowledge and truth in some ultimate reality or 'presence' which is independent of beliefs, culture, values and language. It is the philosophical habit of thinking 'transcendentally', where meaning is seen as residing in a presence or centre outside language, in that which absolutely is, that which makes the final determination (or closure) of meaning possible. This is what we seek to discover when we engage in empirical research and analytic argument. It is the desire and search for certainty or an authorizing centre, which will fix or ground explanations.

The logic of supplementarity ensures that this is an endless search with a never-ending substitution of transcendental signifieds (meanings that can be fixed, thus avoiding the disseminative play of language) where permanent hierarchies and rigid boundaries are erected in a continual attempt to halt the play of difference and institute the fixity and permanence of the one and the self-same. Derrida refers to this process as a 'violence' and characterizes in this way the epistemological knowing of the world, the powerful interpretations that as networks of organized (and thus closed) meaning work through exerting a coercive force.

BINARIES AND HIERARCHIES

Logocentrism involves a process where concepts or terms gain meaning by being linked together in terms of binary opposites. Although these opposites are supposed to be equal pairs, one of the terms in the binary is always privileged; it becomes the positive defining term, with the other term defined negatively in relation to it, i.e. as lacking in the positive attributes possessed by the first term – or to put it another way, it becomes the Other of the defining term. These positive attributes mean that the latter is always associated with that which is 'natural', an origin, source or centre (and therefore outside signification). Thus the organization of meaning in terms of binary oppositions is always a process of positing a centre and, through that, a margin or a marginalization – or in effect, an exclusion. Derrida argues that the prime or 'founding' binary is that of speech/writing. Perhaps more than any other it exemplifies the hierarchical structure and 'violent' structuring effects of binaries. Furthermore, the deconstructive displacement of this binary opens the way for the displacement of all the others and indeed for a challenging of the fundamental categories and impulses of Western thought and philosophy.

Speech has been privileged over writing, in Western philosophy at least, on the grounds that because it is not mediated, meaning is immediate to it. Here we see how the metaphysics of presence works through hierarchical binary oppositions. Speech has been constructed as a 'natural' medium – the notion that in speaking I am 'present' in a direct way to myself. We seem in speech to be putting our very thoughts into words, filling them with meaning, and as we hear ourselves speak we seem to be hearing our thoughts – hence the idea that in speech we are present to ourselves. This primacy accorded to speech is linked to epistemological or foundational notions of knowledge. Knowledge of reality is founded on the idea of truth as a presence that is revealed by speech because the latter is directly present to thought. As Mourad (1997) points out, this is exemplified in the notion that to know the truth is to *speak* the truth – with the emphasis on the speaking.

Derrida argues that there is no such thing as 'self-present' speech and so any privileging of speech over writing collapses. When we speak, it is our words which have been put into thoughts. We must depend on meanings given by language, and it is the pre-existence of language as a signifying system that fills our thoughts with meanings. Because thoughts are 'always already' in language, since it is impossible to escape the mediation and play of language, it is impossible to be fully present to oneself. Furthermore, writing is more than a poor graphic substitute for speech. If we think of writing as more than simply marks on paper but rather as *all that gives rise to inscription*, then writing in this sense subsumes speech.

If writing is inscription, then speech is made possible by writing. The idea that speech is unmediated and thus closer to the originating thoughts in the mind or to the truth of reality is itself presupposed and produced by writing. For Derrida all thought, expression and indeed language is 'always already' inscription; there is no 'before', an origin or pure presence that precedes inscription. In other words, speech is itself inscribed. Thus the notion of knowledge as foundational self-presence – as that which signifies what is essentially present to a methodologically primed knower (the 'scientific' researcher) – is undermined by the 'always' already' of writing. The notion that there is presence in the form of something which is not signification but is an 'authentic' and unmediated grasp of reality becomes highly problematic. What this implies therefore is that signification as an act of naming (knowing) reality is a cultural activity, 'made up', as it were, not a natural necessity, a reflection in the mind of things as they really are.

This also implies that the binary oppositions by which we 'know' and think are not 'natural' or essential and thus their maintenance in the form of privileging hierarchies does not reflect hierarchies already existing naturally but is itself an act of power. Indeed, one could go further and argue that 'violence' in this sense is not a special effect but intrinsic to acts of naming, classifying, dividing, marking of spaces and limits and outlining borders (Lucy 1995: 6–7). Given that the disciplines of the social sciences work in this way, they are themselves not simply bodies of knowledge reflecting the world but knowledges intimately implicated with power – in other words, as Foucault (1980) would put it, they are power–knowledge formations where power is always present in the act of epistemological knowing, Indeed, that power works its effects precisely through its intimate interconnection with knowledge. Research as an activity of knowledge production therefore can be seen as both an enactment of power relations between researchers and the world and an enactment of power relations between researchers and researched. After all, who does the interpreting, who are the sense-makers, who decides what the 'data' mean, who is naming, classifying and putting down limits? Research in the scientific mode denies that these are valid questions, indeed denies the place of values and power, but in this very refusal there is an implicit location of research in a metaphysics of presence.

WRITING AND THE GENERAL TEXT

> If writing is no longer understood in the narrow sense of linear and phonetic notation, it should be possible to say that all societies capable of producing and of bringing classificatory differences into play practice writing in general.
>
> (Derrida 1976: 109)

> It is precisely for strategic reasons that I find it necessary to recast the concept of the text by generalising it almost without limit . . . that's why there is nothing beyond the text. That's why South Africa and apartheid are like you and me part of this general text which is not to say that it can be read as one reads a book. That's why the text is always a field of forces; heterogeneous, differential, open. That's why deconstructive readings are concerned not only with library books . . . they are not simply analyses of discourse. They are also effective or active interventions that transform contexts without limiting themselves to theoretical utterances even though they must also produce such utterances.
>
> (Derrida 1982: 167–8)

When Derrida speaks of 'writing', therefore, he does not mean empirical writing, written marks on a page. Least of all does he equate writing to books or the written down. Equally, when he speaks of 'text' he does not simply mean the written text. Derrida sometimes refers to 'arche-writing', by which he means that which is always already codified through inscription: the system of cultural signs and classifications by which speech as well as empirical writing is determined; the 'limitless network of differentially ordered signs which is not preceded by any meaning or structure but itself constitutes each of these' (Critchley 1992: 38). As the quotation above indicates, for Derrida 'writing' is society's classificatory practices – preceding 'society' but presupposing the social. Culture is therefore a cultural production, a writing itself always 'written' in the sense that there is no precultural or pre-inscribed 'reality' which culture simply and transparently represents.

As we noted earlier, the significance of 'writing' lies not in its empirical sense but in the wider sense of *inscription* and its relationship to knowledge of reality. Since all knowledge is a product of culture and hence 'made up', it must be articulated and recorded in some way: 'everything we know is written or, more accurately, writing produces all our knowledge' (Leitch 1996: 76). Inscription is not just a matter of making marks on paper but the opening up of spaces and the marking of differences (Derrida 1981) – 'the primordial production and recording of all differences, spaces and traces' (Leitch 1996: 28). As Leitch goes on to point out, to recognize the significance of inscription and hence of writing is to foreground relationality and movement, to come to see the world not as a set of lawfully interacting substances and objects but as a contingent and constructed text, open to multiple readings, and furthermore to see knowledge as denatured, historicized, a product of human activity: 'Knowledge in its past and present formations and branches could have been, and may yet be, constituted in other ways . . . our relation to facts, disciplines, departments, and hierarchies of knowledge is less natural or normal than concocted, and thus alterable' (Leitch 1996: 76).

For Derrida 'writing' is not merely something opposed to speech. It is also a metaphor for the 'written' or structured form of all texts (Wolfreys 1998). Concepts and terms do not have meanings in themselves, woven into their very fabric as it were. They do their work as concepts and terms as effects of writing structures – supplementarily structured by other concepts and terms (hence the reason why there are no origins or essences), their meaning given by their difference from these. The consequence of this is that texts are

> never completely logically coherent or homogeneous, but are in some way marked or traced by what we term alterity or otherness: moments which subvert, contradict the logic, figure, traces, conceptualisations for which we cannot account, which our reading cannot fit in with the overall structure.
>
> (ibid.: 66)

Writing always 'reaches out to "grasp" the experience of another' (Revill 1996: 123). As Standish (1995: 131–2) points out, 'we are always then necessarily implicated in something beyond ourselves'.

I mentioned earlier that when Derrida refers to 'text' he has in mind more than a written text. He argues that any articulable human activity is 'textual'. Everything we understand and articulate about the world is by virtue of that understanding endowed with meaning and therefore becomes 'written' as a text. But this should not be understood as a contemporary version of idealism in the sense of a claim that the world does not exist as anything but a *written* text. As Critchley (1992: 39) points out, 'deconstruction is not bibliophilia'. Derrida explicitly says that 'text' refers to 'history, to the world, to reality, to being' (Derrida 1988: 37) and 'all the structures called "real", "economic", "historical", socio-institutional' (ibid.: 148).

Thus a text is any organized network of meaning, a field of contending differential forces (Leitch 1996) whose characteristic is that it is always interpretable, capable of being read and re-read because it is 'heterogeneous, differential and open' (Derrida 1988: 148). The 'always already' of inscription, of discursive structures and systems of significations, and of institutions generally, is referred to by Derrida as the 'general text'. He argues that it is necessary to generalize the notion of the text in this sense, without limit, so that there is 'nothing beyond the text' (ibid.: 136).

That 'text' encompasses more than the written text also implies that ethics and politics are not ignored. Deconstruction is concerned with the politics of institutions and institutional change, not simply with textual (written text) interpretation, or even more simplistically, with 'word-games'. The 'realities' of ethical and political decisions normally thought of as raising questions only of the 'real world', of institutional structures and power beyond the textual, cannot be separately understood from inscription and the hierarchical binary oppositions of Western thought. Derrida (1992a) argues that institutions, like (or as) texts, are sites within a field of forces and thus open to deconstructive readings. Deconstruction therefore becomes institutional critique. Texts, like institutions, are not 'natural' or value-neutral but an *economy* formed by the network of hierarchies through which meaning is formed and conveyed. Deconstruction subverts the restriction of meaning in texts/institutions, a restriction imposed by binary hierarchies, opening them up to show how meaning is structurally organized and what powerful 'authorizing' function that organization serves. Thus 'to deconstruct concepts is to intervene in institutional networks of language and power' (Leitch 1996: 37). Deconstruction then becomes a way of taking a position.

DECONSTRUCTIVE READINGS

> Deconstruction is the name given simultaneously to the stress created in texts (between what they want to say and what they do say) and to the detection of such gaps. A deconstructive reading attends to the deconstructive processes always occurring in texts and always there waiting to be read.
>
> (Payne 1993: 121)

Deconstruction is very often seen as a method, yet to see it in this way is misleading and unhelpful. In so far as it is possible to describe what it is, the notion that it is a critical reading practice is probably most appropriate. However, even this needs further glossing since deconstruction is not the same as, for example, literary criticism or close textual analysis. It is not just a matter of 'taking a text apart'. While it is that, it is also something

more, or at least it is a particular way or strategy of taking a text apart –
and it is the *strategy* which is the most important aspect here since it is
the peculiar nature of the strategy which makes of deconstruction more
than just a method of taking a text apart.

However, although deconstruction can aptly be characterized as a strategy
for reading texts in a particular way, it is a strategy which works where a
deconstructive process is *already* at work in the text – which is why I refer
to it as a 'deconstructive happening'. As noted in the quotation above,
the deconstructive process is to do with a 'stress' constituted by the difference between what a text wants or means to say and what it actually
says or is constrained to mean. What is produced, then, is an aporia – an
irresolvable difficulty or undecidability where texts subvert or deconstruct
themselves so long as they are read in a particular way. Deconstruction
thus works because of the contradiction between the logocentric closure of
meaning which language itself makes possible and the ultimate impossibility
– again a product of language – of the attempt, in itself an impossible
desire, to make present the permanently elusive.

Parker (1997) lists some principal characteristics of deconstruction as
follows:

- Deconstruction only acts upon texts, but 'text' has to be construed in
  both the narrow and the wide sense discussed earlier.
- As a strategy for analysing texts, deconstruction works within the text's
  own structures of rationality and values in a way that makes the text
  work against itself.
- A deconstructive reading of a text does not result in the construction
  of an alternative stronger or 'truer' text. On the other hand, it is not
  a 'destructive' reading. As a strategy it involves a *double* reading: a
  commentary on the dominant interpretation as well as an analysis of
  the weaknesses of its structuring logic.
- Deconstruction assumes that the linguistic vehicle conveying content
  cannot be taken for granted – that content is not independent of the
  way it is expressed, but rather owes its meaning to the particular
  language and the particular stylistic devices in which it is expressed;
  the said cannot be separated from the saying.

As Parker (ibid.) points out, every text presupposes and expresses its meaning
through some underlying rational framework – a framework enabling arguments to be made, evidence deployed and explanations presented. In a
deconstructive reading no attempt is made to emphasize or privilege a text's
central ideas, its unity or its clarity of meaning. In other words, no attempt
is made to privilege and reinforce the underlying rational framework. Rather
the deconstructive task is to show how the text's unity is fragile, how its
meaning breaks down and how as a text it is constructed through the

suppression or marginalization of unwanted elements – in effect, how a text works through boundary-marking and the 'violence' of marginalizing and excluding, or its implicit metaphysics of presence. Thus what is demonstrated is that any text with an apparently clear and unified meaning, a text which appears to have a mastery of meaning and language, is ultimately based on incoherence and contradiction – in other words, is not masterful at all. Deconstruction turns the underlying rational framework back on itself, showing how it fails to meet its own implied standards of rationality. So the concern is not with the truth of a text but rather with the way it *fails* as a text through the irrationality of its very own rationality. The bringing out of irrationality also shows the text's failure of mastery; although any organized, 'reasoned' argument is obviously an attempt to gain understanding, it is also – and this is less obvious – 'an attempt at mastery and control . . . the writing therefore commits violence upon that which it purports to celebrate' (Revill 1996: 123). Thus the deconstructive happening marks the attempt at mastery – and its failure.

Deconstruction emphasizes the metaphorical nature of texts – not just literary texts but all texts. Indeed, Parker argues that metaphoricity can itself be seen as a metaphor for the uncertainty and indeterminacy of meaning that all texts are subject to because of their implicit structuring; the privileged terms of binary oppositions are themselves metaphors of origins or essence. It is this which is revealed in the deconstructive happening. The implication, then, for research texts, for example, is that rather than being 'scientific' they can themselves be seen as a species of literature, although their metaphorical nature is always concealed through the use of a narrative realist way of writing that makes them appear to be a transparent and faithful representation of the reality they research, and hence 'scientific'. The task of deconstruction therefore is to see texts as literary but not as literal, instead seeking out the concealed metaphors within which their weaknesses are wrapped.

At this stage I want to emphasize a point whose full significance will become apparent later in this text. As Lather points out, a deconstructive strategy does not aim to govern a practice (or to put it another way, impose a new mastery) but 'to theorise it, deprive it of its innocence, disrupt the ideological effects by which it reproduces itself' (Lather 1991b: 49). In any piece of research, all the questions that are normally asked are to do with the validity of outcomes and methods, but deconstruction, by focusing on research as inscription, as a written text in both the narrow and wide sense, foregrounds the enactment of the social relations of the research process as they are written or inscribed in the text and this in turn enables issues of mastery manifested in questions of scientificity, power relations and researcher subjectivity to be more readily foregrounded. The significance of this, then, is that deconstruction should not be seen as a 'negative' critique; it is certainly a disruption (or more accurately, a displacement), but because it involves a double reading it is a disruption predicated on what it would not be unreasonable to characterize as an 'obligation to listen', itself the mark of the failure of mastery. It is in this sense – and I shall develop this more fully later – that deconstruction can be understood as a *responsiveness* to the Other, to an ethics which is always implied or immanent in the research process.

At this point I want to present and comment on two examples of deconstruction at work in research texts. The first, by Alison Lee (1992), entitled 'Post-structuralism and Educational Research: Some Categories and Issues', is an example of deconstructive research with a focus on gendered classroom practice. The second, by Ian Stronach and Maggie MacLure (1997), entitled 'Mobilising Meaning, Demobilising Critique? Dilemmas in the Deconstruction of Educational Discourse', is an example of the use of deconstruction in policy research and critique.

Commentary on Lee's study

Lee (1992) provides an account of a study of a Year 11 Geography classroom with a focus on the construction of gendered identities and relationships. The study addresses how the gendering process works discursively in a specific site and within an everyday practice found in that site. Beyond this, however, the study also speaks about deconstruction as a theoretical perspective and its relationship to educational research. The problematic here addresses the widely held view that deconstruction has little or no relevance to educational research because it is 'too complicated', 'too theoretical' or does not belong in education (p. 1). The study responds to this concern by *exemplifying* the relevance of a deconstructive approach to educational research.

Several features of the research can be highlighted:

- The use of binaries to investigate sites such as classrooms through a mapping of the classroom and curriculum dynamics (p. 4) – a site of contending differential forces. Here there is a deployment of the Derridean position that meanings are structured in terms of binary opposites.
- The acknowledgement of the active role of the researcher, i.e. the researcher as producer rather than finder of knowledge with the research process seen as one of 'fabrication' rather than discovery. This foregrounds researcher 'interestedness', the selectivity inherent in any research – that what data are collected for determines what data are collected (p. 3).
- The difficulty of specifying knowledge claims in any straightforward way. This is not a fault of the study but a characteristic of deconstructive research, which unlike, for example, empirical-analytic research does not present outcomes in a clear-cut and determinate (i.e. masterful) way.

- The exemplification in the study that human subjects are not autonomous, unified and distinct from the circulating discourses which provide possibilities of meaning for making sense of self and world. They both identify with and are identified by their discursive positioning.

The deconstructive notion of the structuring of meaning in terms of binary opposites plays a central methodological role in this study of the classroom as a site of gender construction. The starting point was the primary binary of 'masculine–feminine', but one outcome of the methods used was the generation of further binaries (pp. 5–6) which provided data for analysis. These are referred to as 'initial points of structural intelligibility' in investigating gender relations. The further binaries generated enabled a mapping of the gender dynamics of the classroom. This mapping presented a picture of 'the day-to-day negotiating of a position in the classroom on the part of teachers and students [as] a function of the complex interconnections among the different binaries elicited' (p. 6).

The study is based on a number of deconstructive assumptions which, although not explicitly stated, can nonetheless be readily discerned:

- It is empirical in the sense that a particular 'slice' of the world is investigated, in this case the everyday practices of the classroom, by means of fieldwork in this site. Data are collected through ethnographic methods and analysed by means of techniques of textual analysis.
- There is a rejection of realism, the notion that the researcher naïvely addresses an independently pre-existing world and simply 'discovers' things about it. Instead, the assumption is that there is no unmediated access to the reality of the world – in other words, that there is no metaphysics of presence.
- There is a foregrounding of the centrality of language and discourse in organizing human experience – in this study the emphasis is on language and discourse, the binary structures through which these work and the production of difference which is their outcome.
- There is a refusal simply to assume the fixed polarities of binary oppositions and to accept their power unproblematically. These oppositions are seen instead as relational and interactive, i.e. gender as a site both of personal identity and of social regulation but where the nature of the relationship takes different forms in the specificity of different sites.
- It is assumed that social action is a complex process of negotiating a way through multiple circulating discourses, all of which produce different possibilities of meaning. Subjects are seen not as unified and whole but as multiple and fragmented.

Commentary on the Stronach and MacLure study

In this study the authors investigate the nature of the relationship between policy, a theoretical explanation of that policy and a deconstruction of that explanation (Stronach and MacLure 1997: 86). In the first part a text is generated about the educational discourse of vocationalism that exemplifies a critical reading. This reading presents a conventional critical analysis of that discourse in terms of a notion of 'policy hysteria'. This is then followed in the next part of the study by a deconstructive reading of that critical analysis.

The authors argue that vocationalist discourse can be understood as a 'space' for a 'mobilisation of meaning' (p. 87), a space where meanings are continually shifting and transformed. This is a space of 'policy hysteria', a notion which is used to explain those features characterizing UK educational policy development in the past ten to fifteen years, features such as recurring and overlapping waves of reforms; multiple and overlapping innovations with no single initiative given enough time to succeed; inconsistent and incoherent policy changes; reforms answering the needs of politics rather than education; scapegoating; contested, shifting and confusing meanings. The speed and overlap of reforms, and the lack of success of any one reform, they argue, has led to an endemic crisis of legitimation with a resulting policy turbulence. Education consequently has been in a state of flux at both curricular and management level, the latter aggravated by the introduction of management ideologies into the professional field of education, an example of the shifting of education out of professional arenas where it was considered closed and élitist.

Having now critically analysed, or in a sense 'constructed', vocationalism in terms of 'policy hysteria', the authors then proceed to deconstruct their own construction. Deconstructively reading their own text, they attempt to show that vocationalist discourse can be read differently, in terms of a reading that deconstructs and challenges their own authorial practices that produced the 'policy hysteria' text. They argue that their critical analysis was an attempt to read vocationalist discourse as changing and shifting, not as static and fixed, a space where different movements of meaning take place. It was also meant to be a pragmatic intervention where through the notion of 'policy hysteria' the irrationality of the seeming rationality of policy and policy analysis could be exposed. Through working inside the terms of the discourse, through an immanent critique, the hope was to destabilize the discourse in its own terms. The deconstructive reading is also a working from inside, an immanent critique that destabilizes the critical text. They argue that the latter attempted to represent vocationalist discourse as a space of movement but succeeded only in arresting that movement and imposing a singular meaning, thereby robbing it of its critical thrust.

The critical analysis argued that vocationalist discourse is implicitly struc-tured through certain binary oppositions – object/space, stasis/movement, stability/instability, certainty/uncertainty – with the left-hand term always privileged over the right. In the critical analysis the strategy was to invert these in order to effect a reversal in the privileging of the left-hand term. But this reversal led only to the dominant hierarchies being reinstated in the text as the organizing principles of the case for policy hysteria, 'behind the backs' of the authors. This happened because the reading of vocation-alism in terms of metaphors of movement concealed a pervasive nostalgia for its very opposite – a nostalgia for stability, order, certainty and the present as reality (p. 90) – the absolutely is. For example:

- The notion of shortening cycles of reform encapsulated two nostalgic appeals: first, the ideal possibility of arresting policy so that it avoids repeating itself; second, in 'speeding up' with its implication of depar-ture from a course of orderly development and consequent loss of control and crisis.
- Multiple innovations constructed vocational space as cluttered and disordered against the ideal of orderly arrangement, with a covert appeal to the possibility of singular and coherent progress.
- Frequent policy switches carried the suggestion of an implicit pathology of movement, a reading of oscillation against stasis, of inconsistency against consistency.
- Rotation of themes presented a cynical reading of movement as irrational, of policy as an opportunistic carousel of solutions against the implied ideal where solutions are properly and permanently connected to a rationale.
- Scapegoating represented an improper retreat to the primitive and a nostalgia for rational movement, with the implication that this is the cause of the oscillations between false blame and useless cure.
- Shifting of meanings occurred, with meanings subject to a patholog-ical movement, with an implied nostalgia for a lost condition of stability of meaning.
- Professional discretion was displaced by managerial and centralized control, with the implication of an ideological invasion that disrupts the proper disposition of things and overruns protected spaces.

Manifested in the critical text is what can be termed a 'return of the repressed': at every instant of trying to talk of 'movement', what creeps back is stability and its associated order, propriety and normality. 'Policy hysteria' as a story of shifts and displacements contained repressed fantasies of keeping things in their place and curbing excess. What was constructed therefore in the attempt to depict policy as 'hysteria', as an unhealthy deterioration from an ideal state of policy-making, was a metaphysics of presence – a return to an implicit and 'authorizing' origin or standard which is pure and 'healthy'.

Thus in the critical analysis the contemporary policy scene is read as an aberration from an ideal condition of health, normality and reason. All movements in the vocational space became 'policy hysteria', with hysteria as the negative Other, standing for disorder, instability, abnormality, unpredictability, excess, sickness and unreason. While the critical analysis of vocationalism was supposed to point to the impossibility of such a metaphysics of presence, nonetheless it happened, and it did so because the implicit structuring of the 'hysteria/stability' binary opposition went unchallenged. The deconstructive reading showed that this search for presence (the grounding or ideal state) is always deferred, i.e. never fully realized. Thus that which was 'repressed' ended up taking over the text. The text tried to argue against oppositions but ultimately failed because it could itself work only through a dichotomizing logic. That which was the text's strongest point (its attempted mastery) was also its weakest. The saying contradicted the said.

IN WHAT SENSE IS DECONSTRUCTION AN ETHICS?

> I will even venture to say that ethics, politics and responsibility . . . will only ever have begun with the experience and experiment of the aporia. When the path is clear and given, when a certain knowledge opens up the way in advance, the decision is already made, it might as well be said that there is none to make; irresponsibly and in good conscience, one simply applies or implements a program. . . . It makes of action the applied consequence, the simple application of a knowledge or know-how. It makes of ethics and politics a technology.
>
> (Derrida 1992b: 41)

> Any act of reading which is also always a response to the textual other must aim to respect and respond to that singularity and difference. This is to respond ethically to a text, not imposing upon it some ready-made identity, some family likeness, which domesticates and calms down its play. Those who insist on deconstruction as a method of analysis are already imposing an identity on a heterogeneous range of texts and signatures.
>
> (Wolfreys 1998: 9)

> The ethical moment that motivates deconstruction is this Yes-saying to the unnamable, a moment of unconditional affirmation that is addressed to an alterity that can neither be excluded from nor included within logocentric conceptuality.
>
> (Critchley 1992: 41)

These quotations neatly raise some of the leading issues in the argument that deconstruction is an ethics. I start with the question What, after all, is the point of posing such an argument? What's wrong with seeing deconstruction simply as a method? Derrida warns against making ethics into a 'technology' – into something that is instrumental or 'applied'. He argues that ethics cannot even get off the ground if everything is programmatic or clear-cut and known in advance. The very condition of possibility of ethics is an 'aporia', a recognition of undecidability, something impossible to resolve by the application of a 'program', method or set of rules. Equally, as we have already noted, although it is easy enough to see deconstruction as a method or set of techniques, as a 'program' to be 'applied', it needs to be more readily seen as an obligation to listen that marks the failure of mastery and that involves a particular kind of responsibility and responsiveness to the Other.

At this point we need to leave Derrida for a moment and switch our attention to Levinas's account of ethics (Levinas 1989). For him, ethics is the showing of respect for the Other as what the Other is – i.e. radical alterity. He argues that there has been a failure to recognize this because our relationship with the Other (here most readily understood as the world, including the world of others) has been understood primarily in epistemological terms – as the action of the self-present subject getting accurate knowledge of an independently existing world. The crucial issue becomes that of methodological certainty where we relate to the Other only as an object of knowledge. In knowing, the otherness is thus conceptualized, classified and made into an instance of the universal. Placed within 'logocentric conceptuality', the Other loses any singularity and radical alterity. Furthermore, we not only make the Other into an object of knowledge, but seek a certainty in this knowledge about the Other by means of a 'program' or set of rules, along 'a path that is clear and given'. In this attempt to master otherness, we lose sight of that which is 'unnamable' or unsayable in the Other and thus our sense of ethical responsibility by this attempted mastery.

This is why ethics can be understood as a 'yes-saying to the unnamable', the addressing of the singularity of the Other and a recognition that the Other is, as it were, always to come, always exceeding 'logocentric conceptuality', instrumental calculation and programmaticity. For Levinas it does not matter who or what the Other is in relation to me. It is not a matter of reciprocity, what the Other has or has not done, what the Other may or may not do. I have to be for the Other whether the Other is for me or not. That is why it is the singularity of the Other that matters. The relationship is not universalizable and cannot be grasped totally because singularity is inevitably lost in the attempt to do this; I am no longer being *for* the Other, I am simply being *with* the Other.

Of course, expressed in this way this is an abstract, not to say austere, conception of ethics. Its practical implications, although immensely significant, are not easy to discern. Levinas's position implies that ethics involves acting without 'the comfort of the already-existing norms and the already-followed rules' as a guide (Bauman 1993: 52). As Critchley (1992) points out, ethics is normally conceived of as a *system* enabling judgements about action to be formulated and tested, whereas for Levinas ethics is found in the relationship with the Other – a relationship which is constituted by my letting the Other be, by my not trying to assimilate the Other into a pre-existing system, by a refusal to incorporate the Other through programmaticity.

That this is extraordinarily difficult to put into practice is recognized by the reference above to unconditional affirmation being neither included nor *excluded* from logocentric conceptuality. We cannot avoid logocentrism even though we can deconstruct it – but deconstruction, as we have seen, is a double reading where the inevitable logocentrism of the text is first recognized and then deconstructed from an otherness which is itself *within* logocentrism. In this way, deconstruction shows its responsibility and respon-siveness both to logocentric conceptuality and to its Other (and it is in this way that deconstruction cannot be construed as 'wild' reading or 'anything goes', as its critics allege). So too with ethics: while we cannot help but attempt to assimilate the Other through 'innocent' acts of knowing, and believe that by doing so we are celebrating the Other, we can at the same time recognize that this is no innocent celebration. We can recog-nize that every act of knowing is ambivalent – necessary but also a violent act of mastery which contains its own inherent failure. Thus we can recog-nize the aporia of what we are doing, and by this very recognition continue striving to address the singularity of the Other. In effect, this is to recog-nize the necessary failure of masterful acts, to act without the comfort of a firm ground – difficult, certainly, but then without difficulty there would be no ethics anyway.

Critchley (1992) aptly describes deconstruction as an ethical demand – a responsiveness and obligation to the alterity and singularity of the Other, to the singularity of the text by 'not imposing upon it some ready-made identity'. But then the question could be asked – if I can fulfil my obligation to the Other only by resisting conceptualization, by resisting attempts at mastery, does this mean that the Other must remain unknowable? This is precisely the question Derrida puts to Levinas (Derrida 1978). Does not Levinas's ethics make the Other absolutely unrepresentable and is this not itself a form of violence? Is this not an ethics that remains tantaliz-ingly distant, powerfully appealing but forever out of reach (Derrida 1991)?

These questions remind us of the necessity to think in terms of 'both/and' rather than in terms of 'either/or' since the latter only takes us back to the problems that arise from thinking in terms of binary oppositions. We have encountered the logic of 'both/and' when I argued that decon-struction recognizes its ambivalent location as being both inside and outside logocentrism – and by so doing avoids itself becoming a masterful discourse. We cannot escape the need to 'represent' the Other since without this we could not even articulate anything about the Other (including its singularity). There is a sense therefore that I need to relate to the Other as if the Other were me. While this runs the risk of violating the singularity and radical alterity of the Other (one kind of violence), it also means that the ethics of the relationship between myself and Other can encompass dimensions of reciprocal care and justice (thus avoiding another kind of violence).

I want now to return to the deconstructive readings in the previous section and see to what extent they exemplify the ethical moment in deconstruction. First, in relation to Alison Lee's text it is worth noting her comment about enabling a working 'productively with, rather than against, the complexity of human existence' and a working 'with rather than against [the] notion of "zones of uncertainty"'(p. 2). While she makes this comment in relation to post-structuralism, it is applicable also (and this is implied in the text) as a description of what deconstruction *does*. Furthermore, as I pointed out earlier in introducing her text, what she tries to do in it is to provide an exemplification rather than a technical explanation – an emphasis on 'saying' or performing deconstruction rather than an account of what is said about it. Part of this exemplification is to do with the 'complexity of human existence' (in this case that of social differentiation within specific sites) and part is to do with an acknowledgement of a 'zone of uncertainty' – that is, that this complexity cannot be explained in a totalizing and final way; in other words, that there is always an eliminable otherness, marked by a Levinasian relationship of *absence*. The ethical moment is here manifested in a double responsibility – the responsibility both to method and to the Other of method, perhaps best summarized in the comment that post-structuralist (deconstructive) work is explicitly about a *refusal* – 'of unity, of universality, and transcendence, of foundational principles and of particular dominant notions of rationality' (p. 9). This text, in attempting to understand, explain and 'represent' post-structuralism and deconstruction, is clearly an attempt at mastery but at the same time it is a text where the limits and necessary failure of this attempt are demonstrated in and through the text.

To return to the Stronach and MacLure text, in their critical analysis, these authors sought to construct vocationalist discourse as a space of movement where innovation was characterized by the mutability of concepts, innovations and pedagogies. In their deconstructive reading, they showed that rather than opening up a space where the instability of meaning could move, they actually ended up with a closure, an arresting and fixing of meaning. They suggest, however, that rather than leaving it at that, something can emerge from their deconstructive reading – a different kind of account that is not structured around the binary opposition 'hysteria/ stability'. This would not be a definitive account; it would make no appeal to a foundation and would not privilege any pole of a binary opposition. Rather than being a stable, defined meaning or completely dismissed, 'policy hysteria' would be seen as a metaphor for the instability and provisionality of meaning of vocationalist discourse.

They argue that the way through the impasse or aporia opened up by deconstruction is to see movement as inherent rather than as aberration or deviance. This would allow vocationalist discourse to be understood as disordered, but not in the sense of unhealthy ('hysterical'), and would answer the need to address rather than arrest the mobility of meaning which characterizes this discourse. The key to such a reading – a reconstructive reading – is the prevention of a lapse into the nostalgia for order and stability which was the undoing of the critical analysis – in other words, to resist the metaphysics of presence, the temptation to search for an origin or a centre which can act as a foundation, and to resist the attempted mastery of meaning and language.

Stronach and MacLure regard their alternative reading as exemplifying the possibility of deconstruction as a strategy which is not simply negative or reactive. As we have noted, to merely invert a hierarchy is never successful; rather, what is needed is to go beyond that to a displacement that foregrounds the interrelationships, interactivity and interdependence between binary oppositions. Yet this should not be done at the expense of the uncertainty and movement which a deconstructive reading highlights. Of course, most researchers might not be very happy with this position since it seems to open up the abyss of relativism and irresponsibility which is taken to be its consequence – a situation that seems far removed from the ethical moment. But as Stronach and MacLure (1997: 98) argue, 'the charge of irresponsibility is reversed ... it is irresponsible to continue to privilege the escape clauses of a foundational appeal'. What they want to highlight is that there are no escape clauses – that a foundational appeal to certainty can be met only with incredulity. To invoke such clauses therefore becomes ethically problematic. They recognize the need for a responsibility to method but they also refuse to go along with the methodological desire for certainty which is method's failure to recognize Otherness.

IS STYLE THE ENEMY OF ETHICS?

What Derrida's rule sets out to destroy is nothing less than the ethnocentrism and self-referentiality of the West; the mythology that the white man who takes his own logos for the universal form of reason, who transforms his own consciousness into a universal form of appropriation, who makes everything and everyone the 'same' as himself and who makes himself the master of all things.

(Banet 1989: 222)

The way we approach research reflects our inherent beliefs about the world we live in and want to live in. When we do research, what we see reflected is ourselves located in the contemporary world of the postmodern moment – of a decline of absolutes and no longer certain foundations:

> What the postmodern mind is aware of is that there are problems in human and social life with no good solutions, twisted trajectories that cannot be straightened up, ambivalenes that are more than linguistic blunders yelling to be corrected, doubts which cannot be legislated out of existence, moral agonies which no reason-dictated recipes can soothe, let alone cure. The postmodern mind does not expect any more to find the all-embracing, total and ultimate formula of life without ambiguity, risk, danger and error, and is deeply suspicious of any voice that promises otherwise.
>
> (Bauman 1993: 245)

We no longer implicitly assume that following the correct method will guarantee the certainty of true results. The quest for a 'God's-eye view', a disembodied and disembedded timeless perspective that can know the world by transcending it, is no longer readily accepted. The orthodox consensus about how to do research 'scientifically' has been displaced. What we are left with is not an alternative and more secure foundation but an awareness of the complexity, historical contingency and fragility of the practices through which knowledge is constructed. There is thus a loss of certainty in ways of knowing, what is known, and who can be knowers. It is here that Derrida's work is valuable, for he helps us to understand the play of indeterminacy and discontinuity in acts and processes of knowing and in this way to question claims to 'authority' – to a speaking for others which is ethically problematic. This speaking for, no matter what its intent, always has the potential to become too monological, too universalistic, too exclusive and hence oppressive. The world is too complex to be changed purely by rationalistic projects, 'disinterested' research and the one big idea.

There are many research traditions, each with its own epistemology. As noted earlier, deconstruction is not an alternative master discourse for governing research practice, although it does foreground the epistemological commitments and ideological effects which are implicit in all research traditions. So it is not that deconstruction seeks to overthrow research traditions; instead, it argues for a greater awareness of what they do as *cultural* practices of writing and representation.

Underlying this is a scepticism about grand narratives, a distrust of totalizing discourses and of theoretical interpretations with universal pretensions. As Tierney (1994) argues, these have resulted in rigid normative frameworks which have neglected or silenced the Other. As we have seen, it is here that we can begin to discern deconstruction's ethical thrust. Yet critics have argued that deconstruction is problematic precisely because it neglects ethical issues. As Critchley (1992) points out, it is readily assumed that deconstruction, because of its critique of the metaphysics of presence, puts into question the very possibility of ethics. Critics have argued that since deconstruction provides no common standards or criteria which cut across the multiplicity of discourses, in other words no universal and final stand-point, there seems to be no means of making ethical judgements about particular discourses and therefore research traditions.

This is sometimes framed as encouraging nihilism and indifference; a less extreme way of putting this is that deconstruction foregrounds aesthetics rather than ethics. In one sense, this is hardly surprising. There is indeed a foregrounding of aesthetics, given the significance deconstruction accords to style and rhetoric: deconstruction can be understood as a project to transform style, even while this has not been accorded much significance by the academic community (Leitch 1996). Deconstruction addresses the way in which research texts are constructed and how, in particular, mean-ings are organized by discursive practices of representation. It has an in-built reflexivity which demands that attention be paid to the *textuality* of the research text, so *how* the text is written is just as important as what it is about; the saying is as important as the said. In one sense, this is a way of correcting an imbalance that has for too long favoured the anonymity of the researcher-as-author and the neglect of questions of writing in both the narrow and the wider sense. As Revill (1996: 122) points out, 'at the moment when another voice appears to speak with the greatest clarity and highest degree of naturalism in a text, it is arguable that the words most ably express only the literary dexterity of the author'.

Yet it could be argued that there is more to it than this since the aesthetic emphasis is not simply there for its own sake. Derrida shows us that style is institutional. After all, what is the writing of the research text in a 'scien-tific' way? Certainly it is itself a form of rhetoric, a textual organization of meaning, a style; but is it not a style that is also an institution – and a powerful one at that? As Leitch (1996: 35) points out, 'style is productive: how we know what we know results from style . . . what is excluded from knowledge is function of style as well'.

Part of the problem in considering the place and significance of style lies in the framing of the discourse about this in terms of the binary opposi-tion 'ethics/aesthetics' through which a critique is mounted. In the spirit of deconstruction it is therefore necessary to unpick this opposition with its implied privileging hierarchy. Without doing this, it becomes too easy to construct the aesthetic emphasis as yet another example of deconstruc-tion's relativism, superficiality and lack of serious intent.

I would argue that the aesthetic and the ethical cannot be separated in this polarized way; that on the contrary the aesthetic is ethical and ethics must always necessarily have an aesthetic dimension, i.e. a concern with the saying as well as the said, a concern manifested in the foregrounding of style. This means therefore that deconstruction, in emphasizing the aesthetic, is not merely reversing traditional hierarchical opposites but is actually constructing itself as an ethical enterprise. There are two related aspects to this. The first, which I have alluded to earlier in introducing Levinas, and which emerges very clearly from the Banet quotation, is to do with the critique of logocentrism, the white man's logos of universal reason and self-present subjectivity and the patriarchal, ethnocentric and objectifying forms this logos assumes. The consequence of 'universal appropriation' is the marginalization and silencing of the Other, and in addressing this consequence, deconstruction as a critical reading practice privileges the marginal and the silenced, bringing these to the centre of the scene. Yet by not being content with simply reversing the hierarchy, it does so in a way which does not construct another, and potentially oppressive, universal logos. Thus deconstruction, far from valorizing the superficial and far from being indifferent to values, foregrounds the place of values and shows itself to be an enterprise whose aim is ethical. The ethical is neither missing nor 'bolted on' nor applied; deconstruction *is* an ethics.

The second aspect is that deconstruction reconfigures ethics by critiquing the notion of universal standards which traditionally are seen as a necessary ground for ethical judgements. Purpose and context replace these universal grounds. We still have to try to do the right thing, as decentred selves, from where we are located, and in the here and now. As Elam (1994) argues, there are no transcendental alibis for us to fall back on, no essences which will save us from the need to judge on a case-by-case basis. There is no safe ground upon which to base decisions, no pure criteria to be used for judgements; instead there is only radical undecidability (Critchley 1992). We still have to make judgements and come to decisions, but we have to recognize that these are also impossible, given radical undecidability. But undecidability does not imply an abandoning of responsibility: 'Derrida's text leaves us with the infinite responsibility undecidability imposes on us. Undecidability in no way alleviates responsibility. The opposite is the case. We cannot be excused from our own role in history' (Cornell 1992: 169).

The implications for research are that the deconstructive happening is stylistic but necessarily involves ethical issues as integral to the textuality of the research process. It means seeing research, through whichever paradigm it is carried out, as being a rhetoric which is just as much about values as it is about methods and outcomes. In other words, it is to see ethical issues as *immanent* in any act of knowledge production. The foregrounding of the inseparability of knowledge and power and the emphasis on reflexivity are not techniques but a reminder that research is never a purely technical and programmatic process.

THINKING ANEW ABOUT THE RESEARCH PROCESS

> Reality becomes something that is produced in the course of enquiry rather than an object that is essentially separate from the enquiry and that enquiry seeks to discover, accurately represent, and explain. In this sense, knowledge of reality is an irreducible combination of intellectual activity and the things that intellect works with.
>
> (Mourad 1997: 102)

> Academically and culturally, we are trained or conditioned to raise questions which are always mapped for us and ahead of us, within the parameters of a particular discipline or field of thought.
>
> (Wolfreys 1998: 25)

It is clear from what I have argued that there can be no such thing as a deconstructive approach to research in any general sense. Deconstruction is not a methodology – or at least it can become so only by ceasing to be an ethical enterprise. Equally, as we have already seen, deconstruction does not seek to 'govern a research practice', hence it does not seek to overthrow and replace existing research paradigms and traditions. At the same time, however, in a more positive sense deconstruction does have some implications for thinking anew about the research process – and for thinking of it in ways which incorporate the immanence of the ethical dimension. It is to this that I now wish to briefly turn in concluding this chapter.

First, Mourad's notion of postdisciplinary research programmes is worth considering in this context (Mourad 1997). He describes these programmes as a form of intellectual activity that is free-standing in the sense that neither is it contained within nor does it itself constitute a permanent fixed structure of either a disciplinary or an interdisciplinary kind. He envisages these programmes as fluid and mobile, and thus able to work not only with any discipline but also outside disciplines. Unbounded by disciplinary boundaries, a postdisciplinary research programme is a form of enquiry where both the subject and the object of the enquiry are the evolving experience of the enquiry itself and where research becomes a form of learning rather than a search for pre-bounded knowledge. Both complex and open, researchers-as-enquirers become active creators of knowledge through the enquiry process rather than being methodologically primed observers of stable pre-existing disciplinary realities. The research process thus has a greater potential to become both transforming and transformative.

Second, and related to this, there is a need to foreground the place of the researcher. If we think of research in terms of enquiry and if we think of enquiry as *activity*, the researcher is constructed as an active agent who causes knowledge to be created and reality to change through the process of enquiry. The aim becomes that of *exploring* what reality could *become* rather than *explaining* what reality *is*. This way of conceiving research marks a departure from the logocentric and epistemological approach that deconstruction sets out to challenge. Here research is no longer seen as a discipline-bounded and methodologically determined process whose aim is to know reality 'as it really is'. There is no assumption that reality exists independently of enquiry – before and after, and unchanged by the enquiry process. This implies that reality has to be 'captured' and 'mastered' – truly a governing of research practice – and thus in ethical terms this is incompatible with notions of the research process as responsiveness to reality's otherness. If, however, there is an acknowledgement that knowledge is being created by the researcher in the research process, that reality changes through the research process, then there is a displacement of logocentrism (although not a total departure) and at least a recognition of the need to be responsive to reality's dimension of Otherness.

Third, any thinking anew of the research process needs to rethink the place of method in the context of research as writing or textuality. Barthes expresses the problem as follows:

> The invariable fact is that a piece of work which ceaselessly proclaims its determination for method is ultimately sterile; everything has been put into the method, nothing is left for writing. . . . At a certain point therefore it is necessary to turn against Method, or at least to treat it without any founding privilege as one of the voices of plurality – as a view, as a spectacle mounted in the text.
>
> (Barthes 1977: 201)

Method 'forgets' that research is writing, the production of text in both the narrow and the wide sense. As such, it is, however, but an aspect of logocentrism, system-building and programmaticity in general which we have noted earlier. The 'forgetting' of writing is but an attempt to name the unnameable and say the unsayable, the attempt to account for everything and resolve all problems, to 'master' reality as it really is – and thus to fail in that responsibility to the Other which is ethics. Barthes is arguing, however, that method is actually a 'spectacle mounted in the text' – a function of writing, a performative that warrants or legitimizes, a rhetorical practice that persuades 'the reader of systematicity and trustworthiness . . . that the work has been done and that the work is adequate to the claims to be made' (Lee 1999). But at the same time as Barthes argues for the need to recognize the irreducible place of writing – and hence the responsibility to the Other – he also argues for a 'responsibility' in research to method on the grounds that it allows for an awareness of a language which is 'not forgetful of itself' (1977: 201) – hence another kind of responsibility to the Other. Here, then, we have an ethics immanent in the research process which is also a 'double' ethics – an ethics which parallels the double reading, the 'both/and', of deconstruction; an ethics that places a responsibility on the researcher both towards method and to writing, the Other of method.

I end with a quotation from Lather which, it seems to me, encapsulates what the immanent ethical moment in the research process points us towards. This is the point where she refers to the need for 'an altogether different approach to doing empirical enquiry which advocates the creation of a more hesitant and partial scholarship in a world marked by the elusiveness with which it greets our efforts to know it' (Lather 1991b: 15).

Bibliography

Adelman, C. (1998) 'Photocontext', in J. Prosser (ed.) *Image-based Research: A Sourcebook for Qualitative Researchers*, London: Falmer Press.

Adler, M. and Raab, G.M. (1988) 'Exit, Choice and Loyalty: The Impact of Parental Choice on Admissions to Secondary Schools in Edinburgh and Dundee', *Journal of Educational Policy* 3, 2: 155–79.

Agresti, A. and Finlay, B. (1997) *Statistical Methods for the Social Sciences*, 3rd edition, Upper Saddle River, NJ: Prentice-Hall.

Aitken, M, Bennett, S.N. and Hesketh, J. (1981) 'Teaching Styles and Pupil Progress: A Re-analysis', *British Journal of Educational Psychology* 51: 171–86.

Altman, D.G. (1980) 'Statistics and Ethics in Medical Research, I. Misuse of Statistics Is Unethical; II. Study Design; III. How Large a Sample; IV. Collection and Screening Data; V. Analyzing Data; VI. Presentation of Results; VII. Interpreting Results', *British Medical Journal* 281: 1182–4, 1267–9, 1336–8, 1399–401, 1473–5, 1542–4, 1612–14.

—— (1981) 'Statistics and Ethics in Medical Research, VIII. Improving the Quality of Statistics in Medical Journals', *British Medical Journal* 282: 44–6.

American Statistical Association (1998) *Ethical Guidelines for Statistical Practice* (revised edition based on the *1989 ASA Ethical Guidelines for Statistical Practice* and the *1985 Declaration on Professional Ethics of the International Statistics Institute*).

Anderson, C. and Benson, T.W. (1988) 'Direct Cinema and the Myth of Informed Consent', in L. Gross, J.S. Katz and J. Ruby (eds) *Image Ethics*, New York: Oxford University Press.

Arnot, M. (1998) *Recent Research on Gender and Educational Performance*, London: The Stationery Office.

Aronowitz, S. and Giroux, H. (1991) *Postmodern Education*, Minneapolis: University of Minnesota Press.

Aronson, E., Ellsworth, P.C., Carlsmith, J.M. and Gonzalez, M.H. (1990) *Methods of Research in Social Psychology*, New York: McGraw-Hill.

Atget, E. (1992) *Atget Paris*, Paris: Hazan.

Bagley, C. (1968) 'The Educational Performance of Immigrant Children', *Race* 10, 1: 91.

Ball, S. and Gewirtz, S. (1997) 'Is Research Possible? A Rejoinder to Tooley's "On School Choice and Social Class"', *British Journal of Sociology of Education* 18, 4: 575–86.

Ball, S., Maguire, M. and Macrae, S. (1998) 'Education Markets in the Post-16 Sector of One Urban Locale', paper presented as part of the Learning Society programme, King's College, London.

Banet, E.T. (1989) *Structuralism and the Logic of Dissent*, London: Macmillan.

Barthes, R. (1977) *Image–Music–Text*, Oxford: Fontana.

Bartholomew, D.J. (1996) *The Statistical Approach to Social Measurement*, San Diego, CA: Academic Press.

Bauman, Z. (1991) *Modernity and Ambivalence*, Cambridge: Polity.

—— (1992) *Intimations of Postmodernity*, London: Routledge.

—— (1993) *Postmodern Ethics*, Oxford: Blackwell.

Beauchamp, D. and Klaidman, R. (1988) 'The Uncounted Enemy: A Vietnam Deception', in L. Gross, J.S. Katz and J. Ruby (eds) *Image Ethics*, New York: Oxford University Press.

Beck, U. (1992) *Risk Society*, London: Sage.

Beck, U., Giddens, A. and Lash, S. (1994) *Reflexive Modernization*, Cambridge: Polity.

Becker, H.S. (1988) 'Foreword: Image, Ethics, and Organisations', in L. Gross, J.S. Katz and J. Ruby (eds) *Image Ethics*, New York: Oxford University Press.

—— (1998) 'Visual Sociology, Documentary Photography and Photojournalism: It's (Almost) All a Matter of Context', in J. Prosser (ed.) *Image-based Research: A Sourcebook for Qualitative Researchers*, London: Falmer Press.

Beder, H. (1991) 'Mapping the Terrain', in *Convergence* XXIV, 3, ICAE, Ontario.

Beloff, H. (1985) *Camera Culture*, Oxford: Blackwell.

Benjamin, M. (1990) *Splitting the Difference: Compromise and Integrity in Ethics and Politics*, Lawrence: University Press of Kansas.

Benner, P. (1991) 'The Role of Experience, Narrative and Community in Skilled Ethical Comportment', *Advances in Nursing Sciences* 14, 2: 1–21.

Bennett, N. (1976) *Teaching Styles and Pupil Progress*, London: Open Books.

Bennett, N. and Entwistle, N. (1977) 'Rite and Wrong: A Reply to "A Chapter of Errors"', *Educational Research* 19, 3: 217–22.

Bila, F.V. (1998) 'Xitepisi', *Botsotso, Contemporary South African Culture* 9 (Summer): 6.

Bourdieu, P. and Wacquant, L. (1992) *An Invitation to Reflexive Sociology*, Oxford: Polity Press.

Bowden, P. (1997) *Caring: Gender Sensitive Ethics*, London: Routledge.

Bowe, R., Ball, S. and Gold, A. (1992) *Reforming Education and Changing Schools: Case Studies in Policy Sociology*, London: Routledge.

Bowe, R., Gewirtz, S. and Ball, S. (1994) 'Captured by the Discourse? Issues and Concerns in Researching Parental Choice', *British Journal of Sociology of Education* 15, 1: 63–78.

Bradley, W. and Schaefer, K.C. (1998) *The Uses and Misuses of Data and Models: The Mathematization of the Human Sciences*, Thousand Oaks, CA: Sage.

Brewin, T.B. (1985) 'Truth, Trust and Paternalism', *Lancet* (31 August): 490–1.

British Educational Research Association (1992) *British Educational Research Association Ethical Guidelines*, London: BERA.

Brittan, E. (1976) 'Multiracial Education, 2. Teacher Opinion on Aspects of School Life, Part 2. Pupils and Teachers', *Educational Research* 18, 3: 182–91.

Brophy, J. (1986) 'Teacher Influences on Student Achievement', *American Psychologist* 41, 10: 1069–77.

Brown, M. (1998) 'The Tyranny of the International Horse Race', in R. Slee and
    G. Weiner, with S. Tomlinson (eds) *School Effectiveness for Whom? Challenges to
    the School Effectiveness and School Improvement Movements*, London: Falmer Press.
Burgess, R.G. (ed.) (1984) *The Research Process in Educational Settings: Ten Case Studies*,
    London: Taylor and Francis.
—— (ed.) (1989) *The Ethics of Educational Research*, Lewes: Falmer Press.
Burnett, F.M. (1962) *The Integrity of the Body*, Cambridge, MA: Harvard University
    Press.
Busher, H. and Clarke, S. (1990) 'The Ethics of Using Video in Educational
    Research', in *Using Video-Recording for Teacher Professional Development*, School
    of Education, University of Leeds.
Calderwood, J. (1988) *Teachers' Professional Learning*, London: Falmer Press.
Callan, E. (1992) 'Tradition and Integrity in Moral Education', *American Journal
    of Education* 101, 1.
Campbell, J.R. and Beaudry, J.S. (1998) 'Gender Gap Linked to Differential
    Socialization for High-achieving Senior Mathematics Students', *Journal of
    Educational Research* 91, 3: 140–7.
Caputo, J.D. (1993) *Against Ethics: Contributions to a Poetics of Obligation with
    Constant Reference to Deconstruction*, Bloomington: Indiana University Press.
Carlson, R. (1975) 'Environmental Constraints and Organisational Consequences',
    in J. Baldridge and T. Deal (eds) *Managing Change in Educational Organisations*,
    Berkeley, CA: McCutchan.
Carroll, S. and Walford, G. (1997) 'Parents' Response to the School Quasi Market',
    Research Papers in Education 12, 1: 3–26.
Cartier-Bresson, H. (1952) *The Decisive Moment*, New York: Simon and Schuster.
Centre for Contemporary Cultural Studies (1982) *The Empire Strikes Back*, London:
    Hutchinson.
Chonko, L.B. (1995) *Ethical Decision-Making in Marketing*, London: Sage.
Christie, P. (1994) *The Right to Learn*, Johannesburg: SACHED/Ravan.
Cohen, L. and Manion, L. (1994) *Research Methods in Education*, 4th edition,
    London: Routledge.
Collier, J. and Collier, M. (1986) *Visual Anthropology: Photography as a Research
    Method*, Albuquerque: University of New Mexico Press.
Collingwood, R.G. (1924) *Speculum Mentis, or The Map of Knowledge*, Oxford:
    Clarendon Press.
Comey, D.D. (1972) 'Logic', in C. Kernig (ed.) *Marxism, Communism and Western
    Society*, New York: Harder and Harder.
Connolly, P. (1992) 'Playing It by the Rules: The Politics of Research in "Race"
    and Education', *British Educational Research Journal* 18, 2: 133–48.
Coolican, H. (1994) *Research Methods and Statistics in Psychology*, 2nd edition,
    London: Hodder and Stoughton.
Cornell, D. (1992) *The Philosophy of the Limit*, London: Routledge.
Creswell, J.W. (1994) *Research Design: Qualitative and Quantitative Approaches*,
    Thousand Oaks, CA: Sage.
Critchley, S. (1992) *The Ethics of Deconstruction*, Oxford: Blackwell.
Daly, M. (1973) *Beyond God the Father: Towards a Philosophy of Women's Liberation*,
    Boston: Beacon Paths.
Danziger, J. and Conrad, B. (1984) *Interviews with Master Photographers*, London:
    Paddington Press.

Davian, R.M. (1991) 'Integrity and Radical Change', in C. Card (ed.) *Feminist Ethics*, Lawrence: University Press of Kansas.

David, M. (1997) 'Diversity, Choice and Gender', *Oxford Review of Education* 23, 1: 77–88.

Davie, T.B. (1954) 'The Function of a University in a Multi-racial Society', in *The Idea of the University: A Symposium*, Johannesburg: South African Insitute of Race Relations.

Dennett, D. (1976) 'Conditions of Personhood', in A. Rorty (ed.) *The Identities of Persons*, Berkeley: University of California Press.

Denzin, N.K. and Lincoln, Y.S. (1998) *The Landscape of Qualitative Research: Theories and Issues*, Thousand Oaks, CA: Sage.

Derrida, J. (1976) *Of Grammatology*, Baltimore: Johns Hopkins University Press.

—— (1978) *Writing and Difference*, Chicago: University of Chicago Press.

—— (1981) *Positions*, Chicago: University of Chicago Press.

—— (1982) *Margins of Philosophy*, Brighton: Harvester Press.

—— (1988) *Limited Inc.*, Evanston, IL: Northwestern University Press.

—— (1991) 'At This Moment in This Work, Here I Am', in R. Bernasconi and D. Wood (eds) *The Provocation of Levinas: Rethinking the Other*, London: Routledge.

—— (1992a) 'Mochlos, or The Conflict of the Faculties', in R. Rand (ed.) *Logomachia: The Conflict of the Faculties*, Lincoln: University of Nebraska Press.

—— (1992b) *The Other Heading: Reflections on Today's Europe*, Bloomington: Indiana University Press.

Deshler, D. and Selener, D. (1991) 'Transformative Research: In Search of a Definition', in *Convergence* XXIV, 3, ICAE, Ontario.

Devlin, B. (ed.) (1997) *Intelligence, Genes, and Success: Scientists Respond to the Bell Curve*, New York: Springer-Verlag.

Dockrell, W.B. (1988) 'Ethical Considerations in Research', in J.P. Keeves (ed.) *Educational Research, Methodology, and Measurement: An International Handbook*, Oxford: Pergamon.

Edelman, M. (1977) *Political Language: Words That Succeed and Policies That Fail*, New York: Academic Press.

Elam, D. (1994) *Feminism and Deconstruction*, London: Routledge.

Engels, F. (1934) 'Beyond Caring: The De-moralisation of Gender', in M. Hanen and K. Neilson (eds) *Science, Morality and Feminist Theory*, Calgary: University of Calgary Press.

Field, J. (1985) 'From Trade Union Education to Work with the Unemployed', *Trade Union Studies Journal*, 2, London: Workers' Educational Association.

Fieldhouse, R. (1992) 'Tradition in British University Adult Education and the WEA', in C. Duke (ed.) *Liberal Adult Education: Perspectives and Projects*, Coventry: Continuing Education Research Centre, University of Warwick.

Figueroa, P. (1975) 'West Indian School-Leavers in London: A Sociological Study in Ten Schools in a London Borough, 1966–1967', unpublished PhD thesis, London School of Economics and Political Science, University of London (submitted 1974, examined 1975).

—— (1986) 'Student-Teachers' Images of Ethnic Minorities: A British Case Study', paper given at the World Congress of Sociology, New Delhi, August (published in an edited version in 1989).

—— (1989) Student-Teachers' Images of Ethnic Minorities: A British Case Study',
in S. Tomlinson and A. Yogev (eds) *Affirmative Action and Positive Policies in the
Education of Ethnic Minorities: International Perspectives on Education and Society*,
vol. 1, Greenwich, CT: JAI Press (edited version of the 1986 paper).

—— (1991) *Education and the Social Construction of 'Race'*, London: Routledge.

Figueroa, P. and Nehaul, K. (1999) Full Report of Research Activities and Results
(ESRC funded project, 'Parenting, Academic Success and Caribbean Heritage
Pupils', award no. R000222386, End of Award Report).

Fine, M. (1992) *Disruptive Voices*, Ann Arbor: University of Michigan Press.

—— (1994) 'Dis-stance and Other Stances: Negotiations of Power inside Feminist
Research', in A. Gitlin (ed.) *Power and Method*, London: Routledge.

—— (1998) 'Working the Hyphens: Reinventing Self and Others in Qualitative
Research', in N.K. Denzin and Y.S. Lincoln (eds) *The Landscape of Qualitative
Research*, Thousand Oaks, CA: Sage.

Fischer, C.S. (1996) *Inequality by Design: Cracking the Bell Curve Myth*, Princeton,
NJ: Princeton University Press.

Flax, J. (1990) *Thinking Fragments: Psychoanalysis, Feminism and Postmodernism in
the Contemporary West*, Berkeley: University of California Press.

—— (1993) *Disputed Subjects: Essays on Psychoanalysis, Politics and Philosophy*, New
York: Routledge.

Fonow, M.M. and Cook, J.A. (eds) (1991) *Beyond Methodology Feminist Scholarship
as Lived Practice*, Bloomington and Indianapolis: Indiana University Press.

Fordham, P., Poulton, G. and Randle, L. (1979) *Learning Networks in Adult
Education*, London: Routledge and Kegan Paul.

Foskett, N. (1996) 'Conceptualising Marketing in Secondary Schools:
Deconstructing an Alien Concept', in *Proceedings of the 'Markets in Education,
Policy, Process and Practice' Symposium, Southampton*, Southampton: Centre for
Research in Education Marketing.

—— (1998) 'Linking Marketing to Strategy', in D. Middlewood and J. Lumby
(eds) *Strategic Management in Schools and Colleges*, London: Paul Chapman
Publishing.

Foskett, N. and Hemsley-Brown, J. (1999) *Teachers and Careers Education: Teachers'
Awareness of Careers outside Teaching*, Southampton: Centre for Research in
Education Marketing.

Foskett, N. and Hesketh, A. (1996) 'Knowing When and Knowing How:
Touchstones of the FE Market Place', *Education Marketing* 7: 24–6.

—— (1997) 'Constructing Choice in Contiguous and Parallel Markets: Institutional
and School Leavers' Responses to the New Post-16 Market Place', *Oxford Review
of Education* 23, 3: 299–320.

Foster, P. (1990) *Policy and Practice in Multicultural and Anti-racist Education*, London:
Routledge.

—— (1992) 'What Are Connolly's Rules? A Reply to Paul Connolly', *British
Educational Research Journal* 18, 2: 149–54.

—— (1999) 'Some Critical Comments on the BERA Ethical Guidelines', *Research
Intelligence: Newsletter of the British Educational Research Association* 67 (February):
24–7.

Foster, P., Gomm, R. and Hammersley, M. (1996) *Constructing Educational Inequality:
An Assessment of Research on School Processes*, London: Falmer Press.

—— (1997) 'A Response to the Reviews', *British Journal of Educational Studies* 45, 4: 419–23.

Foucault, M. (1977) *Language, Counter-Memory, Practice*, Ithaca, NY: Cornell University Press.

—— (1980) *Power/Knowledge: Selected Interviews and Other Writings*, Brighton: Harvester Press.

Francis, L.J. and Grindle, Z. (1998) 'Whatever Happened to Progressive Education? A Comparison of Primary School Teachers' Attitudes in 1982 and 1996', *Educational Studies* 24, 3: 269–79.

Fraser, L. (1986) 'Reflections on Research', in K. Ward and R. Taylor (eds) *Adult Education and the Working Class*, London: Croom Helm.

Fraser, S. (ed.) (1995) *The Bell Curve Wars: Race, Intelligence, and the Future of America*, New York: Basic Books.

Freire, P. (1972), *Pedagogy of the Oppressed*, Harmondsworth: Penguin.

Friedman, M. (1987) 'Beyond Caring: The De-Moralisation of Gender' in M. Hanen and K. Neilson (eds) *Science, Morality and Feminist Theory*, Calgary: University of Calgary Press.

Gewirtz, S., Ball, S. and Bowe, R. (1995) *Markets, Choice and Equity in Education*, Buckingham: Open University Press.

Gillborn, D. (1995) *Racism and Antiracism in Real Schools: Theory, Policy, Practice*, Buckingham: Open University Press.

Gilligan, C. (1982) *In a Different Voice*, Cambridge, MA: Harvard University Press.

Glass, G.V. and Hopkins, K.D. (1996) *Statistical Methods in Education and Psychology*, 3rd edition, Boston: Allyn and Bacon.

Glatter, R., Woods, P. and Bagley, P. (eds) (1996) *Choice and Diversity in Schooling: Perspectives and Prospects*, London: Routledge.

Goffman, E. (1961) *Asylums: Essays on the Social Situation of Mental Patients*, Garden City, NY: Doubleday Anchor.

Goldstein, H. (1997) 'Methods in School Effectiveness Research', *School Effectiveness and School Improvement* 8, 4: 369–95.

Goldstein, H. and Myers, K. (1996) 'Freedom of Information: Towards a Code of Ethics for Performance Indicators', *BERA Research Intelligence* 57: 12–16.

Gomm, R. (1993) 'Figuring Out Ethnic Equity', *British Educational Research Journal* 19, 2: 149–65.

Gorard, S. (1997) 'A Choice of Methods: The Methodology of Choice', *Research in Education* 57, 1: 45–56.

—— (1999) '"Well, That About Wraps It Up for School Choice Research": A State of the Art Review', *School Leadership and Management* 19, 1: 25–47.

Gore, J. (1992) 'What We Can Do for You? What Can We Do for You? Struggling over Empowerment in Critical and Feminist Pedagogy', in C. Luke and J. Gore (eds) *Feminisms and Critical Pedagogy*, New York: Routledge.

Gouldner, A. (1975) *For Sociology: Renewal and Critique in Sociology Today*, Harmondsworth: Penguin.

Graef, R. (1980) 'The Case Study as Pandora's Box', in H. Simons (ed.) *Towards a Science of the Singular*, Occasional Publication No. 10, Centre for Applied Research in Education, University of East Anglia.

—— (1989) 'Privacy and Observational Film', *Anthropology Today* 5, 2: 1–2.

Gray, J. and Satterly, D. (1976) 'A Chapter of Errors: "Teaching Styles and Pupil Progress" in Retrospect', *Educational Research* 19, 1: 45–56.

—— (1981) 'Formal or Informal? A Re-assessment of the British Evidence', *British Journal of Educational Psychology* 51: 187–96.

Greenwood, J. (1984) 'Nursing Research: A Position Paper', *Journal of Advanced Nursing* 9: 77–82.

Gross, L., Katz, J.S. and Ruby, J. (eds) (1988) 'Introduction: A Moral Pause', in L. Gross, J.S. Katz and J. Ruby (eds) *Image Ethics*, New York: Oxford University Press.

Grosz, E. (1990) 'Philosophy', in S. Gunew (ed.) *Feminist Knowledge: Critique and Construct*, London: Routledge.

Grundstein-Amado, R. (1992) 'Differences in Ethical Decision-Making Processes among Nurses and Doctors', *Journal of Advanced Nursing* 17: 129–37.

Hall, B. (1981), 'The Democratization of Research', in P. Reason and J. Rowan (eds) *Human Inquiry: A Sourcebook of New Paradigm Research*, Chichester: Wiley.

Hammersley, M. (1992) *What Is Wrong with Ethnography? Methodological Explorations*, London: Routledge.

—— (1993) 'Research and "Anti-racism": The Case of Peter Foster and His Critics', *British Journal of Sociology* 44, 3: 429–48.

Hammersley, M. and Atkinson, P. (1983) *Ethnography: Principles in Practice*, London: Tavistock.

Hampshire, S. (1983) *Morality and Conflict*, Cambridge, MA: Harvard University Press.

Haraway, D. (1988) 'Situated Knowledges: The Science Question in Feminism and the Privilege of Partial Perspective', *Feminist Studies* 14, 3: 575–97.

Harding, S. (1987a) 'Conclusion: Epistemological Questions in Feminism and Methodology', in S. Harding (ed.) *Feminism and Methodology: Social Science Issues*, Bloomington, IN: Indiana University Press.

—— (1987b) 'Is There a Feminist Method?', in S. Harding (ed.) *Feminism and Methodology: Social Science Issues*, Bloomington, IN: Indiana University Press.

—— (1997) 'Is Modern Science an Ethnoscience? Rethinking Epistemological Assumptions', in E.C. Eze (ed.) *Postcolonial African Philosophy*, Oxford: Blackwell.

Harpham, G. (1995) 'Ethics', in F. Lentricchia and T. McLaughlin (eds) *Critical Terms for Literary Study*, 2nd edition, London: University of Chicago Press.

Harris, E.E. (1954) 'The Idea of a University', in *The Idea of the University: A Symposium*, Johannesburg: South African Institute of Race Relations.

Hart, E. (1995) 'Developing Action Research in Nursing', *Nurse Researcher* 2, 3 (March): 14.

Hart, E. and Bond, M. (1995) *Action Research for Health and Social Care: A Guide to Practice*, Buckingham: Open University Press.

Healey, J.F. (1996) *Statistics: A Tool for Social Research*, 4th edition, Belmont, CA: Wadsworth.

Hekman, S. (1990) *Gender and Knowledge Elements of a Postmodern Feminism*, Oxford: Polity Press.

—— (1995) *Moral Voices Moral Selves: Carol Gilligan and Feminist Moral Theory*, Oxford: Polity Press.

Held, V. (ed.) (1995) *Justice and Care: Essential Readings in Feminist Ethics*, Boulder, CO: Westview Press.

Hemsley-Brown, J. (1996) 'Marketing Post-16 Colleges: A Qualitative and Quantitative Study of Pupils' Choice of Post-16 Institution', unpublished PhD thesis, University of Southampton.

Hemsley-Brown, J. and Foskett, N. (1999) Young People's Perceptions of Modern Apprenticeships, Southampton: Centre for Research in Education Marketing.

Herrera, C.D. (1996) 'An Ethical Argument against Leaving Psychologists to Their Statistical Devices', Journal of Psychology 130, 3: 125–30.

Herrnstein, R.J. and Murray, C. (1994) The Bell Curve: Intelligence and Class Structure in American Life, New York: Free Press.

Hinton, P.R. (1995) Statistics Explained: A Guide for Social Science Students, London: Routledge.

Hoagland, S.L. (1988) Lesbian Ethics: Towards New Values, Palo Alto, CA: Institute of Lesbian Studies.

Hodkinson, P. (1995) 'How Young People Make Career Decisions', Education and Training 37, 8: 3–8.

Hodkinson, P., Sparkes, A. and Hodkinson, H. (1996) Triumphs and Tears: Young People, Markets and the Transition from School to Work, London: David Fulton.

Hodkinson, P. and Sparkes, A. (1997) 'Careership: A Sociological Theory of Career Decision-Making', British Journal of Sociology of Education 9, 1: 42–55.

Home Department (1999) The Stephen Lawrence Inquiry: Report of an Inquiry (The Macpherson Report), London: The Stationery Office (CM 4262–1, presented to Parliament February 1999).

House, E.R. (1993) Professional Evaluation: Social Impact and Political Consequences, London: Sage.

Howell, D.C. (1997) Statistical Methods for Psychology, 4th edition, London: Wadsworth.

Hyatt, J. and Simons, H. (1989) 'Cultural Codes: Who Holds the Key? The Concept and Conduct of Evaluation in Central and Eastern Europe', Evaluation: The International Journal of Theory, Research and Practice 5, 1: 23–41.

Inner London Education Authority (1968) The Education of Immigrant Pupils in Primary Schools, Report 959, London: ILEA, February.

International Statistical Institute (1986) 'Declaration on Professional Ethics', International Statistical Review 54: 227–42.

Jarvis, P. (1992) 'Reflective Practice and Nursing', Nurse Education Today 12, 3: 174–98.

Jephcote, M., Salisbury, J., Fletcher, J., Graham, I. and Mitchell, G. (1996) 'Principals' Responses to Incorporation: A Window on Their Culture', Journal of Further and Higher Education 20, 2: 33–48.

Johnson, D. (1994) Research Methods in Educational Management, Harlow: Longman.

Johnston, R. (1981) 'A Network Approach to Educational Work with Unemployed People', in J. Reading and C. Elphick (eds) The Political Papers 9, London: City Lit.

—— (1987) Exploring the Educational Needs of Unwaged Adults, Leicester: NIACE Replan.

—— (1991) 'Education with Unwaged Adults as Community Adult Education', unpublished thesis, University of Southampton.

—— (1992) 'Education and Unwaged Adults: Relevance, Social Control and Empowerment', in G. Allen and I. Martin (eds) Education and Community: The Politics of Practice, London: Cassell.

Jonathan, R. (1990) 'State Education Service or Prisoner's Dilemma: The Hidden Hand as Source of Education Policy', *Educational Philosophy and Theory* 22, 1: 16–24.

Jones, P. (1996) 'Academic Cultural Imperialism', *Matlhasedi*, April/May 1996.

Kadane, J.B. (1996) *Bayesian Methods and Ethics in Clinical Trial Design*, New York: Wiley.

Kane, P. (1994) 'Putting Us All in the Picture', *The Sunday Times*, Section 10, 28 August.

Katz, J.S. and Katz, J.M. (1988) 'The Ethics of Autobiographical Film', in L. Gross, J.S. Katz and J. Ruby (eds) *Image Ethics*, New York: Oxford University Press.

Keitel, C. and Kilpatrick, J. (1999) 'The Rationality and Irrationality of International Comparative Studies', in G. Kaiser, E. Luna and I. Huntley (eds) *International Comparisons in Mathematics Education*, London: Falmer Press.

Kekes, J. (1983) 'Constancy and Purity', *Mind* 92: 449–515.

Kelly, B. (1990) 'Respect and Caring: Ethics and Essence of Nursing', in M. Leininger (ed.) *Ethical and Moral Dimensions of Care*, Detroit: Wayne State University Press.

Kelman, H.C. (1967) 'Human Use of Human Subjects', *Psychological Bulletin* 67, 1: 1–11.

Kemmis, S. and McTaggart, R. (1981) *The Action Research Planner*, Victoria: Deakin University Press.

Kennedy, H. (1998) *How to Widen Participation: A Guide to Good Practice*, London: Further Education Funding Council.

Kincheloe, J.L. (ed.) (1996) *Measured Lies: The Bell Curve Examined*, New York: St Martin's Press.

Kirkwood, G. and Kirkwood, C. (1989) *Living Adult Education*, Buckingham: Open University Press.

Kirp, D.L. (1979) *Doing Good by Doing Little: Race and Schooling in Britain*, Berkeley: University of California Press.

Koehn, D. (1998) *Rethinking Feminist Ethics: Care, Trust and Empathy*, London: Routledge.

Kohlberg, L. (1981) *The Philosophy of Moral Development*, San Francisco: Harper and Row.

Krenz, C. and Sax, G. (1986) 'What Quantitative Research Is and Why It Doesn't Work', *American Behavioral Scientist* 30, 1: 58–69.

Kromrey, J.D. (1993) 'Ethics and Data Analysis', *Educational Researcher* 22, 4: 24–7.

Kuflick, A. (1977) 'Morality and Compromise', in J.R. Pennock and J.W. Chapman (eds) *Compromise in Ethics, Law and Politics*, New York: New York University Press.

Kushner, S. (2000) *Personalising Evaluation*, London: Sage.

Lal, J. (1996) 'Situating Locations: The Politics of Self, Identity, and "Other"', in D.L. Wolf (ed.) *Feminist Dilemmas in Fieldwork*, Boulder, CO: Westview Press.

Larrabee, M.J. (ed.) (1993) *An Ethic of Care: Feminist and Interdisciplinary Perspectives*, London: Routledge.

Lather, P. (1986) 'Research as Praxis', *Harvard Educational Review* 56, 3: 257–77.

—— (1991a) 'Post-critical Pedagogies: A Feminist Reading', *Education and Society* 9, 1–2: 100–11.

—— (1991b) *Getting Smart: Feminist Research and Pedagogy with/in the Postmodern*, London: Routledge.

Lauretis, T. de (1984) *Alice Doesn't: Feminism, Semiotics, Cinema*, London: Macmillan.

Le Grand, J. and Bartlett, W. (1993) *Quasi Markets and Social Policy*, London: Macmillan.

Lee, A. (1992) 'Post-structuralism and Educational Research: Some Categories and Issues', *Issues in Educational Research* 2, 1: 1–11.

—— (1999) 'Discourse Analysis and Cultural (Re)writing', in A. Lee and C. Poynton (eds) *Culture and Text: Discourse and Methodology in Social Research and Cultural Studies*, Sydney: Allen and Unwin.

Leitch, V. (1996) *Postmodernism: Local Effects, Global Flows*, Albany: State University of New York Press.

Lemert, C. (1997) *Postmodernism Is Not What You Think*, Oxford: Blackwell.

Levinas, E. (1989) *The Levinas Reader*, ed. S. Hand, Oxford: Blackwell.

Lucy, N. (1995) *Debating Derrida*, Melbourne: Melbourne University Press.

Luke, C. (1994) 'Women in the Academy: The Politics of Speech and Silence', *British Journal of Sociology of Education* 15, 2: 211–30.

Lumby, J. and Foskett, N. (eds) (1999) *Managing External Relations in Schools and Colleges*, London: Paul Chapman Publishing.

MacDonald, B. (1974) 'Evaluation and the Control of Education', in B. MacDonald and R. Walker (eds) *SAFARI I: Innovation, Evaluation, Research and the Problem of Control*, Norwich: Centre for Applied Research in Education.

—— (1987) 'Evaluation and the Control of Education', in H. Torrance and R. Murphy (eds) *Issues and Methods in Evaluation*, London: Paul Chapman.

McFall, L. (1987) 'Integrity', *Ethics* 98: 5–20.

McIntyre, D. (1976) 'Review of "Teaching Styles and Pupil Progress"', *British Journal of Teacher Education* 2, 3: 291–7.

MacIntyre, T. (1997) 'Gender Differences in Cognition: A Minefield of Research Issues', *Irish Journal of Psychology* 18, 4: 386–96.

MacKinnon, C. (1987) *Feminism Unmodified*, Cambridge, MA: Harvard University Press.

MacKintosh, N.J. (ed.) (1995) *Cyril Burt: Fraud or Framed?*, Oxford: Oxford University Press.

McQuillan, J. (1998) *The Literacy Crisis: False Claims, Real Solutions*, Portsmouth, NH: Heinemann.

Martin, M.O. and Kelly, D.L. (eds) (1996) *TIMSS Technical Report*, Vol. I: *Design and Development*, Chestnut Hill, MA: Center for the Study of Testing, Evaluation, and Educational Policy, Boston College.

—— (eds) (1997) *TIMSS Technical Report*, Vol. 2: *Implementation and Analysis*, Chestnut Hill, MA: Center for the Study of Testing, Evaluation, and Educational Policy, Boston College.

Martin, M.O. and Mullis, I.V.S. (eds) (1996) *TIMSS Quality Assurance in Data Collection*, Chestnut Hill, MA: Center for the Study of Testing, Evaluation, and Educational Policy, Boston College.

Merleau-Ponty, M. (1945) *Phénoménologie de la perception*, Paris: Gallimard (*Phenomenology of Perception*, trans. Colin Smith, 1962, London: Routledge and Kegan Paul).

Mertens, D.M. (1998) *Research Methods in Education and Psychology: Integrating Diversity with Quantitative and Qualitative Approaches*, Thousand Oaks, CA: Sage.

Miles, R. (1982) *Racism and Migrant Labour*, London: Routledge and Kegan Paul.

Mirza, M. (1995) 'Some Ethical Dilemmas in Field Work: Feminist and Antiracist Methodologies', in M. Griffiths and B. Troyna (eds) *Antiracism, Culture and Social Justice in Education*, Stoke-on-Trent: Trentham.

Mitchell, C. and Weber, S. (1998) 'Picture This! Vernacular Portraits and Lasting School Impressions of School', in J. Prosser (ed.) *Image-based Research: A Sourcebook for Qualitative Researchers*, London: Falmer Press.

—— (1999) *Reinventing Ourselves as Teachers: Beyond Nostalgia*, London: Falmer Press.

Mkatshwa, S. (1985) 'Keynote Address', Report on National Consultative Conference on the Crisis in Education, Johannesburg: University of the Witwatersrand.

Mourad, R. (1997) *Postmodern Philosophical Critique and the Pursuit of Knowledge in Higher Education*, Westport, CT: Bergin and Garvey.

Murray, B.K. (1988) *Wits – The Early Years: A History of the University of the Witwatersrand and Its Precursors (1896–1939)*, Johannesburg: University of the Witwatersrand Press.

Nagel, T. (1979) 'The Fragmentation of Value', in T. Nagel (ed.) *Mortal Questions*, Cambridge: Cambridge University Press.

Neuman, S.B. and McCormick, S. (1995) *Single-Subject Experimental Research: Applications for Literacy*, Newark, DE: International Reading Association.

Newman, M. (1978) 'Unemployment: The Response of an Adult Education Centre', in J. Wallis (ed.) *Adult Education: Urban Initiatives*, London: Educational Centres' Association.

NIACE, National Institute of Adult Continuing Education (1984), Leicester, DES Programme for the Adult Unemployed, May 1984.

Noddings, N. (1984) *Caring: A Feminine Approach to Ethics and Moral Education*, Berkeley: University of California Press.

Nowell, A. and Hedges, L.V. (1998) 'Trends in Gender Differences in Academic Achievement from 1960 to 1994: An Analysis of Differences in Mean, Variance, and Extreme Scores', *Sex Roles* 39, 1–2: 21–43.

Pagano, R.R. (1994) *Understanding Statistics in the Behavioral Sciences*, 4th edition, St Paul, MN: West Publishing.

Pallegrine, E. and Tomasina, R. (1981) *A Philosophical Basis of Medical Practice*, New York: Oxford University Press.

Parekh, B. (1986) 'Britain's Step-citizens', *New Society*, 1 August: 24–5.

Parker, S. (1997) *Reflective Teaching in the Postmodern World*, Buckingham: Open University Press.

Patai, D. (1991) 'U.S. Academics and the Third World Women: Is Ethical Research Possible?', in S. Berger Gluck and D. Patai (eds) *Women's Words: The Feminist Practice of Oral History*, New York: Routledge.

Payne, M. (1993) *Reading Theory*, Oxford: Blackwell.

Peers, I.S. (1996) *Statistical Analysis for Education and Psychology*, London: Falmer Press.

Perceptions of Wits: Tomorrow Begins at Wits Today. The Role of the University in a Changing South Africa (1987), Johannesburg: University of the Witwatersrand Press.

Perloff, R. and Perloff, E. (1980) 'Ethics in Practice', in R. Perloff and E. Perloff (eds) *New Directions for Program Evaluation*, vol. 7: *Values, Ethics and Standards in Evaluation*, San Francisco: Jossey-Bass.

Plato (1973) *Phaedrus*, trans. W. Hamilton, Harmondsworth: Penguin.

Plewis, I. (1997) *Statistics in Education*, London: Arnold.

Porter, S. (1993) 'Nursing Research Conventions: Objectivity or Obfuscation', *Journal of Advanced Nursing* 18, 1: 137–43.

Power, S., Halpin, D. and Whitty, G. (1997) 'Managing the State and the Market: "New" Education Management in Five Countries', *British Journal of Educational Studies* 45, 4: 342–62.

Prosser, J. (1989) 'The Nature of School: An Ethnographic Case Study', unpublished DPhil thesis, Department of Educational Studies, University of York.

—— (1992) 'Personal Reflections on the Use of Photography in an Ethnographic Case Study', *British Educational Research Journal* 18, 4: 397–411.

—— (1998) 'The Status of Image-Based Research', in J. Prosser (ed.) *Image-Based Research: A Sourcebook for Qualitative Researchers*, London: Falmer Press.

Qabula, A.T. (1995) 'It Has Been Such a Long Road', *South African Labour Bulletin* 19, 6 (December): 14.

Rand, A. (1964) *The Virtue of Selfishness*, New York: Signet.

Reading, J. and Elphick, C. (1981) *The Political Papers No. 9*, London: City Lit.

Reason, P. and Rowan, J. (1981) *Human Inquiry: A Sourcebook of New Paradigm Research*, Chichester: Wiley.

Reeves, F. (1983) *British Racial Discourse*, Cambridge: Cambridge University Press.

Reinharz, S. (1992) *Feminist Methods in Social Research*, New York: Oxford University Press.

Revill, G. (1996) 'Reading "Rosehill": Community, Identity and Inner-City Derby', in M. Keith and S. Pile (eds) *Place and the Politics of Identity*, London: Routledge.

Riley, R.W. (1998) 'The State of Mathematics Education: Building a Strong Foundation for the 21st Century', Speech to the Conference of American Mathematical Society and Mathematical Association of America, Baltimore, Maryland, Thursday, 8 January 1998. Text available in *Notices of the American Mathematical Society* 45: 487–90 (1998).

Robinson, A. and Long, G. (1987) 'Marketing Further Education: Products or People', *NATFHE Journal*, March.

Robitaille, D.F. and Garden, R.A. (eds) (1996) *Research Questions and Study Design*, Vancouver: Pacific Educational Press.

Rogers, A. (1992) *Adults Learning for Development*, London: Cassell.

Rowe, K.J. and Hill, P.W. (1995) 'Methodological Issues in Educational Performance and School Effectiveness Research: A Discussion with Worked Examples', *Australian Journal of Education* 39, 3: 217–48.

Ruddick, S. (1989) *Maternal Thinking*, Boston: Beacon Press.

Russell, C. (1993) *Academic Freedom*, London: Routledge.

Ryten, J. (1981) 'Some General Considerations as a Result of an Ecuadorian Case Study', *Bulletin of the International Statistical Institute* (Proceedings of the 43rd Session) 49, 2: 639–65.

Sackett, D.L. (1979) 'Bias in Analytical Research', *Journal of Chronic Diseases* 32: 57–63.

Sammons, P. (1989) 'Ethical Issues and Statistical Work', in R.G. Burgess (ed.) *The Ethics of Educational Research*, Lewes: Falmer Press.

Sander, A. (1986) *Citizens of the Twentieth Century*, Cambridge, MA: MIT Press.

Sax, G. (1986) 'The Ethics of Quantification and Why It Doesn't Work; or Life among the Numerologists, Innumerates, and Qualitatives', paper presented at the 70th Annual Meeting of the American Educational Research Association, San Francisco, CA, 16–20 April 1986.

Schon, D. (1983) *The Reflective Practitioner*, New York: Basic Books.

Scott, J.W. (1992) 'Experience', in J. Butler and J.W. Scott (eds) *Feminists Theorize the Political*, New York and London: Routledge.

Shanahan, P. and Ward, J. (1995) 'The University and Empowerment: The European Union, University Adult Education and Community Economic Development with "Excluded Groups"', in G. Craig and M. Mayo (eds) *Community Empowerment*, London: Zed.

Shipman, M.D. (1997) *The Limitations of Social Research*, 4th edition, London: Longman.

Simons, H. (1984) 'Negotiating Conditions for Independent Evaluations', in C. Adelman (ed.) *The Politics and Ethics of Evaluation*, London: Croom Helm.

—— (1987) *Getting to Know Schools in a Democracy: The Politics and Process of Evaluation*, Lewes: Falmer Press.

—— (1989) 'Ethics of Case Study in Educational Research and Evaluation', in R. Burgess (ed.) *Ethics of Social Research*, Lewes: Falmer Press.

Singer, P. (1979) *Practical Ethics*, Cambridge: Cambridge University Press.

Slee, R. and Weiner, G. (eds) (1998) *School Effectiveness for Whom? Challenges to the School Effectiveness and School Improvement Movements*, London: Falmer Press.

Smith, D., Scott, P. and Lynch, J. (1995) *The Role of Marketing in the University and College Sector*, Leeds: Heist Publications.

Sophocles (1965) 'Antigone', in *Sophocles, The Theban Plays*, translated by E.F. Watling, Harmondsworth: Penguin.

Stacey, J. (1988) 'Can There Be a Feminist Ethnography?', *Women's Studies International Forum* 11: 21–7.

Standish, P. (1995) 'Postmodernism and the Education of the Whole Person', *Journal of Philosophy of Education* 29, 1: 121–35.

Stasz, C. (1979) 'The Early History of Visual Sociology', in J. Wagner (ed.) *Images of Information: Still Photography in the Social Sciences*, Beverly Hills, CA: Sage.

Stimie, C. and Geggus, C. (1972) *University Education in the Republic of South Africa*, Report No. 16, Pretoria: South African Human Sciences Research Council.

Strawson, P.F. (1985) *Scepticism and Naturalism: Some Varieties*, New York: Columbia University Press.

Stronach, I. and MacLure, M. (1997) *Educational Research Undone: The Postmodern Embrace*, Buckingham: Open University Press.

Sylva, K. (1994) 'School Influences on Children's Development', *Journal of Child Psychology and Psychiatry* 35, 1: 135–70.

Tate, W.F. (1997) 'Race–Ethnicity, SES, Gender, and Language Proficiency Trends in Mathematics Achievement: An Update', *Journal for Research in Mathematics Education* 28, 6: 652–79.

Taylor, C. (1976) 'Responsibility for Self', in A. Rorty (ed.) *The Identities of Persons*, Berkeley: University of California Press.

Taylor, G. (1981) 'Integrity', *Aristotelian Society Supplementary* 55: 143–59.

Taylor, R. (1985) 'Radical Developments in University Adult Education in England: Refining the Liberal Tradition', in R. Taylor, K. Rockhill and R. Fieldhouse (eds) *University Adult Education in England and the USA: A Reappraisal of the Liberal Tradition*, London: Croom Helm.

Tempels, P. (1959) *Bantu Philosophy*, Paris: Présence Africaine.

Thomson, J.A.K. (1953) *Ethics of Aristotle*, Harmondsworth: Penguin.

Tierney, G. (1994) 'On Method and Hope', in A. Gitlin (ed.) *Power and Method*, London: Routledge.

Titchen, A. and Binnie, A. (1993) 'Research Partnership: Collaborative Action Research in Nursing', *Journal of Advanced Nursing* 18: 858–65.

Tomaselli, K.G. (ed.) (1989) *Rethinking Culture*, Belville, South Africa: Anthropos.

—— (1996) *Appropriating Images: The Semiotics of Visual Representation*, Højbjerg, Denmark: Intervention Press.

Tomaselli, K.G., Shepperson, A. and Eke, M. (1995) 'Towards a Theory of Orality in African Cinema', *Research in African Literatures* 26: 18–35.

Tomlinson, S. (1983) *Ethnic Minorities in British Schools: A Review of the Literature, 1960–82*, London: Heinemann.

Tooley, J. (1997) 'On School Choice and Social Class: A Response to Ball, Bowe and Gewirtz', *British Journal of Sociology of Education* 18, 2: 217–30.

Troyna, B. (1991) 'Underachievers or Underrated? The Experience of Pupils of South Asian Origin in a Secondary School', *British Educational Research Journal* 17, 4: 361–76.

—— (1993) *Racism and Education: Research Perspectives*, Buckingham: Open University Press.

—— (1995) 'Beyond Reasonable Doubt? Researching "Race" in Educational Settings', *Oxford Review of Education* 21, 4: 395–408.

Troyna, B. and Carrington, B. (1989) '"Whose Side Are We On?" Ethical Dilemmas in Research on "Race" and Education', in R.G. Burgess (ed.) *The Ethics of Educational Research*, London: Falmer Press.

Troyna, B. and Hatcher, R. (1992) *Racism in Children's Lives: A Study of Mainly-White Primary Schools*, London: Routledge.

Urban Walker, M. (1998) *Moral Understandings: A Feminist Study in Ethics*, New York: Routledge.

Vaughn, S. and Lyon, G.R. (1994) 'Ethical Considerations When Conducting Research with Students with Learning Disabilities', in S. Vaughn and C. Bos (eds) *Research Issues in Learning Disabilities: Theory, Methodology, Assessment, and Ethics*, Berlin: Springer-Verlag.

Verwoerd, H. (1953), Minister of Native Affairs, Speech to the South African Parliament, *Hansard* 83: 3576–86.

Walden, R. and Walkerdine, V. (1985) *Girls and Mathematics: From Primary to Secondary Schooling*, Bedford Way Paper 24, London: Institute of Education.

Ward, K. and Taylor, R. (eds) (1986) *Adult Education and the Working Class*, London: Croom Helm.

Warnock, M. (1991) 'Equality Fifteen Years On', *Oxford Review of Education* 17, 2: 145–53.

Waslander, S. and Thrupp, M. (1996) 'Choice, Competition and Segregation: An Empirical Analysis of a New Zealand Secondary School Market', in A. Halsey,

H. Lauder, P. Brown and A. Wells (eds) *Education, Culture, Economy and Society*, Oxford: Oxford University Press.

Wax, M.L. and Cassell, J. (1981) 'From Regulation to Reflection: Ethics in Social Research', *American Sociologist* 16: 224–9.

Webb, C. (1989) 'Action Research: Philosophy, Methods and Personal Experiences', *Journal of Advanced Nursing* 14: 403–16.

—— (1990) 'Partners in Research', *Nursing Times* 86, 32: 40–4.

Weber, S.J. and Mitchell, C. (1995) *That's Funny, You Don't Look Like a Teacher! Interrogating Images and Identity in Popular Culture*, London: Falmer Press.

Weiler, K. (1996) 'Freire and a Feminist Pedagogy of Difference', in R. Edwards, A. Hanson and A. Raggatt (eds) *Boundaries of Adult Learning*, London: Routledge.

Weiner, G. (1998) *Getting Published: An Account of Writing, Refereeing and Editing Practices*, Final Report to the United Kingdom Economic and Social Research Council.

Weiss, C.H. (1975) 'Evaluation Research in the Political Context', in E.L. Struening and M. Guttentag (eds) *Handbook for Evaluation Research*, Vol. 1, Beverly Hills, CA: Sage.

Wheatley, E.E. (1994) 'How Can We Engender Ethnography with a Feminist Imagination?', *Women's Studies International Forum* 17, 4: 403–16.

Williams, B. (1973) 'A Critique of Utilitarianism', in J.J.C. Smart and B. Williams (eds) *Utilitarianism: For and Against*, Cambridge: Cambridge University Press.

—— (1979) 'Conflict of Values', in B. Williams (ed.) *Moral Luck*, Cambridge: Cambridge University Press.

—— (1985) *Ethics and the Limits of Philosophy*, Cambridge, MA: Harvard University Press.

Winston, B. (1995) *Claiming the Real: The Documentary Film Revisited*, London: British Film Institute.

—— (1998) '"The Camera Never Lies": The Partiality of Photographic Evidence', in J. Prosser (ed.) *Image-based Research: A Sourcebook for Qualitative Researchers*, London: Falmer Press.

—— (1988) 'The Tradition of the Victim in Griersonian Documentary', in L. Gross, J.S. Katz and J. Ruby (eds) *Imagine Ethics*, New York: Oxford University Press.

Wolfreys, J. (1998) *Deconstruction: Derrida*, London: Macmillan.

Woodrow, M., Lee, M.F., McGrane, J., Osborne, B., Pudner, H. and Trotman, C. (1998) *From Elitism to Inclusion: Good Practice in Widening Access to Higher Education*, London: Committee for Vice Chancellors and Principals.

Woods, P., Bagley, C. and Glatter, R. (1998) *School Choice and Competition: Markets in the Public Interest?*, London: Routledge.

WSD: Workers' School Documents, Unpublished documents of the Workers' School.

WSI: Workers' School Minutes, Unpublished interviews of members of the Workers' School.

Yarling, R. and McElmurray, B. (1986) 'The Moral Foundation of Nursing', *Advances in Nursing Science* 8, 2: 63–73.

Index